Change They *Can't* Believe In

Change They Can't Believe In

THE TEA PARTY AND REACTIONARY POLITICS IN AMERICA

Christopher S. Parker

★

Matt A. Barreto

PRINCETON UNIVERSITY PRESS

PRINCETON & OXFORD

Published by Princeton University Press, 41 William Street, Princeton, New Jersey
08540
In the United Kingdom: Princeton University Press, 6 Oxford Street, Woodstock,
Oxfordshire OX20 1TW

press.princeton.edu
Book designed by Marcella Engel Roberts

Library of Congress Cataloging-in-Publication Data

Parker, Christopher S., 1963–
Change they can't believe in : the Tea Party and reactionary
politics in America / Christopher S. Parker and Matt A. Barreto.
pages cm
Includes bibliographical references and index.
ISBN 978-0-691-15183-0 (hardcover)
1. Tea Party movement. 2. Political participation—United States—History—
21st century. 3. Government, Resistance to—United States—History—21st century.
4. Protest movements—United States—History—21st century.   I. Title.
JK2391.T43P37 2013
322.4'40973—dc23
2012046763

British Library Cataloging-in-Publication Data is available

This book has been composed in Sabon LT Std, and Helvetica Neue LT Std

Printed on acid-free paper. ∞

Printed in the United States of America

1 3 5 7 9 10 8 6 4 2

CONTENTS

FIGURES AND TABLES

Figures in the Main Text

Appendix Figures

Appendix Tables

PREFACE AND ACKNOWLEDGMENTS

THIS BOOK BEGAN ACCIDENTALLY. After promotion, Parker designed what he thought would make an ideal survey on race and politics. By happenstance, the survey coincided with the brewing controversy surrounding what has come to be known as the Affordable Care Act (aka Health Care Reform), when the Tea Party's resistance made national (and international) headlines. Barreto thought it a good idea to ask a question about the extent to which people supported the Tea Party. This was January 2010. Two months later, Tea Party supporters marched on Washington to oppose the bill, during which derogatory posters of President Obama were on display for all to see. Even as the Tea Party claimed their efforts were aimed at shrinking government and restoring fiscal responsibility, their critics charged them with racism. Much has been written about the Tea Party. However, this book departs from many others in at least one important way: it draws on social science as a means to adjudicate the above-mentioned claims and counterclaims about the motivations of the Tea Party, and the ways in which they affect contemporary American politics.

As any honest author will tell you, writing a book forces one to incur many, many debts. It's no different in this case. This manuscript has benefited from the comments of the following colleagues: Alan Abramowitz, Christopher Adolph, Shaun Bowler, Devin Burghart, Tony Chen, Karam Dana, Michael Dawson, Christopher Federico, Luis Fraga, Zoltan Hajnal, Ashley Jardina, Jose Marichal, Peter May, Naomi Murakawa, Spencer Piston, Gabriel Sanchez, Mark Sawyer, Lee Scheingold, David Smith, Mark Smith, Jack Turner, and Janelle Wong.

Preliminary results were presented at a number of institutions. Ultimately, the book benefited from spirited discussions at the following universities: Michigan, Minnesota, Oregon, Southern California, California-Berkeley, California–Santa Barbara, Emory, and Stanford. The workshop participants at each place provided timely feedback. We'd like to thank Vince Hutchings, Joe Lowndes, Jane Junn, Cynthia Kaplan, Michael Leo Owens, and Gary Segura for the invitations.

At Margaret Levi's invitation, Parker also presented the research in Australia at the University of Sydney and Australian National University. Workshop participants were both vigorous and generous with their comments at each stop.

We would also like to recognize the hard work of several people at the University of Washington who contributed to this project. Christopher Towler and Betsy Cooper supervised the three surveys conducted through the Survey Research Lab at the University of Washington. Other residents of the Washington Institute for the Study of Sexuality, Ethnicity, and Race (WISER) also contributed, including Francisco Pedraza, Loren Collingwood, Rachel Sanders, Benjamin Gonzales, Kiku Huckle, Sergio Garcia-Rios, and Kassra Osskooii. Parker would also like to thank Towler (again), as well as Rachel North, a precocious undergraduate. These folks logged long hours and provided exceptional research assistance down the stretch. Steve Dunne, our tech guy, kept the servers humming in the survey lab, and Ann Buscherfeld was a big help on the administrative side. Finally, the UW-based Royalty Research Grant provided financial assistance.

We remain indebted to Chuck Myers, our editor at Princeton. He championed the project from the start, shepherding it through the process with ease. Chuck also deserves credit for selecting excellent reviewers.

Beyond the many colleagues who we have acknowledged already, we also wish to thank our families for their unwavering support during the long process of finishing this manuscript. Barreto would like to thank his parents, Kathy and Guillermo Barreto, and his children, Dan and Clara Barreto. Most of all, he would not have been able to complete this project without the love and support of his wife, Julie Straub-Barreto, who went above and beyond in everything he could ask. He would like to dedicate this book to her.

Parker would like to thank his teachers at San Diego City College, especially Dr. Candace Waltz. He would also like to acknowledge the patience, support, and love of his daughters, Brittani and Bryanna Parker, and even the family pet, Daisy. He now has more time to spend with them. Finally, this book is dedicated to his late cousin and longtime UCLA official, Dr. Winston Churchill Doby, who continues to show him the way.

Change They *Can't* Believe In

Introduction

Who Is the Tea Party
and What Do They Want?

F ROM THE BEGINNING, the Tea Party movement, as a loose confederation of leaders, activists, and sympathizers, has said it's about conservative principles: small government, the free market, and governmental fiscal responsibility. On February 26, 2011, at a Tea Party gathering in Portland, Oregon, a thoughtful Tea Party spokesman was heard quoting the famous French social observer Alexis de Tocqueville on liberty, and recommending the audience read Frederick von Hayek's well-known paean to small government, *The Road to Serfdom*. In his address to the audience in the Shiloh Inn's ballroom, Rob Kuzmanich averred, "Conservatives are trying to conserve the liberating ideas of the American Revolution . . . [that while] we retain our moral values, the Tea Party unites around three principles: limited government and the rule of law, free-market capitalism, and fiscal and personal responsibility. The Tea Party slogan is 'No public money for private failure.' "[1]

In addition to these largely mainstream conservative claims about the proper place of government in American life, people associated with the Tea Party movement have often referred to President Obama in plainly racialized terms. For instance, barely a month after the meeting in Portland, another Tea Party gathering was convened in Coeur d'Alene, Idaho, where activists avoided discussions of the bailouts, stimulus, and taxes—issues that form the core of Tea Partiers' grievances. This meeting had something different on its agenda. Devin Burghart, an onsite observer, reports that "Instead [of discussing fiscal issues], speakers at this Tea Party event gave the crowd a heavy dose of racist 'birther' attacks on President Obama [and] discussion of the conspiracy problem facing America." Radio talk show host and Tea Party activist Laurie Roth, based in the eastern part of the state, tore into the president, comparing Obama to the Democrats who preceded him in the Oval Office: "This was not a shift to the Left like Jimmy Carter or Bill Clinton. This is a worldview clash. We are seeing a worldview clash in our White House. A man who is a closet secular-type Muslim, but he's still a Muslim. He's no Christian. We're seeing a man who's a socialist communist in the White House, pretending to be an American . . . he wasn't even born here."[2]

The contrast between the two meetings is striking. The first, consistent with the now familiar retronym the party has adopted, Taxed Enough Already (TEA), speaks to the symbolic nature of its opposition to big government. More to the point, as political scientists Theda Skocpol and Vanessa Williamson argue, invoking the Tea Party calls forth images of "the original American colonial rebels opposing tyranny by tossing chests of tea into Boston Harbor."[3] If conservative commentators such as Peggy Noonan and Juan Williams are correct, that at its core the Tea Party is a group of concerned, mainstream—if angry—Americans who are principally worried about bloated government and fiscal irresponsibility,[4] and if sources sympathetic to the Tea Party are right to argue that the party stands for a reduced role of the federal government, more fiscal responsibility, lower taxes, a free market, and a commitment to states' rights, then we should understand the Tea Party as part of a long-running conservative reaction to the perceived encroachment of Big Government upon Americans' freedoms.[5]

The difference between the two meetings is obvious, so much so that it begs the question: What causes some people to support the Tea Party? Is it, as mentioned at the Tea Party gathering in Oregon, about ideological conservatism: small government, the rule of law, and fiscal responsibility? Of course, this is something to which Tea Party elites, such as retired House heavyweight Dick Armey, have always held fast.[6] Or is it more about a general intolerance of "Others," a rejection of out-groups, something that was suggested at the Tea Party gathering in Idaho? In *Change They Can't Believe In*, we go to great lengths to explore sources of the Tea Party movement. We also consider the consequences of Tea Party support, that is, the ways in which support for the Tea Party affects American social and political life.

Our argument is very simple. We believe that people are driven to support the Tea Party from the anxiety they feel as they perceive the America they know, the country they love, slipping away, threatened by the rapidly changing face of what they believe is the "real" America: a heterosexual, Christian, middle-class, (mostly) male, white country.[7] We think it likely that they perceive such change is subverting their way of life, everything they hold dear. They not only wish to halt change; if we are correct, Tea Party supporters actually wish to turn the clock back. They hope to return to a point in American life before Barack Obama held the highest office in the land, before a Latina was elevated to the Supreme Court, and when powerful members of Congress were all heterosexual (at least publically). Still, the emergence of a Tea Party–like reaction to change isn't altogether new.

Indeed, we argue that its emergence is simply the latest in a series of national right-wing social movements that have cropped up in America since the nineteenth century. In fact, our perspective on the Tea Party is very much in line with a concept developed by the late historian Richard Hofstadter in his path-breaking work *The Paranoid Style in American Politics*. Hofstadter argued that some members of dominant social groups will use any means at their disposal to forestall what they believe is a loss in social prestige as social change takes root.[8] For him, the paranoia wasn't a clinical diagnosis. Rather, he used it as a means of describing the ways in which dominant groups, and the right-wing movements to which they become attached, perceived social change as an attempt to subvert their group's status in American society. At the crux of the paranoid style, according to Hofstadter, is the perception of a "vast and sinister conspiracy . . . set in motion to undermine and destroy a way of life." In response to such threats, in order to protect itself from "forces of almost transcendent power," Hofstadter suggests that right-wing movements must dispense with the "usual methods of political give-and-take." Instead, "an all-out crusade" is needed to defeat the enemy.[9] Oddly enough, exaggerating the perceived threats from their political enemies causes the paranoid to resort to policy preferences that threaten the very system they claim to cherish.[10] Ultimately, Hofstadter's interpretation received some empirical support from the work of sociologist Seymour Martin Lipset twenty-five years later.[11]

Hofstadter and Lipset's comprehension of the Far Right helps us understand the emergence of right-wing movements, including the nativist Know-Nothing Party of the 1850s, the white supremacist (and nativist) Ku Klux Klan as a national movement in the 1920s, and the rise of the anticommunist John Birch Society (JBS). The Know-Nothings, also known as the American Party, were, among other things, concerned with the growing presence of immigrants. They feared the immigrants' attachment to Catholicism as a political and moral threat, and perceived them prone to criminality, something that threatened the security of the country.[12] The Klan and its supporters perceived a threat from blacks, Jews, Catholics, labor unions, and the increasing independence of women. In each case, members of the Invisible Empire, as the Klan was also known, believed themselves to be vulnerable to the emergence of these groups.[13] Similarly, members and supporters of the JBS believed the "American way" of life to be under siege, arguing that the expansion of the federal government threatened to subvert their freedom and transform the United States into a totalitarian country.[14]

If the Tea Party is in any way similar to right-wing movements of the past, we think it likely that President Obama represents a threat to the mostly male, middle-aged and older, middle-class, white segment of the population on par with the ethnocultural and political threats that motivated participation in right-wing movements. Consider the fact that a recent study issued by Democracy Corps reports that 90 percent of Tea Party supporters believe President Obama to be a socialist; as such, they view him as the "defining and motivating threat to the country and its well-being."[15] As American history suggests, this is the same kind of conspiratorial language often deployed by the Far Right when it perceives change of some kind is taking place.

Ultimately, we think it's possible that the Tea Party and its supporters may perceive social change as subversion, and come to fear it.[16] A much-celebrated (or derided, depending on where you sit) column by former *New York Times* columnist Frank Rich crystallizes the point in his observation that "the conjunction of a black president and a female speaker of the House—topped off by a wise Latina on the Supreme Court and a powerful gay Congressional committee chairman—would sow fears of disenfranchisement among a dwindling and threatened minority in the country no matter what policies were in play . . . When you hear demonstrators chant the slogan 'Take our country back!,' these are the people they want to take the country back from."[17] This account suggests that the change witnessed in America in the past three years is simply too much change for some people; social change is also reinforced by allowing gays and lesbians to serve openly in the U.S. Armed Forces. As Rich indicates, these people believe their country is being stolen from them, the connection to their beloved America is rapidly dissolving.

When all is said and done, we argue that support for the Tea Party is motivated by something beyond the more conventional view of conservatism in which economic freedom and small government as well as social and fiscal responsibility are prized. We also believe it isn't completely motivated by hostility toward out-groups in which people of color, immigrants, and sexual minorities are the objects of derision.[18] Instead, we argue that people who are attracted to the Tea Party are *reactionary* conservatives: people who fear change of any kind—especially if it threatens to undermine their way of life. Similar to other motivations that shape the ways in which people see politics, reactionary conservatism is a product of social learning. By this, we mean to say that the impulse to believe that change represents subversion of some kind, a threat to all that one holds dear, is part of a socialization process inculcated during childhood.[19]

As we will soon make clear, reactionary conservatives differ in a number of ways from more conventional conservatives, including the way in which change is viewed. While it's true that more conventional conservatives don't embrace social change, they realize incremental, *evolutionary* change is sometimes necessary as a means of preventing *revolutionary* change. The reactionary conservative doesn't want to stop at the prevention of change: he prefers to reverse whatever progress has been made to that point. He hopes for America's return to a point in history during which the cultural dominance of the group to which he belongs remained unchallenged.[20] This appears consistent with the Tea Party's desire to "take their country back."[21]

CONVENTIONAL EXPLANATIONS FOR TEA PARTY SUPPORT: CONSERVATISM AND RACISM

Now that we have outlined our approach to sources of Tea Party support, we want to expand on the conventional views upon which we've briefly touched. We have already referenced Noonan's rationale for the existence of the Tea Party, as well as Williams's. Indeed, even the most casual perusal of Tea Party websites support their contention that the Tea Party sits astride conservative principles. Ideological conservatism derives its validity from long-standing American values, including a preference for small government, the rule of law, and fiscal responsibility. However, as we shall see, intolerance of perceived out-groups has an equally long history in American social and political life, in which racism, among other in-group/out-group distinctions, has long divided Americans. For illustrative purposes, we return to the vignettes.

We begin with the Tea Party meeting in Oregon. The ideas presented at this gathering represent core conservative, even libertarian, principles, very much in keeping with traditional American political culture. Debates over the size of government, economic freedom, and fiscal responsibility are easily traced to the Founding Fathers, some of whom thought too much government would leave the new nation scarcely better off than what it was under the thumb of the British Crown.[22] The same principles spurred the negative reaction to President Franklin D. Roosevelt's New Deal; for instance, many conservative elites thought the programs and agencies created by Roosevelt encroached much further on American freedoms than necessary.[23] Similarly, some conservatives in the early 1960s thought government had overreached with civil rights legislation and the Great Society programs, and they pushed back. Of course, the Tea Party's reaction to Barack Obama and his policies can be interpreted in the same way: they believe he's overreaching.

The meeting convened in Idaho represents another way to interpret the Tea Party's resistance. However, the source of their resistance is quite different from the above-described, largely conservative perspective, but with its own historical lineage, one rooted in race and racism. This perspective suggests that the Tea Party represents bigotry. By now, charging the Tea Party with racism is old news. In fact, a principal architect behind the movement, Mark Williams, was banished for penning an overtly racist letter, from the "Coloreds" to "Abe" (Abraham Lincoln), in which he went out of his way to ridicule the NAACP.[24] But even with Williams gone, Tea Party rallies remain known for participants' many caricatures of President Obama, which often depict him as a primate, an African "witch doctor," and a modern-day Hitler, among other things. Quite recently, California Republican Party official and Tea Party activist Marilyn Davenport portrayed the president as a chimpanzee.[25]

Moreover, claims that President Obama is an alien of some kind, that is to say, that he was born in Kenya or Indonesia and is a practicing Muslim, are advanced by activists at rallies. The leader of the congressional Tea Party caucus, Michele Bachmann, refuses to deny them.[26] Furthermore, the Tea Party was a driving force behind Arizona's immigration legislation, which many believe will ultimately result in the targeting of Latino citizens for racial profiling. The Tea Party supported similar legislation in Georgia and South Carolina. Another bill, recently made law in Alabama, essentially calls for the racial profiling of Latino schoolchildren. If we take seriously the ways in which race and racism has helped shape American social and political life, none of this should come as a surprise.

Beginning with the American colonial period, racism permitted many settlers to view American Indians as savages, incapable of making good use of their land much less possessing the intellectual and cultural resources necessary for citizenship. Viewing American Indians in this light made it possible for the settlers to make war against them and drive these people from their ancestral homes.[27] Of course, by the mid-seventeenth century, racial arguments—not wholly unrelated to the ones that permanently disqualified American Indians from national membership—were deployed to justify the institutionalization of chattel slavery during which Africans and their descendants were permanently branded inferior. In the late eighteenth century, the Naturalization Act of 1790 took racism to new heights (or lows), restricting naturalization (citizenship) to "free whites of good moral character." Eventually, the intersectional rivalry between North and South over slavery shook the nineteenth century, culminating in the Civil War. The war settled the issue of slavery and *national* citizenship for the time being. However, the South ultimately remained wedded to its racist practices, finding ways to avoid compliance with the law of the land, which eventually resulted in the Jim Crow laws that would regulate black Southerners well into the next century.

Racism also provided a rationale for the appropriation of more than half of Mexico's territory in 1848 (including California and Texas), and the mistreatment of the (now) Mexican Americans who opted to remain as the Mexican border moved south.[28] The early twentieth century saw the objects of racism continue to spread beyond the mainly black-white model to include people of Asian descent who were barred from immigrating to the United States. Even after the law was adjusted to permit Asian immigrants to naturalize, racism permits native-born American citizens of Asian extraction to be seen as aliens in their own country.[29] Needless to say, the effects of racism have endured far beyond the beginning of the twentieth century, giving rise to a range of suboptimal outcomes for people of color. These include relatively high rates of unemployment, incarceration, and poverty, as well as wealth and educational disparities, to name just a few.[30]

Tea Party activists and spokespeople deny that racism or outgroup hostility of any kind have anything to do with either the motivations or objectives of the Tea Party movement. Indeed, it may well be the case that the meeting to which we referred in Idaho is part of a group of fairly isolated incidents, ones that don't fairly represent the sentiments of the millions of Tea Party leaders, activists, and supporters across the country. Still, based on the enduring impact of race on American social and political life,[31] we must consider how, if at all, it may influence arguably the most vigorous movement in the last thirty years. Indeed, similar to the arguments that Americans continue to have over the size of government and economic freedom (among other types of freedom), racism and out-group hostility are also foundational to American life.[32] In fact, award-winning historian Barbara J. Fields insists that race is *the* dominant theme in American life.[33]

In sum, it's not hard to see why people perceive that the Tea Party may be motivated by either conservatism or racism: both have structured American social, economic, and political life from the beginning.[34] Even so, we don't think these are the only explanations for Tea Party support. As we discuss below, we think it's possible that other factors animate not only the Tea Party, but right-wing social movements more generally.

■ ■ ■

To reiterate, this book strives to answer two questions. First, can the apparent negative reaction to the presidency of Barack Obama, and what it's believed to represent, add anything meaningful to the discussion about what drives people to sympathize with the Tea Party? If the history of right-wing movements is in any way indicative of the dynamics of the Tea Party, it suggests that its supporters are motivated by both politics and racism. The vignettes support this claim. However, this raises the issue of whether or not the anxiety associated with Obama's presidency can meaningfully inform how people feel about the Tea Party beyond what we believe will be the powerful influence of racism and politics. We also think it's important to apprehend the social and political consequences of Tea Party support. Hence, our second question: Does the anxiety associated with the change in America represented by the election of Barack Obama have the potential to affect American politics? In other words, does it have the capacity to influence how people think about public policy and how people vote, *independent* of typical explanations, ones related to long-standing social and political predispositions such as political ideology, political partisanship, and how one feels about out-groups?

If we are correct, the answer to both questions is yes. If there is any validity to our contention that the Tea Party is in the tradition of right-wing movements of the past, supporters of the Tea Party are driven by their *reaction* to Barack Obama's presidency, and what they believe it represents. Our explanation draws on symbolic politics to explain why people support the Tea Party, and why sympathy for the movement shapes their preferences beyond more conventional explanations, including ideology, partisanship, and hostility directed toward out-groups.[35] That is, beyond the ways in which politics can affect material and cultural status, it becomes a means through which people may express hopes and fears. Often, these emotions are projected onto political objects, including high-ranking public officials and important political issues. So, for many people, politics is more about what the issues *represent* in the way of larger social conflict, than anything else.[36] For reasons we discuss in chapter 1, we suspect that Barack Obama *represents* change in which the Tea Party, and their many supporters, cannot believe; change they don't support. Because, as we argue, his rise, and everything perceived to be associated with it, threatens to displace the segment of America that the Tea Party has come to represent: mostly white, middle-class, middle-aged men.

PERSPECTIVES ON THE TEA PARTY

An avalanche of Tea Party–related books, many of them journalistic accounts, supports both the purely political approach as well as the more racialized account of the Tea Party.[37] Academics have recently joined the debate, bringing with them more rigorous analytical frameworks within which to analyze the Tea Party. Even so, their accounts appear to mirror the alternative interpretations of the Tea Party offered by the aforementioned, more journalistic renderings of the movement.

For instance, historian Jill Lepore's interpretation of the Tea Party confirms Hofstadter's impression that those on the Far Right are dogged in their determination to restore America's greatness by turning to times past as a means of addressing contemporary problems. Lepore's Tea Party features an anti-intellectualism that has a hard time with both political and social difference, an interpretation that reminds us of the tendency in America to derogate out-groups. Florida International University law professor Elizabeth Price Foley has a different interpretation of the Tea Party. Rather than seeing the Tea Party as motivated by an aversion to change remedied by a return to the past, she believes the movement is animated by enduring fidelity to three constitutional principles: limited government, U.S. sovereignty, and constitutional originalism. Ultimately, this reminds us of the fights Americans have had from the beginning over the role the national government should play in American life.[38]

Other scholarship appears to split the difference, offering a more balanced portrait of the Tea Party. For instance, political scientists Theda Skocpol and Vanessa Williamson reveal often thoughtful, knowledgeable, and resourceful people and groups among Tea Party supporters.[39] It's fair to say, therefore, that this set of observations is compatible with Foley's version of the Tea Party. Still, Skocpol and Williamson were taken aback by the willingness of Tea Party members, many of whom were relatively well educated, to believe incredible rumors and anecdotes about the Obama administration and its liberal supporters. Of course, this confirms the anti-intellectual tendency reported by Lepore. They also describe the zeal with which Tea Party members and activists demonized people with whom they disagreed politically and those perceived as different from them in some way: the poor, illegal immigrants, and Muslims.

These are all valid explanations of what motivates Tea Party activists. In *Change They Can't Believe In*, we too, aim to understand the motivations and beliefs of the people who identify with the Tea Party. Still, our work departs from existing scholarship on the Tea Party in at least five important ways. First, unlike current work on the Tea Party that explores the motivations associated with membership and activism, we examine sympathizers. We do so because we wish to consider the broader political impact of the movement beyond those who have the time, resources, and availability to become activists or members. As we shall see below, restricting our analysis to Tea Party members and activists permits us to say less about social and political outcomes than the approach other scholars have taken.

Second, we develop an original theory of Tea Party support, one irreducible to racism or politics (i.e., ideology and party identification). Third, unlike examinations of the Tea Party that precede ours, we follow Hofstadter's work: we take seriously the fact that the Tea Party is nothing new. Following his model, we believe the Tea Party represents an extension of right-wing movements of the past. This leads to the fourth way in which our book departs from our predecessors' work on the Tea Party. As we develop our theory for the sources of Tea Party support and beliefs associated with it, we do so with the objective of developing a more general analytical framework, one we think capable of explaining sources of support for right-wing movements in general, beyond the Tea Party. Moreover, our framework will also permit a better understanding of the social and political implications of supporting right-wing movements. Fifth, given the array of evidence we marshal, this book represents the most rigorous analysis to date of the sources and consequences of Tea Party support, one that accounts for several competing explanations, including politics, conservatism, racism, and more general intolerance.

WHY THIS BOOK?

This book is timely for at least two reasons. In the first place, there is no denying the political force that has come to be known as the Tea Party in American politics. Consider its impact on the 2010 midterm elections. The six major Tea Party factions backed ten Republican senators, in addition to eighty-five members of the House,[40] and are credited by some as key to Republicans' success.[41] More recently, the impact of the Tea Party has been evident in Indiana's Republican Senate primary as well as elections in Wisconsin, where Governor Scott Walker, and "other Tea Party–supported candidates were victorious."[42] The party has at least 350,000 core members who are part of one of its six major factions.[43] This number is supplemented by the three million or so who aren't members per se but who have attended a rally, donated to one of the factions, or purchased Tea Party literature. Perhaps most important, we cannot discount those who support the goals of—or sympathize with—the Tea Party. According to a recent Pew poll, 20 percent of American adults "agree" with the Tea Party.[44] In raw numbers, this means that roughly forty-five million Americans are Tea Party sympathizers.[45] As the recent fight over increasing the debt ceiling suggests, if support for the Tea Party remains at such robust levels, it will continue to pull the Republican Party to the right, making political compromise—and therefore governance—much more difficult by increasing the polarization of the parties. Moreover, the Tea Party, and its supporters, are a driving force in both the Voter Identification efforts that threaten to disenfranchise at least 5 million voters across more than a dozen states, and the erosion of women's rights.[46]

This volume's immediate purpose is to investigate the sources of support for the Tea Party and how it informs mass attitudes and behavior. We also hope to contribute to a broader conversation in which we may better understand why people identify with reactionary movements. Research on right-wing movements stretches back several decades. Thanks to interpretive work relying on historical accounts, we have a firm grasp of the macrohistorical forces that provoke the emergence of right-wing movements. At the individual level, however, beyond race, ethnicity, class, and religious orientation, we know relatively little about why people are drawn to right-wing movements. We know even less about whether or not supporting right-wing movements can explain social and political attitudes and preferences beyond the influence of other factors, including ideology, partisanship, and racial group membership. In *Change They Can't Believe In*, we bring an array of evidence to bear on the study of right-wing movements and their sympathizers. In doing so, we are able to tease out the sources and consequences of supporting right-wing movements as no other investigation has to date.

We understand if some readers object to our lumping the Tea Party in with right-wing movements, including the Know-Nothings, the Klan of the 1920s, and the John Birch Society. Quite frankly, however, we run the risk of intellectual dishonesty by avoiding what seems to us an obvious comparison. The following suggests why the comparison is appropriate. Right-wing movements, according to sociologist Rory McVeigh, are "social movements . . . act[ing] on behalf of relatively advantaged groups with the goal of preserving, restoring, and expanding the rights and privileges of its members and constituents. These movements also attempt to deny similar rights and privileges to other groups in society . . . [something that] distinguishes right-wing movements from progressive movements."[47] Sarah Diamond, another sociologist, adds to our understanding of right-wing movements by describing them as "political activists who . . . bear a coherent set of policy preferences," including the protection of free market capitalism, the desire for a strong national defense and the maintenance of American international hegemony, and the "preserv[ation] of traditional morality and the supreme status of native-born white Americans."[48]

Recent research has shown that the Tea Party's supporters belong to relatively advantaged groups. They tend to earn more money on average, are less likely to be unemployed, are overwhelmingly white, and predominantly male. They are also more likely than other people to favor strong military presence, support stricter moral codes, back free market capitalism, reject government policies that give minorities a shot at equality, and prefer to maintain the advantaged status of native-born whites more than non–Tea Party supporters.[49] Further, as we illustrate in chapter 1, the Tea Party has more in common with these prior right-wing movements than demographics. As middle-class white males with a stake in America—both cultural and economic—members and supporters of the Klan, the JBS, and the Tea Party committed (and commit) to fighting what they perceive(d) as tyrannical forces. Moreover, they defended freedom in the face of what they argued were unjust laws and court decisions, ones they cast as oppressive. Finally, each suggested that sometimes intolerance is necessary to protect liberty.[50]

APPROACH: TEA PARTY SUPPORTERS AS MOVEMENT SYMPATHIZERS

Our goal is to gain a better understanding of the broader impact the Tea Party movement is enjoying, beyond the participation of members and activists. We think the best way to accomplish this is through an examination of Tea Party sympathizers. Consider the gains made by the Republican Party in the 2010 midterms. In several states, U.S. senators were elected with the backing of fairly small groups of Tea Party *members*: Florida, a state with approximately 20 million residents and 12,000 members of the Tea Party, elected Marco Rubio; Wisconsin, with approximately 6 million residents and 1,800 members of the Tea Party, elected Ron Johnson; and Pennsylvania, 12 million strong, which has more than 5,400 members of the Tea Party, elected Pat Toomey. It's hard to believe that Tea Party–backed candidates would have achieved this level of success in the midterms absent of support from sympathizers. Remaining confined to movement members doesn't come close to explaining the success the Tea Party achieved in these races. Only if we consider those who sympathize with the Tea Party can we begin to appreciate these results. The fact that social movement *sympathizers* tend, in general, to outnumber social movement *members* by a factor of *twenty* helps to explain the above-cited outcomes in Florida, Pennsylvania, and Wisconsin, among many other places.[51] For this reason—one that suggests the broader impact of social movements on attitudes and behavior—we think it wise to cast our lot with Tea Party sympathizers versus activists and members.

Myriad reasons help to explain why an individual may choose to remain a sympathizer rather than become a member or activist in a social movement. (One doesn't have to be a member to be an activist.) Generally speaking, sympathizers "take a positive stand toward a particular movement,"[52] but may not know anyone connected to the movement, or may not have been targeted by a local organization—that is, they may not be part of a recruitment network. Then there are always cases in which the perceived costs of participating outweigh the benefits.[53] Even if one is connected to someone in the movement and thinks participation is worthwhile, other barriers such as family obligations or work may prevent activism. Even if these barriers are overcome, research suggests that for one to move from supporter to activist, the person who has yet to make the transition must have encouragement from someone who already identifies with movement goals. Equally important, if the potential activist is to eventually participate in movement activity, he or she normally *cannot* face strong opposition from people in the wider network. A spouse or sibling who fails to share the potential activist's identification with the movement makes it difficult for the sympathizer to participate.[54]

Needless to say, surmounting all of these barriers, to participate is difficult even for those who have positive feelings about a movement's goals and objectives. Thus, we argue that people's inability to free themselves of the constraints prohibiting activism does not render their attitudes or behavior irrelevant, nor should those who believe that the cost associated with activism exceeds the benefit be ignored. For one thing, if Clyde Wilcox's research on the Moral Majority is any indication, right-wing sympathizers are markedly less conservative than right-wing members and activists, who tend to be on the Far Right. Indeed, activists and members' attitudes and behavior are more in tune with movement goals than those who are sympathizers, because issue positions are solidified *after* one becomes a member or an activist.[55] Our point is simply that our task is all the more difficult because we aren't focusing on members and activists whose opinions and behavior are easily distinguished from the broader public. By all rights, we should find no differences between Tea Party sympathizers and the broader public, because sympathizers tend to be less extreme than movement members and activists.

Again, we argue that the election of Barack Obama to the presidency, his policies, and what he represents have driven many people to support the Tea Party. We also believe that supporting the Tea Party has important social and political consequences. We bring considerable evidence to bear on our claims, which allows us to rule out rival explanations for both why people support the Tea Party and on the ways in which it influences how people think about politics. Along the way, our data permits us to gauge what Tea Party elites and activists are saying, and the way(s) in which their discourse informs how rank-and-file supporters think about social and political life in America. In sum, our evidence allows us to draw firm conclusions about what Tea Party sympathizers believe, and why they believe it.

At this point, we'd like to take a moment to stress that this book is intended to account for reasons why people are sympathetic to the Tea Party, and some of the consequences associated with such an orientation. While we think accounting for the rise of the Tea Party as a movement—including the development of its intellectual and financial infrastructure—is important, it remains beyond the scope of this book. In like fashion, *Change They Can't Believe In* isn't about why people *join* the Tea Party or become activists per se. These, too, are questions worthy of pursuit, ones that we hope to answer in the near future. For the moment, though, we leave these questions aside in order to pursue the broader social and political implications attached to support for the Tea Party.

Chapter Preview

As social scientists addressing an issue of great public interest and vital national importance, we take great care to base all of our claims on social scientific evidence and historical patterns. Chapter 1 outlines our theoretical approach, but not before placing the Tea Party movement in historical context. In chapter 2, we test the claim that Barack Obama, and what he is perceived to represent, plays a key role in why people support the Tea Party. In chapter 3, the emphasis shifts from explaining support for the Tea Party to assessing the ways in which it informs political attitudes and behavior. We begin by examining how closely people who sympathize with the Tea Party adhere to themes the movement often promotes: patriotism and freedom. Chapter 4 explores claims made by the Tea Party's critics, who argue that the movement is one rooted, at least partly, in bigotry. In chapter 5, we consider the extent to which a positive orientation toward the Tea Party influences attitudes and opinions about the president, beyond ideology, partisanship, general out-group hostility, and racism. Chapter 6 explores the proposition that the Tea Party promotes political mobilization beyond other factors known to promote activism. In the conclusion, we close with a summary of our findings and a discussion of the implications.

1

Toward a Theory of the Tea Party

WE OPENED THE BOOK with a comparison of two Tea Party meetings. There were vast differences between the meeting held in Oregon and the one convened in Idaho. The gathering in Oregon was, at its core, about some basic conservative principles: small government and fiscal responsibility. The one in Idaho appeared to be little more than an expression of intolerance and bigotry in which President Obama was painted as an alien of some kind. As we mentioned, these currents have been part of the American social and political milieu from the beginning. Indeed, we freely acknowledge that a commitment to conservative principles may well be associated with sympathy for the Tea Party. Similarly, we think it likely that hostility (resentment, anger), largely based on intolerant attitudes though not exclusively so, also motivates people to support the Tea Party. Still, we think there's room for an alternative understanding of Tea Party support, one that stands analytically apart from politics and racism, though for all practical purposes may be related to both.

We have two objectives in the present chapter. First, we outline a theory of why people support the Tea Party. We argue that one of the reasons why some folks are sympathetic to the goals and objectives of the Tea Party rests upon their discomfort with Barack Obama as the president. Before going any further, we wish to make it clear that the president isn't the only reason why people support the Tea Party. In fact, in chapter 2, we show that many other factors push people to support, if not necessarily join, the Tea Party movement. Our point is simply that in addition to ideology and, say, partisanship, the fear and anger associated with the presidency of Barack Obama is an additional factor. We argue that similar to the Klan, who believed that Jews, Catholics, and blacks threatened to subvert the America to which they had become accustomed, and the John Birch Society, who worried about communists destroying their country, so, too, is this the case with the Tea Party and Obama.

In fact, this is a consistent theme at Tea Party rallies and on Tea Party websites, with signs depicting Obama and proclaiming, "Socialism is not an American value," and bumper stickers reading, "Al-Qaeda wants to destroy America—Obama is beating them to it!" In short, we entertain the possibility that he represents a threat to the America they've come to know, in which American identity is commensurate with being white, male, native-born, English-speaking, Christian, and heterosexual.[1] Ultimately, we draw on social psychology to illustrate why President Obama is believed to be an agent of change in which neither the Tea Party nor its supporters can believe.

Using the Tea Party as an example, we ask the following: Are right-wing movements merely conservative? In other words, are they about maintaining order and stability while allowing at least incremental change as a means of avoiding revolutionary change? Or are they radical, even extreme reactions to change of some kind in which the preferred course of action isn't the status quo but regression to the past? Our second objective in this chapter is to test an oft-made claim of the Tea Party and their sympathizers: that they're simply conservative, nothing more. The Tea Party's rhetoric suggests otherwise. Many years ago, long before the rise of the Tea Party, Richard Hofstadter, drawing on the work of Theodor Adorno and his colleagues, pointedly charged that right-wing movements were "pseudo-conservative." We take this to mean that they used conservative rhetoric as a means of pursuing nonconservative ends, ones at odds with timeless conservative principles such as order and stability, among others.

Hofstadter went on to argue that a telltale sign of pseudo-conservatism is reliance on conspiratorial discourse in which the "enemy" is out to destroy society.[2] This is fairly close to our claim that the Tea Party represents a reaction to the election of Barack Obama and the perceived threats of the policies he seeks to implement. We entertain the possibility that the fear and anxiety associated with Obama's presidency generates a paranoia that is easily observed through the conspiratorial discourse employed by Tea Party activists, something we investigate in some detail below.

Drawing on content analysis of elite discourse, and a survey-based experiment, we conduct a preliminary test of these alternative points of view in this chapter. In short, if the Tea Party and its supporters are conservative, we should see no difference between what they say and believe and what conservatives say and believe. If, however, we observe a marked difference between the groups, it suggests that conservative journalists, such as *Washington Post* columnist Kathleen Parker, are correct for worrying about the ways in which the Tea Party may be damaging the conservative brand. Indeed, if her observation that "the behavior of certain Republicans who call themselves Tea Party conservatives makes them out to be the most destructive posse of misguided 'patriots' we've seen in recent memory" represents the sentiments associated with mainstream conservatives,[3] we should witness discernible differences between Tea Party conservatives and conservatives that remain unsympathetic to the movement. After comparing the discourse of Tea Party activist-elites to conservative elites, we find no support for the proposition that the Tea Party adheres to more mainstream conservative principles. This general conclusion is reinforced among the masses, where Tea Party conservatives are far more likely than more mainstream conservatives to believe that the president of the United States is out to "destroy the country."

But before we take a stab at explaining our version of why people support the Tea Party, and subjecting it to preliminary tests, we first need to prepare the way by placing the Tea Party movement in historical context. This serves at least two purposes. First, it demonstrates that the emergence of the Tea Party as a right-wing, reactionary movement is nothing new. Second, drawing on the two most influential right-wing movements of the twentieth century, the Ku Klux Klan of the 1920s and the John Birch Society,[4] provides the grist for a much-needed analytical framework on which to base our appraisal of the Tea Party movement and its supporters. To the extent that right-wing movements are, at least in part, fueled by conspiracy theories, we stress the emphasis that the Klan and the JBS placed upon perceived subversion of some kind.[5] As suggested by the late conservative political theorist Clinton Rossiter, such paranoia is indicative of the reactionary tendencies of right-wing movements, impulses driven by the inability of some people to accept the reality of social change. These are people who long for a bygone era in which American society, in some way or another, was better, and who refuse to accept the social and economic changes that have been essential to American progress.[6]

RIGHT-WING MOVEMENTS IN THE TWENTIETH CENTURY

Leaving aside for the moment the social and demographic factors that motivate involvement in political participation of any kind, including age, education, and income, most of the scholarly work on right-wing movements boils down to anxiety associated with change of some kind as the principal ingredient, one that pushes people to join such movements. More pointedly, right-wing movements are driven by a reaction to what is perceived as threatening change, a sentiment captured by Hofstadter, who said that members of the "right wing . . . [feel as though] America has been largely taken away from them and their kind, though they are determined to try to repossess it and to prevent the final destructive act of subversion."[7] For this reason, right-wing movements are, to borrow a term from Lipset and Raab, "preservatist" in that they seek to "narrow the lines of power and privilege."[8] Right-wing movements are often mobilized by conflicts in which fundamental values are at stake—ones, as history suggests, bounded by perceptions of what Americans should believe, how Americans should behave, and how, phenotypically, Americans should look.[9] Right-wing movements and their supporters are committed to the preservation of these ideals.

Anxiety associated with perceived change was clearly manifest in the Ku Klux Klan of the 1920s, the largest and most influential of the Klan's three incarnations.[10] William Simmons of Stone Mountain, Georgia, founded the Second Klan in 1915. Members of the Invisible Empire, an alternative moniker by which the Klan was known, were relatively well educated, held relatively high occupational-status jobs, tended to be family men, and were native-born.[11] In fact, at least one person referred to Klan members as "if not the 'best people' at least the next best . . . the good, solid middle-class citizens."[12] Unlike its late-nineteenth-century predecessor or the mid-twentieth-century version that succeeded it, the Second Klan was truly a national movement. At its zenith in the mid-1920s, it boasted a membership of one to five million and had spread to all forty-eight states. (Alaska and Hawaii both joined the Union in 1959.) The Second Klan claimed to represent "pure Americanism, patriotism, old-time religion, and morality."[13]

According to its worldview, threats to these values had

cropped up everywhere, coming particularly from blacks, Jews, women, and Catholics. World War I had transformed blacks into the "New Negro," more race-conscious and therefore more assertive than ever. Blacks—especially veterans—refused to "stay in their place" after the war, and the fact that black soldiers had been intimate with French women didn't help matters. Black migration to southern cities, and to places beyond the South threatened white dominance. So called "race mixing" posed another threat to it. Ultimately, Klan members feared black mobility, black assertiveness, and interracial relationships would topple white supremacy.

The Klan also feared Jews and Catholics. Klan members ascribed all sorts of nefarious motives and actions to Jews. First and foremost, Jews served as scapegoats for the vicissitudes of capitalism. They were accused of putting profit before anything else, including the country, as well as cheating "hardworking" Americans. The Klan charged that Jews limited the economic opportunities available to Christians, and were taking over America through their dominance in the financial sector. For their part, Catholics were feared not for their religious practices, but for their allegiance to the Old Country, particularly to the pope. The Klan imagined the possibility of papal influence in American politics, arguing that the pope wanted to play a role in American politics. Believing that Catholics voted in accordance with the wishes of the Vatican, the Klan held Catholicism to be anti-Democratic, at odds with political freedom. It didn't help matters much that Jews and Catholics hung on to Old World habits, established foreign-language newspapers, and were perceived to support what many thought were corrupt political machines.[14]

Klan members were also concerned about maintaining their economic position. Concentration of capital in the hands of industrialists from above and the increasing power of labor from below frightened Klan members who were, by and large, drawn from small business and skilled labor.[15] Those who were members of the skilled-labor class worried about decreasing demand for their skills due to mechanization, and the small-business class grew nervous over competition with large chain stores capable of taking over market share even at a distance from their central hubs in the big cities.

Like political competition, economic competition became intertwined with nativism, insofar as the new wave of immigrants didn't speak much English and tended to retain traditions from the Old Country. Jews, as we have already mentioned, represented the scourge of capitalism and big chain stores. Ethnic and religious economic threats from above and below prevented serious class divisions from taking place among Klan members, who rallied around their identity as white native-born Protestants. Still, even as the bulk of Klan members were squeezed between capital and labor, many of them held fast to the tenets of *economic* individualism and the sanctity of private property, both of which were seen as part of the great American tradition.[16]

Finally, the Klan appointed itself a moral police force. To the extent that drinking affected a man's family and his ability to show up to work every day, and was linked to ethnicity (i.e., immigrants), the Klan tried to curb this type of vice.[17] Members similarly policed the sexuality of females in their respective families. Male family members were charged with maintaining family honor, a significant portion of which rested upon the sexual conduct of the family's women. In short, for the Klan of the 1920s, men were responsible for maintaining the integrity of the family name.

Some thirty years later, the John Birch Society (JBS), another national mass movement, resisted the erosion of what members held to be society's most sacred values. Named in honor of an American missionary murdered by Chinese communists in the days following World War II, the organization was founded by retired candy manufacturer Robert Welch in 1958. At its height, the John Birch Society boasted a membership of eighty thousand and had four to six million sympathizers.[18] In the mid-1960s, the JBS spread from coast-to-coast, divided into approximately five thousand local chapters.[19] Its members and sympathizers were firmly middle-class. Approximately 33 percent of JBS activists had completed college, and almost two-thirds had attended some college, versus 10 percent and 12 percent, respectively, among the general public. Occupationally, only 14 percent of JBS members were classified as manual laborers versus 49 percent of the general public, and approximately 51 percent were forty years of age or older.[20]

Welch preached small government, but it was his insistence upon the existence of a vast communist conspiracy that brought him the most notoriety. He believed the federal government was full of communist agents who were actively attempting to subvert the American people and their way of life. Almost no one was spared being tarred with the JBS brush, including sitting president and war hero Dwight D. Eisenhower, and every justice on the Supreme Court. Welch accused the president of treasonous behavior based in part on Eisenhower's decision to settle for peace instead of victory in Korea. He charged the court, and Chief Justice Earl Warren in particular, with treasonous activity, mostly because of how it ruled in *Brown v. Board of Education*, which outlawed segregation in public schools. Welch argued that the court had sided with the communists because the civil rights movement was nothing more than a communist plot to sow dissent in America.

Beyond serving as an ideological competitor to Western emphasis on the free market, communism did a lot of work for the JBS. Many right-wingers, including Welch and his followers, labeled as "communist" any values and policies with which they disagreed.[21] During the heyday of the JBS, right-wingers lay the blame for moral decay, the rising crime rate, pornography, lack of respect for authority, and the avoidance of individual responsibility at the feet of communism. These were said to be un-American, as were social welfare policies that aimed to ameliorate the underlying conditions that produced poverty and racial injustice. Communism became the proxy with which middle-class, suburban, relatively educated whites on the right attacked the move away from traditional American values toward new lifestyles and distributions of prestige. In sum, for "Birchers," communism threatened to subvert American economic, political, and social life.[22]

This brief survey highlights a few themes around which the Klan and the JBS appeared to coalesce. Clearly, each group perceived different threats. For the Klan, the threats were primarily ethnocultural, stemming from concerns about the actions of blacks, Jews, Catholics, and immigrants. The JBS was motivated by the perception that an alien ideology would transform America into a totalitarian nation-state. Still, these movements had much in common. Each was organized around the basic principle of defining and policing who and what counted as "American." The Klan emphasized ethnocultural traits and considered ideology only secondary. For the JBS, the emphasis was the other way around. Race was relevant to the JBS only insofar as "Birchers" believed communists used it as a tool to undermine American social, political, and economic life. Regardless of the relative priority of social difference, it was a driving force for both movements. Another important factor the Klan and the JBS had in common was their appeal to white, Protestant, middle-class males. As we outline in chapter 4, these three groups tend to converge upon an exclusive sense of American identity in which departures from membership in these categories are rejected.

Prior to concluding this section, we'd like to make it clear that we don't see these right-wing movements as identical. Religious differences separate them insofar as the Klan was virulently anti-Catholic in its orientation while the JBS had several thousand Catholic members. Another cleavage separating the movements is their respective foci. For the Klan, neopopulist conservatism was driven by a blend of racial and religious nativism yoked to political and moral reform. JBS members were more driven by big government collectivism, which, to some degree, was driven by anticommunist fervor. While it is true that the JBS opposed the civil rights movement, its leader Welch—regardless of his personal feelings—knew better than to embrace overt racism; to do so would harm the movement.[23]

Still, each group managed to fuse what Hofstadter has called "militant nationalism and anti-communism" into an ideology resistant to broader social changes.[24] Nationalism, based upon the "American" way, was (and is) rooted in individual autonomy, coupled with the Protestant ethic of achievement and hard work. Even though dogged belief in individualism violently clashed with the beliefs of Christians and social conservatives, who thought social bonds indispensable, anticommunism tapped into fundamentalist views of the relationship between the state and society, as well as the role of religion and the role played by capitalism, production, and moral character of the individual. Of course, communism was anathema to religion, but "collectivism" also injured the ability of a man to develop habits of mind that would reward the Christian virtues of hard work, temperance, and thrift, among others.[25]

For us, the question is how well the Tea Party fits this model of a right-wing movement. Is it really about striving to retain a country in which small government and traditionalism assume pride of place? Is their resistance to President Obama really about what they perceive as his liberal policies? Or does their resistance to the president transcend disagreements over policy, crossing over into anxiety, fear, and paranoid social cognition? Next, we outline a general theory of right-wing movements, after which we apply it to the Tea Party.

WHY ARE RIGHT-WING MOVEMENTS SO ATTRACTIVE?

Far from the caricatures often drawn of people who support the Far Right, in which they're often depicted as undereducated, unskilled, and untalented, many have been quite the opposite: relatively well educated, skilled, and talented citizens. The question, then, is why such people would support intolerant, mainly antidemocratic organizations? After all, their support of such organizations flies in the face of convention, insofar as education is at least conducive to the appreciation of more democratic values.[26] One answer is the way in which these movements and their sympathizers perceive threat.[27] The Klan and the JBS waged all-out wars of good versus evil against their respective opponents, with winner-take-all stakes: prevail or be destroyed. The Klan believed that Jews, Catholics, "uppity" African Americans, and liberated women would destroy the world as they knew it. Likewise, for the JBS, the fight against communism was a fight to the death. Even if the rank and file didn't buy into Welch's belief that the *entire* government and key civil societal institutions were run by communists and their sympathizers, they believed that they posed a threat to what they held dear: their religion, country, and families. If Welch and fellow patriots failed to halt communism's march, totalitarianism would eventually prevail.[28]

In what follows, we first place the Klan and the JBS within a broader theoretical framework, one that we believe accounts for the attractiveness of right-wing movements. Then, after making adjustments to account for the current political environment, we apply the same framework to Tea Party sympathizers.

Prior work suggests that right-wing movements emerge during periods of immense social change. Indeed, we have already detailed the circumstances under which the Klan and the JBS appeared, times during which the American social landscape shifted. The literature suggests that right-wing movements emerge as a means by which their constituents and supporters may preserve social prestige. As sociologist Joseph Gusfield argues, when society experiences significant change, "the fortunes and the respect of people [or groups] undergo loss or gain. We [intellectuals] have always understood the desire to defend fortune. We should also understand the desire to defend respect." Furthermore, prestige, deference, and respect are based, among other factors, on the perceived qualities of the group. Groups, in turn, may be identified on the basis of racial, ethnic, or religious criteria and the relevant community-based "values, customs, and habits" with which they are associated.[29]

For the most part, conflicts over prestige, centered upon the perceived displacement of one group's values in favor of another's, are about a contest between the forces of modernity versus the forces of tradition.[30] Generally, white, mainly middle-class, Protestant men and their values represent forces of tradition. In most cases, marginalized groups such as racial, ethnic, religious, and sexual minorities, as well as women, represent the forces of modernity and change. Religious and secular fundamentalism, commensurate with Christian morality and economic conservatism, represent the suite of values, norms, and customs of the more traditionalist forces that are believed by their constituents to be under threat from forces associated with marginalized groups and modernity. In fact, the Klan and the JBS both mobilized under the banner of economic conservatism and Christian morality to do battle against the forces of modernity. To the degree that both groups stressed the "American way [of life]," nationalism was essential to their mobilization efforts.

Drawing on the idealization of traditional American values and social practices, in which white Protestant males are the dominant group, right-wing movements and their sympathizers often feel themselves victims of undue persecution. In their view, the opposition is often evil in some way, out to destroy them and their view of the American way of life. With the JBS, the threat to the American way was relatively straightforward: communism was evil, anathema to everything in which Americans believed. Sooner or later, big government would lead to a totalitarian nation-state. In short, members of the JBS thought themselves persecuted by the federal government, or the elites they believed controlled it.

The process was a bit more complicated for the Klan, for it took at least two steps. First, it had to make cultural claims on American identity. From there, it was about identifying groups who failed to conform to the cultural stereotype. For the Klan of the 1920s, Jews and Catholics were out to tear America asunder: the former through finances, the latter through an alliance with the Vatican. The Klan feared a Jewish conspiracy based on capitalism, and a Catholic conspiracy in which the pope would wield political power in America through Catholic immigrants. Whether it's through communism or through Jewish and

Catholic conspiracies, the overriding theme is one of attempted subversion of the "American way of life."

That the Klan and the JBS often depicted the nature of their conflicts with the opposition in apocalyptic terms is no coincidence. Earlier work on right-wing movements suggested that their constituents were perhaps maladjusted in some way. Social psychologists, however, indicate that such people aren't necessarily irrational. Instead, paranoia may be used as a means of understanding and coping with what such people perceive as "threatening and disturbing social environments." Until they figure out their place in the new social environment, these people will be fraught with anxiety as they try to make sense of it. But sensitivity to their position within the system forces them to spend too much time processing information on their position in it, causing them to contemplate their circumstances even more. "Paranoid-like" social misperception and misjudgment is the product generating, psychologist Roderick Kramer suggests, the belief that one is the target of persecution. In short, other members of the system are perceived to be in cahoots, conspiring against the persecuted party.[31]

Blaming external parties for negative outcomes is also associated with victimhood, what has come to be known as "poor me" paranoia. Scholars who have researched this type of paranoia suggest that as a means of preserving self-esteem, people will blame others for bad outcomes, not themselves. Moreover, because persecution is perceived as undeserved, the target (i.e., the aggrieved party) believes that the persecutor(s) intentionally cause negative events. As a consequence, the aggrieved party becomes angry.

At the root of paranoia, including paranoia-related social cognition, is a sense of powerlessness and distrust. If an out-group holds far more power than an in-group, threatening the latter's sense of "control and competence," the in-group becomes anything but content. To cope, people in the less powerful in-group tend to manufacture stereotypes of the power-holding out-group, ones including a perceived "out-group conspiracy."[32] In short, people become anxious when they perceive their desire to belong to a social group is threatened. As a consequence, the in-group bands together, expressing its solidarity, asserting its superiority.[33] This situation may escalate into conflict, especially if the in-group perceives the social position to which they feel themselves entitled is slipping away to an undeserving out-group.[34] In other words, they perceive themselves as losing control, something that promotes conspiratorial thinking.[35]

Again, if "American" values were at stake with the Klan and the JBS, our analytical framework offers an explanation for why perceived, rapid social change may have contributed to the formation of right-wing movements, and attracted sympathy beyond members and activists. The social psychological approach we've outlined appears to fit the historical facts. With the Klan, the maturation of industrial capitalism and the declining need for skilled labor, dilution of the group's political power, and the increasingly assertive New Negro after World War I, among other things, may have caused at least some members to feel less secure of their position within the social order. Indeed, the Klan perceived threats from many quarters. Still, these groups had at least one thing in common: members were perceived as either racially or ethnically un-American. Or their religious beliefs failed to align with dominant "American" religious doctrine. For members, activists, and sympathizers of the JBS, perhaps they felt their position as guardians of the American way slipping vis-à-vis the intellectual elites in the eastern United States who they believed were leading America down the road to totalitarianism.

We concede that the Tea Party isn't identical to the right-wing movements outlined above. Nonetheless, we believe the Tea Party is very *similar* to them. Our analysis of the Klan and the JBS suggests the economy was more stable than in the present climate. At the height of the Klan's reign in the 1920s, the real per capita gross domestic product (GDP) increased every year from 1921 through 1929. While unemployment spiked in 1921 at 9 percent, by 1926 it had declined to 4 percent. During the height of the JBS, in the early 1960s, real per capita GDP rose each year from 1960 to 1965, and unemployment for the decade averaged 5 percent. This suggests that economic decline is not a necessary condition for the rise of right-wing movements. Contrast this with the rise of the Tea Party: since 2008, real per capita GDP has declined each year, and unemployment has been at least 8 percent. The difference in the economic climate is, therefore, perhaps the greatest departure in the emergence of the Tea Party from that of its right-wing predecessors. This suggests that the state of the economy isn't a necessary condition for the rise of right-wing movements.[36] In other words, it appears that the state of the economy can tell us little about the likelihood of the emergence of right-wing movements.

Yet, even here, the similarities between the Tea Party and what we believe to be its predecessors, are greater than their differences. Like their forebears, Tea Party supporters tend to be white, Christian, middle-class men over forty-five years of age.[37] Further, 18 percent of American households earn $100,000 per year or more, while 20 percent of Tea Party households earn that amount; thus, they better represent the top 10 percent of income distribution than does the general public. This suggests that where perceptions of macrolevel economic factors fail to shed much light on the rise of right-wing movements, one's personal economic situation may provide a few clues.

Perhaps the most important similarity, at least for our purposes, is the presence of change: the displacement of the white, Christian, male-dominated, native-born American. We have already highlighted the change associated with the Klan and the JBS. In other words, the Klan was concerned with ethnocultural change; the JBS was preoccupied with ideological change. Even so, both groups believed their country was slipping away from them. With the Tea Party, we believe the election of Barack Obama, the first black president of the United States, represents that change. As such, we see the Tea Party's attitudes and behavior as a reaction to this event.

TOWARD A THEORY OF THE TEA PARTY

So far, we have argued the possibility that right-wing movements are, at least in part, reactions to a perceived slip in the dominance of their group. However, we think it necessary to provide a mechanism by which this takes place. We have already outlined an approach we think works well to explain the emergence of right-wing movements in general, but we've yet to explain the Tea Party's reaction to Obama. To do so, we follow Pamela Conover and Virginia Gray's work on feminism and the Far Right, in which feminism *represented* a threat to the right-wing's understanding of the family.[38] In like fashion, we also take a symbolic politics approach (something we explain below) as a means of understanding the sources and consequences of support for the Tea Party.

In what follows, we first propose a path through which the Tea Party and its sympathizers come to fear and resent the president. We argue that these sentiments are driven by anxiety associated with the perception that Obama and his confederates are subversive forces, ones that threaten to steal "their" country. If this is change, if this is progress, "real" Americans want no part of it. We follow our account with one in which the Tea Party, and its supporters, are no more than ordinary conservatives. They're simply concerned with encroaching government and the regulation with which it's associated, the erosion of traditional values, and the relative decline of America's position as the sole superpower.

Tea Party Supporters as Pseudoconservatives

We believe that President Obama, by virtue of his position as president, and the fact that he's the first nonwhite person to hold the office of president, represents to some an assault upon a specific ethnocultural conception of American identity and everything for which it stands. In short, Obama and his policies threaten the America that has come to be identified with white, middle-class, middle-aged, Christian, heterosexual, mostly male indentity.[39] By virtue of his ascent to the Oval Office, becoming in theory the most powerful man in the world, it represents a decline in the lifestyle associated with that segment of the historical constituency of the American right wing, one that now includes the Tea Party.

In the United States, the president holds the dual position of chief executive and head of state. As chief executive, the president wears many hats: commander in chief of the armed forces, chief law enforcement officer, and so on. In short, as President Harry Truman famously said, "the buck stops here [with the president]." Through these official duties, the president is often the repository for the nation's hopes and fears. He is called upon to lead the nation through times of national grief, providing reassurance to millions of Americans who are concerned, for instance, about terrorism, or who are nervous about the economy. The president is also called upon to represent America to the world. In his role as chief diplomat, he is the voice of the American people. For these reasons, the president is recognized as a representation of the American government.[40] Indeed, the president is America personified.

The American presidency, in our estimation, is a political symbol for many Americans. Generally, symbols communicate complex arrays of stimuli from which meaning is extracted. In short, they concretize abstract values. Political symbols are arrayed on a continuum from the more abstract to the more tangible, ranging from representations of the political community, such as the Constitution or the Stars and Stripes, to the ways in which specific policies represent the priority of an administration, like health care reform. Key institutions, such as the presidency, Congress, and the military, are important to many Americans. But the presidency stands above the rest because the president is a figure with whom Americans are fascinated from childhood. As one of the principal figures of authority that is visible early on in children's lives, kids develop an affective bond to the office, a bond that is fairly stable over the life course. More important, among children the president stands as *the* symbol of government.[41] The president, as a political leader, is important insofar as he has a proven ability to cope with adversity while in office and is capable of providing a measure of comfort in tough times.[42]

The meanings of symbols are informed by how people feel and think about them. In turn, this is based on the ways in which people are socialized, and their personal experiences.[43] For this reason, we believe Tea Party members, activists, and supporters react to Obama the way they do because his presence as the face of *their* country, as the commander in chief of *their* armed forces—all that the presidency represents—undermines their sense of social prestige. We mention this because Tea Party activists often refer to themselves as "real Americans." As it turns out, people who consider themselves real Americans tend to have a fairly bounded idea of who counts as a real American. Drawing on results from a national survey, Elizabeth Theiss-Morse found that people who identify most with America see "real Americans" as white, English-speaking, native-born, and Christian.[44] This provides a reasonable, if partial, explanation for Tea Partiers' resistance to Obama's presidency. As we show in chapter 3, President Obama fulfills only one of the four criteria, according to them: he speaks English.

From the beginning, we have argued for the possibility that the Tea Party and its sympathizers are quite possibly successors of the Klan and the JBS in the sense that each of them resist(ed) change, preferring to turn the clock back in time. Applying the framework we outlined earlier, one in which we theorize the emergence of the aforementioned right-wing movements, we can fashion an argument for the emergence of Tea Party support. Remaining mindful of the symbolic importance of the president, it's not hard to imagine that people who embrace both normative and phenotypical stereotypes of American identity may believe their way of life is under threat of displacement, and that they are no longer in receipt of the deference to which they have become accustomed.

This is a new, very different America in which some Americans find themselves. Referencing the social psychological literature cited herein, it's possible that Tea Party sympathizers are trying to negotiate their way in an America where a non-white man is the president, the face of the country. With this in mind, we think it fitting to extend the paranoid social-cognition paradigm to Tea Party sympathizers. This mirrors Hofstadter's impression that perceived persecution extends beyond the individual and attaches to a wider, like-minded community. Under these circumstances it's possible that Tea Party supporters feel themselves the victims of a conspiracy. They feel unduly persecuted by President Obama, who is thought of as conspiring with liberals and minorities to subvert the American way, ultimately stealing the United States from them, its rightful heirs. Perhaps this is why almost half of Tea Party supporters, despite doing relatively well economically, are pessimistic about the future of white people in America.[45] More than pessimism, however, the often-aggressive reaction to Barack Obama suggests Tea Party supporters may feel insulted, even disrespected by his emergence.[46]

Perhaps this is one way of explaining why the Tea Party and its supporters reject, in the strongest terms, Obama and his policies. They violently resisted the stimulus package, an expensive (as opponents see it) piece of legislation at an estimated $831 billion, but a measure that registered some success. To illustrate, the Congressional Budget Office (CBO) reports that, as of May 2011, the stimulus had decreased unemployment on average 1.2 percent and increased real GDP by 2.1 percent.[47] For 2012, the CBO reports that the stimulus is projected to increase GDP, on average, by 0.5 percent, and produce as many as 1.1 million jobs.[48] Next came the controversial health care reform legislation, a law that opponents claim will only enlarge the federal deficit, though supporters say long-term savings may be significant. Obama's health care reform aims to insure 31 million Americans who would've otherwise gone without coverage, and it will do so at a savings of $124 billion over ten years (2010–19), according to the nonpartisan CBO. In contrast, repealing it would add $210 billion to the deficit (2012–21). As political psychologist Michael Tesler's work suggests, it may be the case that no matter the policy domain, even ones that have nothing to do with race, Obama's support is guaranteed to spark opposition in many quarters.[49]

We submit that the strength of the Tea Party opposition has something to do with, frankly, the threat associated with a non-white commander in chief and what he represents to supporters of the Tea Party: a threat to the cultural dominance of "real Americans." To put it differently, the emergence of Obama, and the rise of other marginalized groups, represents, as Daniel Bell once called it, "dispossession." Referring to the John Birch Society and their actions in the early 1960s, Bell observed the following: "the Radical Right . . . gains force from the confusion within the world of conservatism regarding the changing character of American life. What the right as a whole fears is the erosion of its own social position, the collapse of its power, the increasing incomprehensibility of a world . . . that has changed so drastically within a lifetime."[50] Bell's description of the JBS sounds identical to how we see the Tea Party. Still, to the rest of America, Obama's emergence heralds progress.[51] This refusal to embrace change, even progress, is a surefire sign of pseudoconservatism, something on which we elaborate shortly.

Tea Party Supporters as Conservatives

Another—equally credible—explanation for the emergence of the Tea Party and its supporters is the fact that 73 percent are self-identified conservatives.[52] This is important because conservatives have always had strong opinions about the appropriate size of government: generally, the smaller, the better. Perhaps this explains the hostility to Obama. In other words, it's not the election of the first black president, an event that threatens to displace them from their rightful place in American hierarchy. Rather, it's the big government, high taxes, and the skyrocketing debt associated with Obama and his policies that is so off-putting to them. It's entirely plausible that this explains why people are sympathetic to the appeals of the Tea Party.

Likewise, Tea Party supporters' opposition to lesbian, gay, bisexual, and transgender (LGBT) rights, and hostility to illegal immigrants, among other issues, may also be explained by their conservative ideology. Social conservatism, for instance, can explain Tea Party supporters' opposition to LGBT rights. Conservatism can also accommodate the hostility directed toward illegal immigrants. After all, they're breaking the law, and law and order is part of the conservative creed. From the purely conservative perspective, it's quite possible that Tea Party supporters' antipathy toward these groups has nothing to do with the perception that as Obama's accomplices, they too have a role to play in the displacement of "real Americans."

In sum, it's quite possible that the hostility we observe toward Obama and his policies is really a function of people's commitment to conservative principles. Indeed, unlike the possibility we raised in which Tea Party sympathizers traffic in a conservatism of the reactionary kind, one committed to resisting, even retarding, social change, perhaps it's the case that they simply hew to conservative doctrine. We turn now to explore this proposition.

ARE TEA PARTY SUPPORTERS REALLY CONSERVATIVES?

Now that we have outlined a theory of Tea Party support, accomplishing our first goal of the present chapter, we now pivot to the second: providing a preliminary test of our theory. In the introduction to our book, we made a point of illustrating the Tea Party's commitment to conservative principles. But as we have mentioned, we think it's possible that the Tea Party is the most recent representation of the Far Right. If true, this calls into question their claim to the same conservative principles promoted by the Founding Fathers,[53] the group to whom Tea Partiers often turn for inspiration. Indeed, over the years, leading conservative intellectuals have questioned the aims of right-wing movements, which suggests that Tea Party objectives weren't consistent with the tenets of conservatism.[54] After we offer a definition of conservatism, we then set out to test the competing claims we've just outlined.

Conservatism Defined (in Brief)

Over the years, conservatives have disagreed among themselves about many things, including the proper balance between rugged individualism and maintaining social bonds, as well as how one negotiates fidelity to conservative principles in a changing world.[55] Despite such schisms, conservatives converge in their belief in the priority of stability and order, for without them, maintaining a free society is all but impossible. Conservatives, in other words, are about "ordered liberty." Institutions, ones capable of balancing the sometimes knee-jerking demands of the masses— motivated by their passion against the long-term maintenance of a free and stable society—are of immense import in the eyes of conservatives. Therefore, anything or anyone that threatens order, stability, and the institutions charged with maintaining them is deemed inconsistent with conservatism, for they (or it) ultimately fail(s) to *conserve* what makes a free society possible.[56]

Based on this definition of conservatism, one that we feel is an accurate—albeit simplified—definition, one can make a case for or against the Tea Party and its supporters. There is no reason to doubt that the Tea Party and its supporters are in favor of small government, individualism, adherence to Christian ethics of traditional moral conduct (social conservatism), and believe in a strong national defense. These beliefs form the core of postwar conservatism. However, the application of the following framework, outlined by the late professor Rossiter's as a means of assessing the application of conservative principles, permits a case to be made against the Tea Party. First, as he indicates, conservatives must be willing to "accept gracefully social and economic changes that have firmly been established in a successful way of life, especially changes in which millions of their fellow citizens have a sizeable stake." This, of course, can be read as a necessary concession to evolutionary change as a means of staving off the possibility of revolutionary change that will likely occur if the masses remain frustrated. In other words, evolutionary change is a means of preserving social order. Moreover, as the late professor argues, conservatives must avoid displaying "a weakness for arguments and methods that unravel the bonds of social unity."[57] Put differently, Rossiter cautions against the practice of demagoguery, something that threatens social order. He isn't alone in this interpretation of conservatism, for the late Russell Kirk, as well as Patrick Allitt, among others, read it in like fashion.[58]

By these criteria, the Tea Party appears to fail on both counts. Its willingness to risk America's economic stability, as it did during the debate over the debt ceiling, likely disqualifies the Tea Party's claim to mainstream conservatism on the first count. Similarly, the Tea Party's push to change the citizenship clause in the Constitution's Fourteenth Amendment, as a means of denying citizenship to the U.S.-born children of illegal immigrants,[59] suggests its refusal to accept change. Of course, perhaps the most important indicator of change in recent memory is the presidency of Barack Obama, something the Tea Party vigorously opposes. The Tea Party would appear to fail the mainstream conservative litmus test on the second count, one that prohibits demagoguery, as well. The way in which Texas governor, recent presidential candidate, and Tea Party favorite, Rick Perry, charged Ben Bernanke, chairman of the Federal Reserve, with treason, is an example.

We now consider the competing claims. Are Tea Party conservatives any different in their outlook from, say, what conservative journalist Sam Tanenhaus, calls "responsible conservatism" (mainstream), a brand of conservatism more concerned with conserving what's good about American social and political life?[60] Or can, say, Sarah Palin and Edmund Burke be lumped together, as political theorist Corey Robin insists?[61] We first turn to an analysis comparing Tea Party websites to the *National Review Online* (NRO). There are at least three reasons why we selected the *National Review* over other conservative publications like the *American Spectator* or the *Weekly Standard*. First, as political scientist Mark Smith makes clear, the *National Re-*

view is the most representative of these conservative publications in that it publishes across the spectrum of conservative thought, from moderates to libertarians.[62] In this sense, the *National Review* is true to postwar conservative "fusionism," in which the libertarian wing of the conservative movement was fused to the socially conservative wing, something made possible because both were opposed to the collectivism associated with communism.[63] Second, the *National Review*, by virtue of its circulation and website hits, is the most influential conservative publication.[64] Third, it represents the single longest-running statement of conservative thought, premiering in 1955, under the stewardship of one of the leading lights of postwar conservatism, William F. Buckley Jr.

Framing and the Meaning of Tea Party Support

As we have already detailed above, the presidency occupies an important, almost sacred symbolic space in American life. Whoever holds the office is the commander in chief of the armed forces and chief law enforcement officer, among many other things. Most important, however, as we pointed out, the president of the United States is the face of the country, someone with whom Americans, since we were all children, have come to identify. We think it's likely that for some, the first nonwhite president may simply be too much to bear. We draw on the use of interpretive frames to help us understand how Tea Party sympathizers, as well as other Americans, make sense of this new landscape.

Interpretive frames, according to sociologists David Snow and Robert Benford, work to simplify the real world by emphasizing objects and other events within one's setting. The frames constructed by movement elites, or in this case activists, direct and assist collective action by providing "shorthand interpretations of the world" that "locate blame" and "suggest lines of action." In short, frames help individuals identify, define, and react to problems emphasized by elites or frame constructors. We use frames to investigate how Tea Party sympathizers, among others, interpret and react to the new political landscape.[65]

John Zaller's work on elites (or opinion leaders), people who are politically active and influential, illustrates their ability to shape how people think about issues through the provision of important cues.[66] In short, elites permit nonspecialists to make sense of the often-complicated world of politics. Also, in order to accurately examine Tea Party elites, we must shift our examination beyond traditional elites—people who have devoted their life to politics—to what Taeku Lee identifies as citizen activists.[67]

Citizen activists play a key role in bridging informational gaps that may exist between the elites and the masses. Citizen activists are engrossed in, and attentive to, politics so that they are able to stay informed in ways that the mass public cannot. Before the 2010 midterm elections, citizen activists dominated the elite Tea Party discussion, for there were only a handful of traditional elites (Dick Armey, Jim DeMint, Michele Bachmann) that had risen out of the movement. For this reason, we consider the members and contributors to major Tea Party websites as citizen activists or, as we call them moving forward, activists. To the degree that they influence rank-and-file Tea Party sympathizers, citizen activists will serve as the central focus of our content analysis of the Tea Party.

Frame Typology and Examples

We drew on eight frames to guide our analysis of the online content from the *NRO* and the major Tea Party websites. (Please see chapter 1 results in the appendix for coding details, sampling, etc.) Our selection of one set of frames was driven by themes associated with postwar conservatism.[68] Recall that postwar conservatism "fused" the belief in small government and individualism to social conservatism's emphasis on tradition and morality. Of course, as we have already mentioned, national security is the third element of postwar conservatism. To illustrate, the small-government strain of conservatism is reflected in dialogue criticizing "big government" and government expansion. One article entitled "Big Government Forgets How to Build Big Projects" in the *NRO* criticizes the stimulus package for expanding government to an unproductive level. Similarly, a post from the Lansing, Michigan Tea Party encourages its supporters to speak out against a government that has "gone over the edge" when it comes to federal spending.[69]

Our selection of another set of frames is designed to test our contention that the Tea Party, and its supporters, represents the most current installment of the Far Right. As the literature of right-wing movements makes clear, the Far Right is often concerned with subversion, something that generates the paranoid social cognition and conspiratorial thinking discussed above. To capture the fear of subversion and conspiratorial aims that we believe Tea Party supporters attach to the presidency of Barack Obama, we examined the percentage of posts and articles that paint President Obama as a socialist or communist.[70] We also found others who believed that Obama would ruin the country. Collectively, we call these "fear of change" frames because they represent the anxiety Tea Partiers associate with the Obama presidency.

We are aware that many conservatives hesitate to embrace change; some may even fear it. Still, as we alluded to above, there is an important distinction between *mainstream* conservatives and *reactionary* conservatives. Mainstream conservatives oppose change that happens too rapidly, or change they perceive as too radical. Nonetheless, they believe that change is organic, evolutionary even, and must be permitted to happen if order is to be maintained. Otherwise, change may take a revolutionary turn, destroying the institutions on which a stable social order has come to rest, an event the mainstream conservative cannot abide.[71] Reactionary conservatives, on the other hand, are more likely to buy into a narrative in which subversion masquerades as change. Thus, change of any kind, even if it leads to tangible progress, is considered bad: it's nothing more than a plot to undermine dominance of the aggrieved group. In sum, there are reasons why conservatives may be apprehensive about change, but the belief that change ultimately disguises subversion of some kind isn't one of them.[72]

Consider the following as an example of the type of frames we sampled from forty-two official Tea Party websites over a two-year period.[73] In the following post on the Colorado Tea Party Patriots website, the author told readers that "We have to stop this President from ruining our country." The Atlanta Tea Party urged supporters to speak out against "Elected officials who support Socialist Government and forced re-distribution of wealth." These sentiments were echoed on the Alabama Tea Party Patriot website, which asked for a "vital third voice . . . that can challenge the relentless drift into socialism that is destroying America," a voice able to stop "the runaway freight train of government insanity that dominates Washington today." Other posts accuse the Obama-led government of "socialist tyranny" and call members of the administration less-than-flattering names such as "socialist monkey nuts" who are destroying the constitution.[74] A final set of frames examines the hostility directed toward President Obama and other out-groups, including "taking the country back" from these groups.

Tea Party Conservative = Responsible Conservative?

To begin, figure 1.1 confirms our prior comments about the *National Review Online*: it reflects the aims of mainstream, "responsible" conservatism. Indeed, 76 percent of the content is centered on core conservative issues. Much of the content, 33 percent, focuses on issues relating to "big government" or argues for states' rights. Fully 33 percent of posts and articles focus on foreign policy or national security. Overall, 10 percent of the content focuses on values and morals. All told, then, 76 percent of the *NRO* content is about core conservative issues. The remaining 24 percent display intolerance of some kind, be it personal attacks on the president, racism, immigration, and/or taking the country back from "Others."

We now invite the reader to contrast the results on display in figure 1.2, the content gleaned from the official Tea Party websites, with the results from figure 1.1. The differences are hard to ignore. Posts and articles that focus on big government or argue

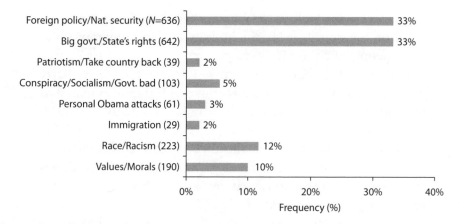

1.1. Content of *National Review Online*

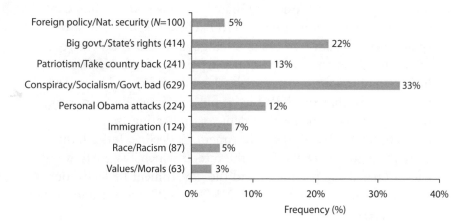

1.2. Content of Tea Party websites

for states' rights account for 22 percent of the Tea Party website content. Another 5 percent focus on issues related to national security and foreign policy. Three percent of the posts discuss issues relating to values and morality. Taken together, 30 percent of all Tea Party websites are concerned with core conservative issues. The remaining 70 percent consist of conspiratorial discourse (33%), "taking the country back" (13%), personal attacks on the president (12%), and attacks on immigrants and other people of color (12% altogether).

Conspiratorial content constitutes 33 percent of the Tea Party website content—the most content of any frame—compared to the content from the NRO, which holds steady at 5 percent. Moreover, there is a 46-point gap between the NRO and Tea Party websites in the space allocated to core conservative issues. These results suggest that Tea Party supporters are different from mainstream conservatives, as they lean more toward reactionary conservatism.

So far our analysis suggests that there is some daylight separating Tea Party conservatives from mainstream conservatives. The citizen activists posting on the Tea Party websites are far more suspicious of President Obama and his policies than conservative elites posting on the NRO. These results suggest that sympathizers believe an Obama-led government is on the road to ruining America. Yet the content posted on the NRO bears little resemblance to what is posted on Tea Party websites. This is not to say that the NRO is completely innocent of posting personal attacks on the president, or indicating that the government he heads will result in America's decline. Indeed, there were posts to this effect. Still, the rate at which Tea Party websites attacked the president, and the government he leads, outstripped similar content on the NRO by 400 percent and 600 percent, respectively.

Our results suggest that the Tea Party and its supporters are reactionaries. Furthermore, it doesn't require much to make the connection from reactionary to right-wing movements. In fact, the tone of believers' sentiments toward Obama reminds us of rhetoric deployed by the JBS against another sitting president: Dwight D. Eisenhower. This was one of several incidents for which William F. Buckley Jr., *National Review* editor and dean of the postwar conservative movement, ejected Robert Welch, and eventually the JBS, from the conservative movement. Anxiety and anger typify the reactions of Tea Party sympathizers at both the activist and mass level. Tea Party sympathizers believe Obama is destroying their country. Our evidence, coupled with the history of right-wing movements, suggests that the Tea Party and its supporters likely view immigrants—illegal and otherwise—and the gay and lesbian community as coconspirators.

As we close this section, we'd like to respond to a possible objection: our use of conspiratorial beliefs as a means of identifying the Tea Party as a reactionary movement, beyond mainstream conservatism. We understand. Still, we'd like to point out that some scholars say conspiracy theories are foundational to American politics. Mark Fenster, for instance, argues that conspiracy theories aren't necessarily bad or beyond the bounds of American politics, and that "Populist concerns about the concentration of public and private power and of foreign control of domestic authority . . . have long animated American practice and governance."[75] In fact, historian David Brion Davis suggests that conspiracies played no small role in the run-up to the Civil War. As an example, he argues that abolitionists believed proslavery aristocrats planned to seize control of the government and gradually subvert "free constitutions" and execute "plans to enslave the people."[76]

The late political scientist Michael Rogin takes it a step further by making the case that *political demonology*, in which monsters are created through the "inflation, stigmatization, and dehumanization of political foes," is the rule, not the exception, when it comes to American political culture.[77] Put simply, each of these scholars suggests that countersubversive movements are as American as apple pie. Still, none of these scholars claim that the so-called paranoid style is consistent with traditional, more "responsible" conservatism. Even the above-mentioned Fenster, who tries valiantly to rescue conspiracy theory in the guise of populism from the pathological behavior to which it is frequently connected, cannot abide the political objectives often associated with conspiratorial discourse. In short, making a case that conspiracy theory is a recurring theme in American political culture is *not* to say that it's free of extremism.

Even so, we cannot afford to get carried away with these results, for if we take a step back, a critic may credibly argue that
we're comparing "apples to oranges." By this we mean that the
National Review is staffed with professional, seasoned journalists.[78] We cannot make the same assumption about the citizen
activists posting on the Tea Party websites.[79] In fact, since they're
writing for a narrower, local readership, it's likely that the citizen activists have more latitude to write more edgy pieces, ones
that will play well at home but not nationally. Still, these findings mesh well with the results of other scholars who have studied Tea Party activists in that they tend to believe and say things
many people may find, quite frankly, hard to believe.[80] Perhaps
most important, at least for our purposes, is that we now see
evidence emerging that makes it difficult for the Tea Party and
its supporters to claim mainstream conservatism. Even so, to
have confidence in our findings, in which Tea Party activists are
closer to reactionary than mainstream conservatives, we need
to devise another test, one that moves beyond elites and citizen
activists to the masses.

ARE TEA PARTY CONSERVATIVES REALLY MORE EXTREME THAN OTHER CONSERVATIVES?

To better capture the attitudes of Tea Party sympathizers at
the mass level, we employ an experiment embedded within our
Multi-State Survey of Race and Politics (MSSRP; 2011), a pro-
cedure we hope will tease out differences already observed between Tea Party supporters and Tea Party sympathizers.[81] Recall
our claim that Tea Party conservatives differ from mainstream
conservatives in that the former are reactionary and therefore
prone to believing conspiratorial, demagogic discourse. To test
this, we asked people in our survey if they believed it was true
that "Barack Obama is destroying the country." Now, admittedly, this is a provocative statement. Asking someone to agree
with this statement, even if people believed it to be true, is difficult. People will hesitate to offer their honest assessment of a

statement like this out of fear that agreement will peg them as a misfit or deviant of some kind. This is precisely why the experiment is necessary: it allows people to overcome the fear associated with giving what some may consider socially undesirable answers to sensitive questions, or becoming overly concerned with making controversial statements.[82] (We leave the details of the experiments for people who are interested. Please see "Experiment Methodology and Results" in the appendix.)

The other part of our analysis includes separating self-identified Tea Party conservatives from self-identified non–Tea Party conservatives. If we are correct, and people who call themselves conservative and sympathize with the Tea Party are really reactionary conservatives, they should be more willing to believe the president will destroy the country than self-identified conservatives who aren't too keen on the Tea Party.

As figure 1.3 makes plain, the difference separating the two groups is quite stunning. First, however, let's take a look at the willingness of all conservatives to say that Obama is destroying the country. We see that slightly more than one-third of conservatives believe that Obama is out to destroy the country. While not insignificant, it's not as high as one would think given the extent to which conservatives have resisted the president's agenda. Once we consider cleavages between self-identified Tea Party conservatives and other conservatives, it leaves little doubt that the percentage reported for all conservatives is driven by the 71 percent of Tea Party conservatives who believe Barack Obama will ultimately ruin the country. Compare this to the 6 percent of conservatives who agree with them, and it's easy to make the claim that Tea Party conservatives are a lot more reactionary than other self-identified conservatives.

These results support the claim that Tea Party conservatives are out of step with more mainstream conservatives, which supports our position that they may fairly be defined as reactionary conservatives. Furthermore, our findings reinforce the conclusions we drew on the basis of our content analysis among the Tea Party activists. This suggests a common thread running

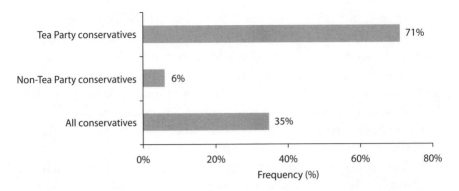

1.3. Percent that believe Obama will destroy country

from Tea Party activists through the masses, the vast majority of whom, as we shall soon see, aren't activists, much less Tea Party members. One may wonder why there is such consistency between the message of Tea Party activists and the masses. An obvious answer is simply that all Tea Party websites are like the ones we just canvassed. Another one, suggested by Skocpol and Williamson, is that Fox News is a clearinghouse for Tea Party–related discourse.[83] By this, we mean that the conservative channel is a means through which Tea Party elites communicate with the masses.

TEA PARTY SUPPORTERS: WHAT DO THEY SAY?

So far, our results suggest that Tea Party–related beliefs—among the elites and masses—are outside of mainstream conservatism. Why do people who support the Tea Party feel the way they apparently feel? What motivates their animosity toward President Obama? Our theory suggests that they are angry and anxious about Barack Obama's occupation of the presidency. It also suggests that Tea Party supporters harbor negative sentiments toward members of out-groups from whom they are trying to save the country: immigrants, illegal and otherwise, and sexual minorities. To get a better handle on the "what" and "why" we turn to open-ended interviews, which allow us to explore how fear and paranoia may structure the attitudes of Tea Party sympathizers.

In what follows, we contrast the views of Tea Party sympathizers with the opinions of people who are skeptical of the movement. Since we have already seen stunning differences among self-identified conservatives, we aren't even going to try and sell the fiction that there's any chance sympathizers and skeptics will see things the same way. To examine anxiety over America's future, we asked a number of Americans, a subset of one of our surveys,[84] about their feelings toward President Obama, illegal immigrants, and sexual minorities. The interviews we conducted drew on a range of emotional cues to examine positive and negative feelings toward the president and the groups from whom Frank Rich indicates the Tea Party is attempting to recover the country.[85] Positive sentiments include pride, inspiration, excitement, enthusiasm, and strength. Negative sentiments include fear, anxiety, and anger.

Our expectation is that Tea Party sympathizers will have a hard time mustering anything in the way of positive sentiment toward the president and the out-groups we reference. We expect those who have no use for the Tea Party to have an opposite reaction; that is, we expect them to express relatively positive emotions toward the president and these groups.[86] (Please see the appendix for sampling and coding details.)

Tea Party Sympathizers Explain Why They Feel the Way They Do

As figure 1.4 makes clear, this is exactly what happened. When compared to people who don't like the Tea Party, and those without any strong opinion, Tea Party sympathizers' feelings toward President Obama, illegal immigrants, as well as gays and lesbians are decidedly more negative; they're worried about the future of their country. For example, a respondent angry with Obama said, "I believe he's trying to ruin everything that you asked me about before [in a previous question] that was good

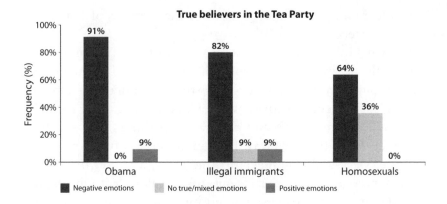

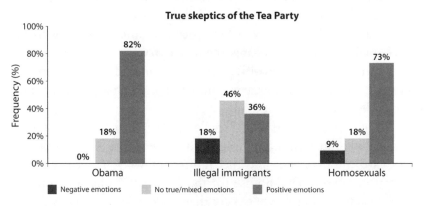

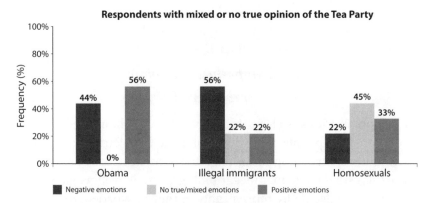

1.4. Emotional responses to open-ended interviews, by Tea Party support
Note: Total $N = 31$, with 11 true believers, 11 true skeptics,
and 9 with mixed or no opinion; no true opinion = had
no well-informed opinion of the Tea Party
Source: MSSRP (2010)

about America." When asked to further elaborate, this person simply "believe[s] that [Obama] is a socialist." Another Tea Party sympathizer expresses similar feelings toward Obama, claiming that, "he's been brought up very badly. Even his grandparents were communist," and that the liberal agenda is "right out of a communist manifesto."

Indeed, as we observed with both the content analysis and the survey experiment, Tea Party supporters aren't shy about expressing their belief that Obama is well on his way to destroying the country. Apparently, many believe his weapon of choice is socialism. Consider the following observation from a Tea Party supporter in the Midwest:

> I think he comes from a very socialist, Marxist background. I think that it's absolutely the way that he leads. I think that he wants to micro-manage individuals as an elitist, looking down trying to make people do what he thinks they should be doing. And I think that's very close to tyranny and I think it's very wrong.

Clearly, this person perceives the president as an autocrat, a leader with a philosophy at odds with the American principles of freedom and democracy. Still, this is a relatively mild rebuke of Obama. For instance, some Tea Party sympathizers went even further, calling President Obama "an enemy of the state," an assessment based on the perception that the president is a "freakin' Communist."

Although the majority of our interviews with "true believers" reflected the above sentiments, not all Tea Party supporters are critical of President Obama. For example, the lone Tea Party supporter who is positive about Obama remains "excited" with his presidency. To elaborate, this person believes that:

> [Obama] is a positive person who has a big vision for the country that goes beyond where we are today. He believes people can be better than they are today.

As we have hoped to make clear, this statement shows that not *all* Tea Party supporters are fearful of, and anxious over, an Obama presidency. Indeed, there are some sympathizers who buy into the "hope and change" meme surrounding Obama during the campaign and the early days of his tenure in office. Still, better than 90 percent of our subsample see the president in a negative light.

We now turn to the task of investigating what sympathizers say about illegal immigrants and sexual minorities. As we inspect the results, it's clear that Tea Party sympathizers wish to keep constituents of these communities at bay. This is justified by the more than 80 percent of sympathizers who remain suspicious of illegal immigrants and the 64 percent of them who have less-than-flattering opinions of sexual minorities. For example, often the voices of those sympathetic appear fraught with anxiety over the presence of illegal immigrants in America. One man laments that after "letting them in the country, they just come in and take over everything. . . . and the criminal acts—there are just a lot of criminal activities they do." Another man is more concerned with surveillance:

> I don't know where they came from or what their past history was or anything like that I guess. I don't know—I just don't know I guess. I think there should be a better way of keeping track of them and what they are doing.

Where the first guy seems overwrought with anxiety over the presence of illegal immigrants in the country, this gentleman seems at least mildly anxious. He's not really concerned about crime, it seems. Indeed, his concerns reside with the unlawful *presence* of illegal immigrants.

We have already noted that almost two-thirds of believers have a negative opinion of sexual minorities. For reasons unknown to us, at least two of the Tea Party sympathizers referred to sexual minorities in relatively epidemiological terms in which both invoked disease, in some fashion, as a way of describing how they felt about gays and lesbians. To illustrate, as one man referred to homosexuality as a "cancer . . . an infectious disease" that "if you live around it long enough, you catch it." His re- action suggests he's afraid of coming into contact with members of the gay and lesbian community. Other Tea Party sympathiz- ers aren't as hostile, but disease is still referenced. Consider the following observation by a female Tea Party supporter:

> I guess because of the HIV I feel very scared. Well, you know, I just believe marriage should be between a man and a woman. I feel that they [gays and lesbians] don't take the responsibility of safe sex. Well, I have a friend from the hospital who was gay, HIV positive and he was very abu- sive with it. He's probably alienated everybody.

This woman isn't as hostile to homosexuality as the above- mentioned guy. Rather, her concerns are more about the conse- quences of homosexuality, and her perception of the behavior that leads to such outcomes.

Not all Tea Party sympathizers are hostile toward illegal im- migrants, nor are they categorically homophobic. In fact, by the numbers, approximately 20 percent are at least sympathetic to illegal immigrants' situation, if not unabashedly in favor of them. One true believer, in fact, thought positively about illegal immigrants, elaborating that "they are just working folks kind of making a life for themselves and better themselves." Another sympathizer agrees, explaining that illegal immigrants are sim- ply doing what they must to survive:

> [Illegal immigrants] take a lot of risk to support their fam- ilies. I met a lot of immigrants from all around the world and they are just trying to make it. If you want to put a negative light on them, that's just not right.

Likewise, some Tea Party sympathizers reject homophobia. For example, one Tea Party supporter describes gays and lesbians as, "remarkable people." Her positive portrayal of gays and lesbians continues as she explains that she has a number of gay and lesbian friends that she just "adores." This is a departure from the all-too-common attacks on sexual minorities on Tea Party websites.

To summarize, Tea Party sympathizers fail to embrace those they believe are beyond the perceived bounds of American identity, especially President Obama. In fact, the president, as well as members of the selected social groups, appears to evoke anxiety among Tea Party sympathizers. Even so, such negative sentiment isn't universal. Indeed, there are some Tea Party sympathizers who respect the president and reject xenophobia and homophobia. Still, it's hard to overestimate just how much Tea Party sympathizers loathe President Obama. We realize of course, that we're not working with a lot of interviews here, an issue we promise to work out later when we make an attempt to understand just how general these sentiments are. For now, though, among Tea Party sympathizers, Obama is the source of more anxiety than sexual minorities and illegal immigrants.

What Are Skeptics of the Tea Party Saying?

Now that we've inventoried a sample of what Tea Party supporters say about the president, as well as illegal immigrants and sexual minorities, we must consider what those who dislike the Tea Party say. While it's true that our focus is on Tea Party supporters, good social science demands that we also observe the opposite end of the spectrum: what it means to reject the Tea Party. If we are correct in our assessment of Tea Party supporters, we should expect that the sentiments of non–Tea Party supporters go in the opposite direction. In other words, non–Tea Party types should embrace the president, as well as sexual minorities and illegal immigrants, more so than Tea Party sympathizers. This is the bulk of what we found.

The most clear-cut case starts with how non–Tea Party types feel about the president. In fact, not a single one of these folks had anything critical to say about the president. They reported being "interested" in Obama, and describe him as "an inspiring speech maker" and "very intelligent." Several others mentioned the pride they've taken in their country for electing Obama. One such example should suffice to make the point. Consider the following observations of a male southerner:

> Well, I'm proud that as a country we have come to the point where the color of your skin is not the most important thing. That he's a bright, intelligent man and that he was elected because people were ready for something like that. And [even] being a black person, or a partially black person, [that] he could be elected, and I'm proud of that.

Non–Tea Partiers also report positive feelings for sexual minorities. In fact, as panel B in figure 1.4 indicates, more than 70 percent of them were sympathetic to the plight of the gay and lesbian community. Most of these people are disturbed by the treatment to which sexual minorities remain subjected, even if they acknowledge some progress has been made. The following comment, proffered by a non–Tea Party type, is an ideal example:

> Well I think they're probably the most persecuted minority in America still. They are still lynching gays, in the last few years even. So, they have had quite a struggle and they are achieving some tolerance—they are now achieving some equality and I'm happy to see that. But, [they] still actually face a lot of bigotry and a lot of hatred against them.

Nonetheless, as the numbers in figure 1.4 suggest, there's no consensus on the way in which folks feel about sexual minorities. As a matter of fact, almost 10 percent failed to have positive feelings associated with gays and lesbians, with approximately 20 percent reporting no opinion at all. One non–Tea Party type is uncomfortable discussing sexual minorities. He explains that "I really don't spend much time thinking about them [sexual minorities]." And, without necessarily agreeing or disagreeing with the lifestyle of gays and lesbians, this person makes it clear that "whatever moral issue there is, is between them and God."

So far, clear majorities of non–Tea Party types have positive impressions of Obama and sexual minorities. We expected as much. Things become more complicated, however, once we shift the analysis to explore the sentiments associated with illegal immigrants. To illustrate, approximately 40 percent of this group has anything in the way of sympathy for illegal immigrants. In fact, only one of the non–Tea Party strata referred to illegal immigrants as a "persecuted population," indicating a sense of compassion for these people. Another skeptic, framing her sympathy in terms of rights, observes that "[illegal immigrants] should be given every right that anybody else has in America."

Other folks claiming membership in the non–Tea Party strata were less sympathetic. Putting numbers to it, approximately 20 percent of this group expressed anger toward illegal immigrants because "they are taking jobs." They continue to describe their fears in detail:

> You know, they'll work for nothing. In Mexico, they don't get about 50 cents a day. I mean, they ain't got nothing over there. The water is nasty. The water ain't no good. Oh, it's terrible. It's horrifying. I mean, I believe everybody should be you know, treated equal, but they are not—I mean, if they weren't born and raised in the United States of America, then they need to have proper assistance to get over here and then if the federal government says they can come over here, then let them come over here. But if the federal government don't allow them to come over here, they need to be put right back where they belong. I mean, because you know, disease is over there that we ain't never heard of.

Clearly, his concerns aren't limited to economic competition and dislocation. To be sure, this guy isn't without sympathy: he recognizes that illegal immigrants are essentially forced to leave (we presume Mexico) if they are to have a shot at a good life. Still, his words imply that he's also concerned about illegal immigrants spreading disease in America.

What Are People with No Definitive Opinion of the Tea Party Saying?

We now turn to folks without a definite opinion of the Tea Party. As figure 1.4 makes clear, they fail to trend one way or the other. By this, we mean they're neither uniformly positive nor uniformly negative. For instance, when it comes to President Obama, approximately 60 percent feel positive about his election versus approximately 40 percent who fail to share this view. To illustrate the point, when asked about President Obama, one respondent without a definite opinion of the Tea Party expressed "pride and admiration," while another reported that the president is "a disgrace to the American people."

Attitudes toward illegal immigrants, for people who have no strong feelings about the Tea Party and no clear opinion of the Tea Party, track in the opposite direction. That is, the sentiment among this group toward illegal immigrants is, on balance, negative. Attaching cold, hard numbers, we estimate that 60 percent of these strata aren't very sympathetic to the plight of illegal immigrants, versus approximately 20 percent who are, and 20 percent who really don't care. An exemplar of those in the majority, one woman feels disgust toward illegal immigrants: "Here they come, they have no insurance. They are draining state governments. We have to provide for them because they are here." Other people held less hostile views. One man, for instance, asked that we "don't judge [illegal immigrants] because they are from somewhere else." His plea continues, encouraging people to "find out what [illegal immigrants] need and help them with it."

Attitudes concerning sexual minorities among people claiming no opinion of the Tea Party are more difficult to make sense of, mainly because a plurality of this stratum either had mixed emotions about the subject or didn't care. Another third of this group harbored positive feelings, and about one in five had less-than-flattering opinions of the gay and lesbian community. For example, one respondent held the right of gays and lesbians in high regard, averring that, "I respect their rights. I respect them and the decision they've made." Someone else, also indifferent to the Tea Party, felt scared of gays and lesbians, mostly because of the common perception that "the HIV" virus is in some way connected to the homosexual lifestyle. Another interviewee without strong feelings one way or another about the Tea Party declares the following: "I think they've got a right to exist, but I don't particularly want them around me."

■   ■   ■

Based on the evidence we've already accrued with respect to the content analysis and the experiment, our findings here aren't very surprising. In fact, the sole purpose of these open-ended interviews is to appreciate why Tea Party sympathizers and their counterparts feel the way they do about the president and other entities believed to be beyond the bounds of the American national community. By talking with both Tea Party sympathizers and those who are less supportive of the movement, we find that the attitudes of Tea Party sympathizers toward President Obama and selected minorities are overwhelmingly negative, revealing a sense of social paranoia consistent with the way in which we have theorized reactionary conservatism. We want to be clear that Tea Party sympathizers don't see all out-groups as bad. Nor do all non–Tea Party folks feel good about all out-groups. Yet we see a *tendency* for Tea Party supporters to harbor more negative feelings toward minorities, feelings that parallel the paranoia and anxiety consistent with the reactionary conservatism we hypothesize, than feelings expressed by non–Tea Party folk. Put differently, relative to Tea Party skeptics, Tea Party supporters believe that President Obama, illegal immigrants, and gays and lesbians represent a change for the worse in America, which gives Tea Party sympathizers reason to be anxious.

We freely admit that a case can be made against seeing illegal immigrants as part of the American community. Nonetheless, it should be hard for anyone to wrap their head around the idea that a sitting president of the United States isn't a part of the political community he personifies. We must approach our findings with a fair bit of caution since people sometimes have a hard time justifying why they feel the way they do about something, and when they do locate a reason, it may not make logical sense.[87] However, since these are strong attitudes (an exception can be made for those with no definite opinion of the Tea Party), we have every expectation that such attitudes are stable indicators of how these people feel.[88]

CONCLUDING THOUGHTS

In this chapter, we sought to accomplish two things. First, we offered a theoretical framework as a means of understanding why people are motivated to support the Tea Party, one based on observations of similar right-wing movements such as the Klan of the 1920s and the JBS. While some may think it inappropriate to compare the Tea Party to these two movements, we hope to have made clear the logical basis for doing so. All three appeal to the same demographic and use similar, if not identical, rhetoric as a basis for mobilization. For these reasons, we drew on our analysis of the Klan and the JBS to derive a theoretical framework, one that we applied to the Tea Party as a means of explaining the movement's attractiveness.

Second, upon concluding that President Obama represents the fear of change we've witnessed in other right-wing movements, we conducted a preliminary test of our theory. If the Tea Party was really about mainstream conservatism, the discourse among the citizen activists should parallel the discourse in the *NRO*. It didn't. It was far less conservative and far more reactionary than the *NRO*. Without too much trouble, we identified the paranoia we expected to find in the discourse examined on Tea Party websites. We conducted another analysis at the mass level among the rank and file in order to examine whether or not conspiratorial discourse filtered down. It did. Considerable differences separated so-called Tea Party conservatives from non–Tea Party conservatives, which validates our claim that the Tea Party and its supporters aren't conservative in the strict sense of the word. Rather, they are indeed reactionaries.

Our final test explored how people expressed their feelings about the president. We also extended the analysis to include certain others who have been part of recent public discourse: sexual minorities and illegal immigrants. These groups serve as a means of validating our claim that Tea Party sympathizers are really reactionary conservatives. Again, there are signs that paranoid thinking among Tea Party sympathizers is directed at the president, but not limited to him. As we observed, people with an affinity for the Tea Party are also concerned with the sexual minorities and illegal immigrants in their midst.

At this very preliminary stage, our theory is supported. While we are off to a promising start, we must, nonetheless, refrain from jumping to conclusions. We remain cautious because there are other factors—ones we have yet to take into account—that may explain the relationship between support for the Tea Party and the paranoia associated with Obama. For those who might say ideology is the key factor involved in support for the Tea Party, we have already eliminated it as a factor insofar as we are able to discriminate between Tea Party conservatives and non–Tea Party conservatives in the extent to which they resent Obama. What other factors remain? Is there anything beyond disdain for Obama and allies that pushes people to support the Tea Party?

Since Tea Party supporters tend to be hard-core Republicans, and Obama is the leader of the Democratic Party, perhaps partisanship can help explain why Tea Party supporters resent Obama. We need to also consider the possibility that people are driven to sympathize with the Tea Party for reasons unrelated to politics. For example, preference for social conformity (authoritarianism), affection for one's own group (ethnocentrism), or the drive to dominate other "subordinate" groups (social dominance orientation) may also motivate people to gravitate toward the Tea Party. In other words, before we have any confidence that anxiety associated with what Obama represents helps to drive the Tea Party and its supporters, we must consider alternative explanations. Upon accounting for these quite reasonable explanations for why people may be sympathetic to the Tea Party, it's possible our claim that Obama is an important reason why people support the movement is no longer valid, a possibility we address in chapter 2.

2

Who Likes Tea? Sources of Support for the Tea Party

I N CHAPTER ONE WE offered a theoretical account of the Tea Party and its supporters. We argued the possibility that if the Tea Party is anything like the Far Right of yesteryear, it's not likely conservative in the more traditional sense. More to the point, we argued that Tea Party activists and supporters are reactionaries, something our findings confirm. Beyond this, however, we still don't know what, if anything else, is associated with support for the Tea Party. The literature on right-wing movements, some of which we discussed in the introduction and chapter 1, furnishes a few clues. Several factors appear to push people to support the Far Right, including age, class, religion, race, and gender. The literature suggests that other factors contribute to support for the right wing, such as political and ideological motivations: partisanship and preference for a limited government. Of course, we cannot ignore the role social psychology plays. Indeed, as we shall soon see, a desire for conformity, what social scientists call authoritarianism, has also been identified as a source of support for right-wing movements.

We agree that these are all worthy of investigation. After all, each has been mentioned time and again by the most renowned scholars of their respective times as key contributors to the rise of right-wing movements. Still, we feel these explanations remain incomplete. Most of the empirical work on right-wing movements was conducted prior to important refinements in the ways in which scholars approach intergroup relations. In the past twenty years, for instance, scholars have made important strides in their efforts to explain the persistence of racism, sexism, xenophobia, and homophobia, all of which are assumed to be associated with support for the right wing. Yet, for one reason or another, these advances haven't been incorporated in studies of the Far Right. We think intergroup relations may be a useful way in which to understand the Tea Party and its supporters. In what follows, we correct this oversight.

Who are the Tea Party supporters and *why* do they support the movement? The Tea Party and its sympathizers insist that they are about small government and fiscal responsibility, thoroughly conservative principles. (We add the caveat that Tea Party conservatism isn't commensurate with mainstream conservatism, a conclusion we drew in chapter 1.) Critics, however, claim that the Tea Party is driven by intolerance. We consider the likelihood that both sets of explanations may push people to support the Tea Party. Indeed, if the past is prologue for right-wing movements, we expect *both* to animate sympathy for the Tea Party. Granting this, we argue that the change represented by the election of Barack Obama increases the attractiveness of the Tea Party to the mainly white, middle-aged, middle-class, relatively well-educated, largely male slice of America who believe he is committed to the destruction of "their" country.

Accordingly, the purpose of the present chapter is twofold. Our first order of business is to establish the meaning of Tea Party support and the characteristics of those who are sympathetic to the movement. We then explore the sources of Tea Party sympathy. More to the point, we examine the extent to which the perceived threat associated with Obama, and what he's perceived to represent, explains support for the Tea Party beyond obvious—though yet tested—factors such as politics and out-group hostility. In the end, our findings confirm that Tea Party supporters tend to be relatively financially secure, white, mostly male, and Protestant—many of whom are evangelicals. Our results also confirm that sympathy for the Tea Party is driven by conservative principles as well as out-group hostility. Most important, we find support for our claim that perceived subversion on the part of President Obama and his policies (as we witnessed in chapter 1) is also associated with support for the Tea Party.

Exploring the Contours of Tea Party Support

Before we get under way with our examination of Tea Party supporters, we'd like to first elaborate on what it means to support the Tea Party. We have already made the claim that the Tea Party movement is akin to the Ku Klux Klan of the 1920s and the John Birch Society (JBS) in that all three appeal to the same demographic and draw on similar rhetoric. Indeed, as we have already mentioned in our citation of other studies, rank-and-file Tea Party supporters (not necessarily activists) are generally middle-class, middle-aged, white males, and this is something we will confirm in this chapter. Moreover, the literature is clear on the fact that these folks were trying, as best they could, to preserve their way of life.

The Klan and the JBS were concerned with change they read as threats to the "American" way of life. The Klan defined the American way of life ethnoculturally: as white, male, and Protestant. The JBS, as we have already mentioned in chapter 1, drew more on ideology to communicate its brand of nationalism than *overt* ethnic or racial intolerance. Anything that failed to support its philosophy, in which small government and traditional social and racial relations dominated, was viewed as part of a communist plot, as un-American. Taken together, then, the Klan and the JBS weren't reacting to a single threat. Instead, the sources of perceived threat were manifold. However, what united Klansmen, and bound many followers of the JBS, was the sum of these threats: perceived subversion of their way(s) of life, and, ultimately, the destruction of "their" country.

We believe a similar logic applies to the Tea Party and its supporters. Consider the results from chapter 1. There, we saw that more than 60 percent of the content posted on official Tea Party websites is based on a perceived threat from President Barack Obama and his policies, from illegal immigrants, and from sexual minorities. What they all have in common is a threat to the American way of life, even as the specific source of threat varies: President Obama and his policies are viewed as un-American, even anti-American, and illegal immigrants are viewed as alien, as is the lifestyle associated with homosexuality.[1] Still, in each case, the threat is grounded in difference of some kind.

Before we begin our assessment of who sympathizes with the Tea Party and who doesn't, we wish to first gauge popular sentiment associated with it. This should give us some insight into why some people get behind the Tea Party and why others fail to do so. To accomplish this, we used a simple, open-ended question near the end of our survey in which we asked people whether or not they believed the Tea Party was, on balance, good or bad for America. This was followed by a question in which we asked the respondents to elaborate. We opted for open-ended questions here because, as polling expert and sociologist Howard Schuman indicates, they are better at providing meaning than the more typical close-ended, forced-choice questions that are often necessary for surveys. Open-ended questions, in other words, permit the participants to offer a rationale, i. e., *why*, they answered a question the way they did.[2] In this particular case, we hope to understand why someone believes the Tea Party is good or bad for America. Generally, the responses were very short, often no longer than two or three sentences in length.

Overall, 56 percent of our survey participants had something positive to say about the Tea Party. As figure 2.1 illustrates, among those who said something positive, a good portion of them, 42 percent, mentioned that the Tea Party added a new,

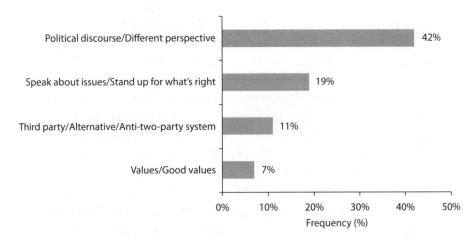

2.1. Positive statements about the Tea Party
(Percent, for those who give opinions, $N = 519$)

much-needed voice to the political discussion. Further, for these people, it furnishes a perspective, they believe, that best represents people like themselves. Another 19 percent favor the movement because of the uncompromising positions it takes on issues. In short, as one of our participants commented, the Tea Party "stands up for what's right."

Approximately 11 percent of those who hold the Tea Party in high regard declare them good for America on the grounds that it challenges the existing two-party system, believing that Republicans and Democrats are incapable of effectively representing anybody's interests. Many of these people believe that the Tea Party is a viable alternative to the existing parties. Another 7 percent report appreciating the Tea Party for the values it represents: hard work and patriotism.[3] As one person said, the Tea Party "shows what good Americans are all about."

A different slice of our participants fail to see the Tea Party in a positive light (see figure 2.2). More to the point, the remaining 44 percent of our participants in the sample believe the emergence of the Tea Party is bad for America. As one can well imagine, then, the responses for the group least attracted to the Tea Party depart markedly from the above responses in tone

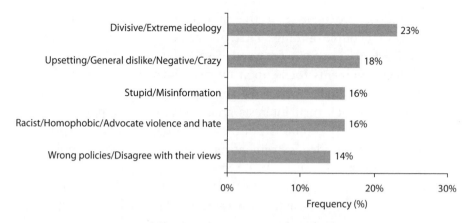

2.2. Negative statements about the Tea Party
(Percent, for those who give opinions, $N = 406$)

and content. For instance, 23 percent of those who think ill of the Tea Party do so on ideological grounds. Simply put, they see the Tea Party as too extreme and too divisive; as one respondent noted, "they're [the Tea Party] way out there." Another 18 percent of this group's critique of the Tea Party is grounded in pure emotion. These people hate the Tea Party because they believe its activists are maladjusted in some way, something that will eventually lead to a crisis of some kind in which "something bad will happen" to the country. Sixteen percent of our respondents in this category believe that the Tea Party is bad for America because its activists are misinformed. In the words of one of our respondents, "these people [the Tea Party] are just plain stupid." Another 16 percent dislike the Tea Party because of the intolerance they believe it has demonstrated. In other words, this segment of our sample is put off by what it perceives as the Tea Party's racism, homophobia, and xenophobia. The final group of people who take a dim view of the Tea Party's influence on America do so for reasons related to policy differences. In short, 14 percent think the Tea Party's position on fiscal and social issues are "dead wrong."[4]

Beyond the fact that open-ended responses permit our participants an opportunity to explain their answers, and allow us a window into their respective thought processes, the content suggests a couple of things. First, for the people who believe that the Tea Party is a force for good (56%), the tone and substance of their comments focus upon intense dissatisfaction with the status quo in some way. They are angry at what they see as a system in which their interests aren't served, where politicians are full of empty promises. For these people, the Tea Party represents a much-needed instrument for course correction to a political system that seems broken. Second, some people fail to share this view of the Tea Party. Detractors of the Tea Party (44%) appear, for the most part, frustrated by the Tea Party. Simply put, these folks don't know what to make of the Tea Party and its activists. In other words, they don't know, and just don't get, what truly motivates the Tea Party and its supporters.

With the possible exception of those who disagree with the Tea Party on policy, many of the comments were also tinged with anger: they're concerned that the Tea Party is tearing the country apart with its attacks on the president. Noticeably absent from the observations of those who have no good use for the Tea Party is the perception of fear. Put differently, no one seemed concerned that the Tea Party's influence in Congress might result in doing irreparable harm to the country. (There's no doubt that these people were angry and resentful toward the Tea Party due, in large part, to the way in which Tea Party activists had recently behaved during the debate over health care.) We conducted these interviews well before the political impact of the Tea Party, and the caucus that represents it in Congress, was felt during the debt-ceiling debate of 2011, in which the country was threatened with the possibility of economic collapse. With this in mind, it's not at all surprising that fear or anxiety isn't a constant theme with those who are frustrated with the Tea Party.

The Depth of Tea Party Support

Now that we know what people in our sample think of the Tea Party, we turn to the task of measuring the depth of its support.

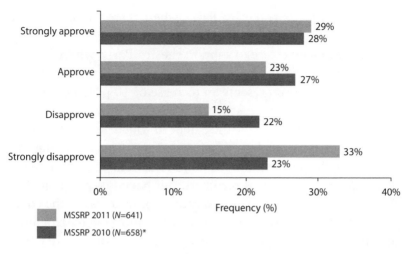

2.3. Tea Party approval, by year
*2010 MSSRP states include: CA, GA, MI, MO, NC, NV, OH

As the Tea Party first began to sweep the country in 2009, gaining momentum in the midst of the debate over health care reform, it seemed its supporters were everywhere. But how much
of the population backs the movement? We begin our examination of the Tea Party with a look at two sources of data we collected, one in 2010, and the most recent in early 2011. Our first
survey covered seven states; the second, thirteen states. (Please
see table A2.1 in the appendix, "Comparison of MSSRP 2011
with contemporaneous national polls by Tea Party support and
selected demographics" for details.) For the current analysis, we
draw on the seven states common to both surveys. As figure 2.3
indicates, our first survey, conducted during the height of the
debate over health care reform in the winter of 2010, reports
that for people with opinions about the Tea Party, more than
one in four Americans (28 percent) in the states we surveyed
"strongly supported" the Tea Party and 23 percent "strongly
disapproved" of them.[5]

If we compare 2010's results, conducted in the winter
(January–March) with the poll we conducted in 2011 during
the same time frame, the results don't change much among those

who strongly support the Tea Party, where there's an increase of 1 percent. Most of the movement occurs elsewhere, especially among those who refuse to support the Tea Party, where 33 percent of the public in the states we surveyed "strongly disapproves" of it. This represents an increase of 10 percent over the previous year.

We now turn to examine the extent to which people who support the Tea Party go beyond approval to formally joining the movement. We also explore the number of folks who aren't willing to declare themselves members, but have taken part in Tea Party–related activities. This is a means for us to assess the commitment of Tea Party supporters to the movement. To gauge membership, we simply asked people whether or not they had joined the Tea Party. We can get a handle on *activism* by asking our respondents if they had done any *one* of the following: attended a Tea Party rally, attended a meeting at someone's home, or donated money. To make things a bit easier as we move forward in this chapter, we divide support for the Tea Party into three categories instead of four. As we press ahead, we make the following designations. We call people who strongly approve of the Tea Party "true believers," those who strongly disapprove of the Tea Party as "true skeptics," and people who don't have strong feelings one way or another, or people who reside between the two poles, as "middle of the road."

Before we move on to our examination of commitment to the Tea Party across levels of support for the movement, let's first explore what it looks like in the general population. As figure 2.4 makes clear, commitment to the Tea Party, captured by whether or not people are members, is pretty small: approximately 2 percent of our respondents are actual *members* of the Tea Party, people who have signed up at some point. The numbers increase once the analysis moves to the question of activism. At 7 percent, the proportion of the population engaged in Tea Party activism of some kind is more than triple the number of people who are official members, which suggests the obvious: membership requires greater commitment.

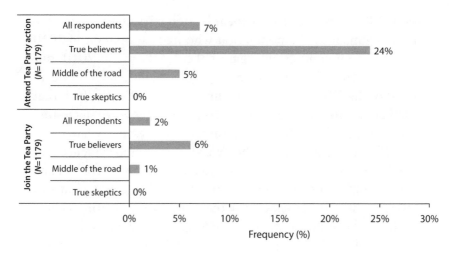

2.4. Tea Party action, by movement approval

Now we turn to explore the connection between sympathy for the Tea Party and commitment to it. It only makes sense that commitment to the Tea Party movement should be greatest among those who we call the true believers, and should be least among true skeptics. The data confirms this. Absolutely none of the skeptics report becoming a member of the Tea Party, and only 1 percent of those in the middle report joining. And while it may not sound like much, 6 percent of believers are official members of the Tea Party. But this is the typical proportion of movement sympathizers who eventually become full-fledged movement members in general.[6] The gaps persist even as the level of movement commitment is relaxed. For instance, none of those who totally reject the Tea Party have engaged in activism of some kind; 5 percent of those in the middle have done so. However, almost one in four true believers (24%) have become active in the movement, even if they have yet to officially join the Tea Party.

So far, we have established the following: in the last year, support for the Tea Party has held fast, but resistance to it has increased. We believe that a chunk of the increased resistance to the Tea Party can be attributed, at least in part, to the difference in the segment of the population who had no opinion in 2010 who are now coming out against the Tea Party. In 2010, our study indicates that approximately 33 percent had either never heard of the Tea Party or had no firm opinion of it. In 2011, that number shrank to 23 percent, a 10-point difference, suggesting that once people without an opinion on the Tea Party had come to hold one, it wasn't favorable. We also presented evidence that true believers are far more committed to the Tea Party than any other group, something that should strike no one as a great surprise. Yet, it's still bracing to witness the gap separating believers from those in the middle, much less the skeptics. So, even though relatively few people are official members of the Tea Party, many more have taken an active part in the movement. Still, only 7 percent of people surveyed said they participated in Tea Party–related activities, and only 2 percent reported actually joining the Tea Party. This is a chief reason why our focus remains solely on Tea Party supporters: doing so allows us to reach beyond the relatively small numbers of committed members and activists.

UNDERSTANDING THE BASICS: SOCIAL AND POLITICAL SOURCES OF TEA PARTY SUPPORT

Up to this point, we have explored what people have to say about the Tea Party, as well as the depth of their support. We found out that people who think well of the Tea Party and its impact on American life (prior to the debate over the debt ceiling) see it as a much-needed corrective to the status quo in which politicians fail to stand on principle, among other things. We also heard mostly bewildered, scornful responses from people who reject the Tea Party and everything for which they believe it stands. They have manifold reasons for dismissing the right-wing movement of the moment. Skeptics are offended, for instance, by what they see as the extreme behavior of Tea Party activists, and the apparent intolerance in which the Tea Party traffics.

We have also made inroads into discovering the depth of Tea Party support, concluding that a bit more than one in four Americans qualify as "true believers," those who "strongly" support the Tea Party. Finally, we have a better understanding of the depth of commitment to the Tea Party. Very few people report membership in the movement; more, however, report engaging in movement activism of some kind. However, as the data indicates, relative to membership or activism, more people in our sample look kindly on the Tea Party and support it. From family obligations to just not being in the right place in one's life cycle, there are many reasons why people aren't in a position to commit to activism, much less movement membership.[7] Still, the inability to join a movement or participate in movement activism shouldn't foreclose identification with a movement and its goals.

So, who are these people who are sympathetic to the Tea Party? Our chief claim, of course, is that people who believe the president represents a subversive force of some kind are sympathetic to the aims of the Tea Party. Prior research has identified several other factors that are associated with support for right-wing movements, some of which we have already discussed in detail in chapter 1: race, gender, class, and religion. Still, we must carefully weigh other considerations, ones beyond categories associated with ascription and achievement. Partisanship and ideology are important insofar as Republicans are more likely to support right-wing movements, as are (reactionary) conservatives, something we validated in chapter 1.

Making use of both interpretive (historical) and more empirical approaches, scholars have examined these factors for years. Yet, the extent to which intolerance of "Others" affects support for right-wing movements remains a relative mystery. How do preferences for one's own group versus other groups, racism, group-based hierarchy, and a preference for social conformity (authoritarianism) encourage support for right-wing movements? Moreover, as chapter 1 illustrates, economic insecurity may also play a role in people supporting right-wing movements. In this section of the chapter, we explore the ways in which support for right-wing movements, in this case the Tea Party, are influenced by the sociodemographic and political factors. We follow up in the next section by exploring what we think are more proximate sources of support for the Tea Party. We turn first to sociodemographics.

Sociodemographic Factors

What are some of the sociodemographic factors that lead one to accept or reject the Tea Party? Could one of them be age? After all, if sympathy for the Tea Party is in any way a reaction to one's way of life, people who are middle-aged and older may be willing to side with the Tea Party because of their discomfort with change, something that generally occurs with advancing age. Class-based explanations, as we discussed in chapter 1, are also important. This work suggests that it's not the poor and un-educated who tend to support right-wing movements but often those in the middle. Since white males are more likely to support right-wing movements, race and gender are also important factors.

Religion is another important factor. In this case we draw on evangelical Protestants, the single largest religious group in the United States. As modern-day successors to fundamentalists, most evangelical Protestants believe in the inerrancy of the Bible, salvation through Christ, and spreading the Gospel.[8] The roots of evangelical Protestantism are grounded in the South, where its adherents have sought to protect their society from forces that would undermine their way of life. Beyond the defense of Christian morality, evangelicalism was nurtured in a belief system that, among other things, celebrated states' rights, white supremacy, and small central government.[9] Moreover, evangelical Protestantism tends to adopt a Manichaean approach to conflict in which differences are reduced to a battle of good versus evil.[10] Hence, anything that fits with their way of life is perceived as good. Anything that doesn't is generally considered evil. In short, there are few gray areas. This line of thinking is often connected to support for right-wing social movements.[11] For this reason we think it relevant to consider its influence on support for the Tea Party.

As figure 2.5 reveals, our results confirm the findings of prior work on the right wing, as well as more recent work on the Tea Party. A 7-point difference separates true believers from true skeptics in the youngest category, where 18 percent of those who reject the Tea Party reside, and 11 percent of those who embrace it are camped out. On the flip side, 7 percentage points separate believers and skeptics among middle-aged Americans and older, where 66 percent of the former group are at least forty-five years of age compared to 59 percent of skeptics. No more than a cursory glance at education and income is needed in order to see that those skeptics with college or graduate degrees outstrip those who are believers in this category by 12 percent (38 percent versus 26 percent). Relative to those on education, our findings for income are inverted, even if the gaps aren't as pronounced. For instance, where 24 percent of the believers make in excess of $100K annually, the number declines to approximately 20 percent among skeptics. Our suspicions for race are also confirmed. Indeed, 84 percent of believers are white versus 10 percent for blacks and 6 percent for Latinos. This is in contrast to the distribution among skeptics in which 60 percent are white, 27 percent are black, and 13 percent are Latino. Shifting to gender, almost 60 percent of believers are men, versus 40 percent of women. The relationship between support for the Tea Party and gender reverses as the focus moves from believers to skeptics, where women constitute approximately 53 percent of the latter group, and men 47 percent.

What are we to make of these preliminary findings? First off, they are very much in sync with much of the work on right-wing movements. In chapter 1, we took care to highlight socio-demographic parallels between the Tea Party and earlier right-wing movements. These findings confirm the similarities. Each of these movements appeals to the same basic demographic: white, middle-class, middle-aged, evangelical Protestant men.

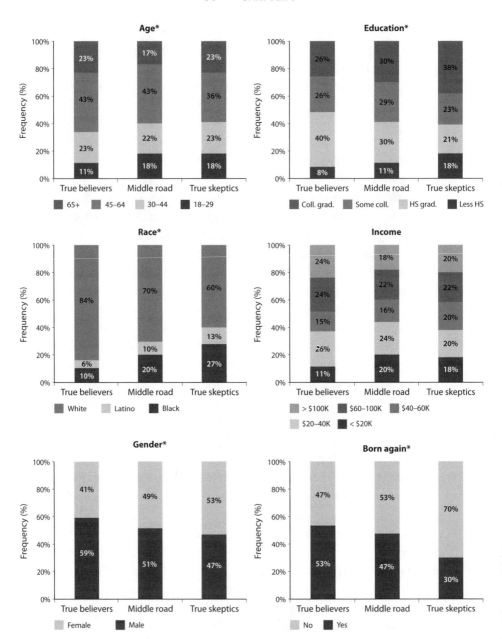

2.5. Sociodemographics, by degree of Tea Party support
Note: Total $N = 1188$, with 308 true believers, 488 middle of the road,
and 392 true skeptics; *significant at $\chi^2 < 0.000$

Second, our findings closely parallel other surveys with content measuring support for the Tea Party, most of which are national polls.[12] There are some variations in the ways in which other surveys tapped support for the Tea Party. Even so, all of the surveys roughly confirm our findings. While our study is confined to thirteen states, the congruence between our results and those of other studies should permit us to draw more general conclusions based on our findings as we move forward.

Politics and Ideology

Now that we have an idea about the relationship between support for the Tea Party and important demographic differences, we must consider politics and ideology. These elements, after all, reside at the core of the Tea Party's philosophy: fiscal responsibility and small government. Of course, these are also core principles of the Republican Party, ones that crystallized around the New Deal. The influence of partisanship on political judgment is undeniable; it influences everything from the way people see foreign and domestic policy issues to the candidates for whom they choose to vote. Because partisanship is largely rooted in who we are—that is, our identity—it serves as a reliable cue, helping us to navigate an increasingly complex political world.[13] Identification with one party over another is a process most recently captured by political scientists Zoltan Hajnal and Taeku Lee's rendering of partisanship. For them, partisanship is the sum of long- and short-term influences: political socialization (the long term) and the content of the current political environment (the short term).

In a nutshell, political socialization combines one's sense of self and how one has been raised, with one's ideological preference. Short-term influences are based on information culled from the current political environment, something that allows people to update party performance in real time and taps their socialization experience as a means of filtering the information.[14] Perhaps this explains why the Republican Party has served as an institutional home for right-wing movements.[15] After all,

Republicans have long been identified as the party of strong national defense, small government, fiscal responsibility, and a commitment to countering what the Far Right would view as subversive threats to American life.[16]

We must also account for the ways in which ideologies inform people's social and political judgment. Ideologies, according to British political scientist Michael Freeden, are connected to the "world of ideas and symbols through which political actors find their way and comprehend their social surroundings . . . inform[ing] their practices and institutions."[17] Like partisanship, ideology's influence on political judgment is also important.[18] But the way in which it influences political judgment is contingent upon the ideological label one chooses to bear. Liberals, for instance, tend to prefer change of some kind, equality, and a "concern with [social] problems." In contrast, conservatives are more preoccupied with fiscal policies, socialism/capitalism, and foreign policy.[19] In the case of right-wing movements, of which the JBS is a good example, this division is taken to extremes.[20] It's also worth mentioning that ideology is an important factor in the party to which one becomes attached: where conservatives tend to align with the Republican Party, and liberals with the Democrats.[21] It stands to reason, then, that since conservatives tend to favor small government and fiscal responsibility, as does the Tea Party, and liberals a social safety financed by tax revenues, consistent with critics of the Tea Party movement, ideology should have much to say about support for the Tea Party. We use ideological self-placement to measure this. (Please see the appendix for details.)

The American belief in small government, a founding American value, is also an important consideration. In fact, political scientist Samuel Huntington argues the following: "opposition to power, and suspicion of government as the most dangerous embodiment of power, are the central themes of American political thought."[22] Of course, this is a matter of interpretation. Still, it's a fact that several of the Founding Fathers feared, and were suspicious of, government power. Most of this sentiment, as his-

torian Bernard Bailyn demonstrates, was based on past experience with the British Crown: excessive taxation, corrupt representation, and standing armies, among other things. Founding
Fathers such as Patrick Henry and George Mason had no reason to believe a powerful central government would stand them
in any better stead than that which they had endured under the
Crown. For, in the end, too much centralized power would un-
doubtedly curb freedom—no matter who held it.

According to Bailyn, who drew on several thousand pages
of published material recorded during the ratification debates
surrounding the U.S. Constitution, a segment of the patriots
feared ceding such power to fallible man. These men believed
that "mankind's selfish neglect of the public good and passion-
ate devotion to the narrow self-interest" would ultimately result in America winding up "either as a military dictatorship
or as a junta of ruthless aristocrats."[23] More than two hundred
years later, suspicion of government persists as a value on which
Americans continue to draw.[24] If we hold the Tea Party at their
word, that a desire for small government is at the top of their
agenda, we should see a strong empirical connection between it
and support for the Tea Party.

So what, if any, relationship do these factors have to do with
Tea Party support? If figure 2.6 is any indication, all of them
inform whether or not one chooses to align oneself with the Tea
Party. Looking first at ideology, vast differences emerge across
levels of Tea Party support.

Close to two-thirds (66 percent) of believers are self-identified
conservatives, 25 percent are moderate, and only 9 percent consider themselves liberal. The pattern is inverted for skeptics:
more than 50 percent of this group identify as liberal. Almost
40 percent (38% to be exact) of skeptics prefer the ideological
center, and barely 10 percent of them are to the ideological right.

Moving to examine party identification does little to narrow
the gap between believers and skeptics. Only 11 percent of believers identify with Democrats; far more, almost one in three,
prefer to align themselves with independents, but 57 percent

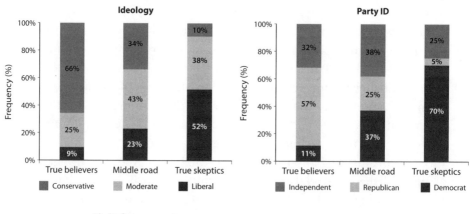

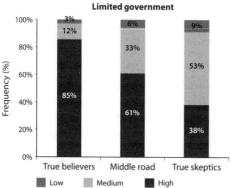

2.6. Political-demographics, by degree of Tea Party support
Note: Total $N = 1188$, with 308 true believers, 488 middle of the road, and 392 true skeptics; relationships significant at $\chi^2 < 0.000$

choose to belong to the Republican camp. Skeptics take a different, even more partisan tack. Fully 70 percent identify with the Democrats, and only 5 percent with the GOP. Twenty-five percent of them fail to commit to either major party, preferring instead to self-identify as Independent. Moving from partisan and ideological attachment to a core value associated with each does nothing to diminished divisions among believers and skeptics.[25] Close to 90 percent of believers score high on preference for small government, something consistent with the Tea Party's platform, a figure that more than doubles support for limited government offered by skeptics, who weigh in at close to only 40 percent. Slightly more than 50 percent of skeptics are more comfortable with a moderate level of government versus 12 percent of believers. Very few in any category support big government, a figure that never exceeds the 9 percent registered by skeptics.

Overall, our findings are consistent with conventional wisdom. Indeed, if the attitudes of Tea Party supporters are any indication, it appears that the Tea Party is everything they have claimed all along: Republican conservatives who prefer small government. Likewise, skeptics tend to prefer Democrats, are relatively liberal, and most are more comfortable with medium-sized government. In a nutshell, we observe differences between believers and skeptics in their partisan loyalty, and their commitment to conservatism, as a function of self-identification, and commitment to at least one conservative principle: limited government. Nevertheless, chunks of both skeptics and believers are in the middle ideologically, as well as when it comes to partisanship.

Toward a More Complex Understanding of Tea Party Support

What we have presented so far confirms what scholars have been saying about right-wing movements for some time. Indeed, our Tea Party sympathizers appear to be relatively older, are doing fine financially, are reasonably well educated, evangelical, and male. These findings go a long way in justifying our comparison of the Tea Party to what we think are their predecessors on the Far Right. Our analysis of Tea Party supporters also confirms the fact that people who are attracted to the Far Right also prefer the Republican Party and conservatism to the Democratic Party and liberalism.

We now investigate other forces that we believe push some people to support the Tea Party. We begin with an elaboration of our position, that the anxiety associated with Barack Obama as president of the United States is a source of Tea Party support. This, we argue, is due to the perception that he's an alien of some kind that poses a threat to real Americans and their way of life. We then highlight the out-group hostility that has helped shape American social and political life. As the following discussion makes clear, out-group hostility takes many forms and is motivated by a range of concerns. We conclude with a brief discussion on the role that economic anxiety might play in influencing people to sympathize with the Tea Party.

Anxiety and the Presidential "Other"

The anxiety associated with the perceived subversive intentions of President Obama and his policies, for us, is key to understanding the motivation of Tea Party supporters.[26] As we have noted, right-wing movements are generally spurred on by fear of change of some kind, something that we verified in chapter 1 when we argued that support for the Tea Party is in part driven by a reaction to Barack Obama as president. Indeed, if political scientsist George Marcus and his colleagues are correct, anxiety is triggered by a threat, or something that we believe is amiss in our environment, something with which we should be concerned.[27] We contend that, at least for Tea Party supporters, Barack Obama's ascendency to the highest office in the land may be construed as both: something amiss and as a threat. More to the point, we believe that the symbolism associated with the presidency, having someone that many perceive as a black foreigner occupying the office, is too much for many Tea Party supporters to bear. If the Tea Party is similar to other right-wing social movements, it perceives social change—in this case the emergence of Obama as president—as a symbol of their declining social prestige. Recall, for instance, our results in chapter 1 in which we reviewed the content of Tea Party websites. We discovered that portraying Obama as un-American, and calling him a socialist or communist on many occasions, was commonplace in true believer discourse.

As we show below, our survey suggests the blog posts were not atypical but rather represent what seems to be a prevalent view among Tea Party supporters, that Obama has a secret, and, one would think, socialist—even subversive—agenda. Further, lest the reader think that the content of the Tea Party websites are produced by a handful of zealous, true-believing activists, we remind the reader that we also observed this way of thinking among the rank and file, the masses. All of the above suggests the following as an appropriate measure for gauging the perceived subversion associated with Obama:

> When it comes to Barack Obama's policies, please tell me which statement you agree with most: (1) I support Obama's current policies; or (2) Obama's policies are misguided and wrong, but they are not socialism; or, (3) Obama's policies are pushing the country toward socialism.

Authoritarianism

We believe that authoritarianism, a preference for social conformity, may also motivate people to support the Tea Party. Theodor Adorno and colleagues' landmark study on authoritarianism, *The Authoritarian Personality*, was first published more than sixty years ago.[28] Originally conceived to better understand anti-Semitism, it eventually morphed into a study of what's commonly known as ethnocentrism, a form of generalized prejudice (something we will discuss below).[29] Authoritarianism, as a psychological theory, was believed to be a product of an upbringing by strict, even punitive, parents during one's childhood. The internal conflict generated by a childhood fraught with such stress, scholars believe, results in social, political, and moral "outsiders" serving as scapegoats for repressed hostility.[30] Recent work conducted by political psychologist Stanley Feldman, and his student Karen Stenner, has refined this approach to authoritarianism. Theoretically, for them, it's a matter of autonomy versus social cohesion. In the end, they argue that authoritarianism is about a desire for social conformity, that any threat to upset the social order is worthy of punishment. Among authoritarians, coercion is favored as a means of regulating what is thought to be deviant behavior of any kind. Intolerance, therefore, is triggered by the failure of people to conform to what are believed to be widespread social norms. The wrath of people disposed to authoritarianism is also directed at political leaders who, through incompetence or malfeasance, are deemed to threaten social stability. (For details on measurement for "Authoritarianism," and the categories that follow below, please refer to "Description of Multi-State Survey of Race and Politics and Telephone Survey Methodology" in the appendix.)

Ethnocentrism

We have mentioned that ethnocentrism is related to authoritarianism, but the two are not the same. The nature of the relationship between the two is one in which ethnocentrism is part of the broader syndrome that characterizes the authoritarian personality. Another difference between the two lies in the way in which each is activated. Authoritarianism is activated upon the perception of threat to the social order; ethnocentrism is activated upon sensing a threat to a specific in-group. Ethnocentrism is also related to prejudice, but transcends prejudice aimed at a specific group. Instead, ethnocentrism is a more "generalized" prejudice directed toward out-groups.[31] It departs from prejudice in another key way: it's not necessarily about out-group hostility. Rather, it emphasizes in-group affection, too.[32] Ethnocentrism partitions the social world into in-groups (us) and out-groups (them), something that occurs both consciously and unconsciously.[33] We believe ethnocentrism is relevant to right-wing movements because—based on the demographic group to which right-wing supporters appeal—anyone who is not white, male, Christian, and middle-class is part of an out-group.

Racism

Racism may also contribute to support for the Tea Party. Consider our examples from other right-wing, reactionary movements: the Ku Klux Klan and the JBS. Of course, preservation of white supremacy was one of the reasons for the Klan's existence. The JBS avoided aligning itself with racism directly. Still, the position it adopted on civil rights, as a Trojan horse for communism, is difficult to square with anything but racism. Since "old-fashioned" racism is no longer, well, fashionable,[34] a new type of black antipathy has replaced it. Instead of saying that African Americans are biologically inferior, some whites' hostility toward blacks is now a matter of joining prejudice with the perception that blacks are in violation of the Protestant work ethic. In fact, recent research by psychologist Cheryl Kaiser and colleagues suggests that the election of Barack Obama may even sharpen the resentment directed at African Americans. Kaiser argues that, for many whites, Obama's election signals that racial injustice is over with: it's a thing of the past. Now, with a little effort, blacks could achieve success,[35] and are securing "special favors" from the government that they scarcely deserve. Whites, then, become "racially resentful." This, scholars believe, explains the manifold reactions to race and race policy held by whites.[36]

There's another way in which racism may contribute to support of right-wing movements. As sociologist Michael Hughes suggests, we can apply this approach to Joseph Gusfield's status politics model that we outlined in chapter 1. Hughes argues that there are parallels between attempts by supporters of the temperance movement to defend their Protestant, middle-class lifestyle from changes wrought by industrialization, and the defense of the white, middle-class lifestyle and status from racial equality abetted by structural changes.[37]

Social Dominance Theory

Another factor we think contributes to support for right-wing, reactionary movements, but is never mentioned in the literature, is the tendency of societies to become divided into dominant and subordinate groups. Psychologist Jim Sidanius explains the persistence of this arrangement, in part by arguing that near universal agreement exists on ideologies responsible for maintaining social hierarchy. In the American context, racism, sexism, and the Protestant work ethic are all ideologies that serve to enhance hierarchy, legitimating discrimination as a means of maintaining a social order in which a group of dominants presides over subordinates. Another set of ideologies such as egalitarianism, in the American context, helps to attenuate inequality. Social dominance orientation (SDO), part of a larger theory of intergroup relations, is a psychological predisposition that describes the extent to which individuals subscribe to these ideologies. In short, SDO is a reflection of one's "preference for inequality among social groups."[38] Someone who has high levels of SDO is likely to buy into the hierarchy-enhancing ideologies, ones that result in the perpetuation of inequality. People who are low on SDO are more likely to promote equality.[39] We contend that people high in SDO, people who are intent on keeping subordinate groups down as a means of maintaining group-based prestige, are likely to support right-wing movements and, therefore, the Tea Party.[40]

Economic Anxiety

Economic anxiety, at least in America, doesn't often successfully push people toward right-wing movements. We have already confirmed that followers of the Far Right tend to be more middle-class than anything else. Still, Rory McVeigh makes a case for the Klan of the 1920s. During times of economic transformations, he argues, people gravitate to right-wing movements. Of course, this is consistent with a more materialist account of support for the Far Right. As capitalism kicked into high gear, instituting a system in which the assembly line took over as the principal mode of production, the need for skilled workers declined. This opened the door to increased demand for unskilled, cheaper labor. It just so happened that this pool of labor included many immigrants. So, a big part of the incentive pushing some Americans to support the Klan, McVeigh argues, is that it pushed for measures that would reduce the supply of unskilled labor. Since immigrants were perceived as a source of economic threat, the Klan, among other organizations, pushed for immigration restrictions. In this sense, the Klan served as a means by which some Americans sought to protect their economic interests.[41] Likewise, it's conceivable that people who support the Tea Party do so because they perceive a threat to their economic position by losing their jobs, and the decreasing value of their homes. In this light, it's a good bet that they feel the Tea Party has the answer.

For good reason, we have advanced claims that each of the aforementioned predispositions (with the exception of economic anxiety, because it's not a predisposition) should influence support for right-wing movements. If, as we imagine, support for the Tea Party is connected to intolerance of some kind, the evidence we present should verify our theoretical claims. While our claims weren't validated across the board, the ones that were are quite illuminating. For ease of presentation, we turn to figure 2.7 where we have divided the factors we believe contribute to support for the Tea Party (authoritarianism, anxiety associated with Obama, ethnocentrism, racism, social dominance, and economic anxiety) into high and low categories where, for instance, "high" indicates the percentage of people in the relevant category that possess high levels of the trait under investigation. For the "fear of Obama" question, "high" indicates the percentage of people who agreed with the response option that "Obama is moving the country toward socialism," versus the other two response options in which people either agree with Obama's policies (low), or think his policies are misguided but not socialist (medium).

As we scan figure 2.7 we see that the relationship between Tea Party support and authoritarianism, as well as ethnocentrism, is weak. We arrive at this conclusion because we expected that as support for the Tea Party shifts from skeptic to believer, the percentage of those who prefer both social conformity (authoritarianism) and their own group (ethnocentrism) should increase. Neither increase in any meaningful way: authoritarianism and ethnocentrism fail to increase at all across levels of support for

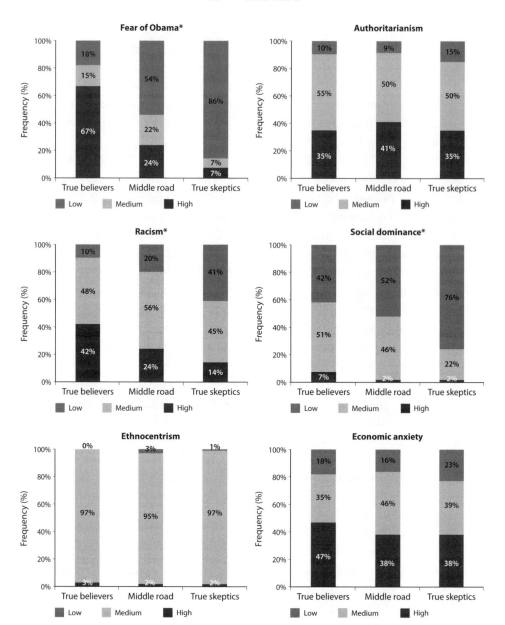

2.7. Attitude orientations, by degree of Tea Party support
Note: Total *N* = 1188, with 308 true believers, 488 middle of the road, and
392 true skeptics; *significant at χ^2 < 0.000

the Tea Party. These results suggest that neither authoritarianism nor ethnocentrism can reliably distinguish between believers and skeptics. Economic anxiety doesn't appear to provide much leverage, either.[42]

This is not the case for another group of explanations. Racism, SDO, and suspicions of Obama's intentions permit us to easily discriminate between believers and skeptics. Consider the predispositions. Beginning with racism, a 27-point gap emerges between skeptics and believers, where only 14 percent of those who have no use for the Tea Party are racist versus 41 percent of those who are sympathetic to the right-wing movement. Similar disparities are visible with SDO, where 76 percent of skeptics embrace equality, but only 42 percent of believers do so: a 34-point gap. The difference between believers and skeptics only widens as we shift from long-standing predispositions to what we think is the most proximate cause of Tea Party support: threat perceived from the president and his policies. Where only 7 percent of skeptics think Obama's policies are socialist, a jarring 67 percent of believers think so, a whopping 60-point difference.

This analysis allowed us to accomplish at least two things. First, it permitted us to explore the extent to which our claim— that at least one reason people might support the Tea Party is related to the perceived threat associated with Obama's presidency—may be valid. In fact, if these results are in any way instructive, the anxiety incited by Obama as president bears the strongest relationship with support for the Tea Party. Second, our decision to consider the association between racism and SDO, and support for the Tea Party, appears justified. It's still too early to make any definitive judgments. Still, for now at least, it seems that whether or not one supports the Tea Party is also associated with racial intolerance and a desire for group-based inequality.

We think another finding bears mentioning. Since the Tea Party gained momentum during the economic downturn, it's reasonable to assume that believers' attraction to the Tea Party is driven by economic anxiety. Yet the other right-wing movements we have cited flourished during relative economic boom times, suggesting that people were drawn to the Klan and the John Birch Society for nonmaterial reasons. That is, these movements were more about the preservation of their respective ways of life.

In the analysis we just conducted, we did find a weak relationship between economic anxiety and support for the Tea Party. But when we confined the analysis to whites (in a separate examination), interesting results emerge. It seems that whites who are anxious about their economic stability are *less* likely than nonwhites who are economically anxious to support the Tea Party.[43] These results suggest that whites are less likely to be drawn to the Tea Party for material reasons, suggesting that, relative to other groups, it's really more about social prestige. This is consistent with Hofstadter and Gusfield's claims and, therefore, supports ours.[44]

POLITICS, OUT-GROUP HOSTILITY, OR FEAR OF A PRESIDENTIAL "OTHER"?

At this point we have examined the relationship between support for the Tea Party and various explanations for it. Across several domains we are able to distinguish between believers and skeptics. Sociodemographics, age, years of formal education, gender, race, and evangelicalism all help us to discriminate between skeptics and believers. In like fashion, differences in partisanship, ideology, and the appropriate size of government all permit us to designate believers and skeptics. Finally, social dominance orientation, racism, and the belief that Obama and his policies are socialist and/or harmful make it easy to distinguish believers from skeptics.

So far, our claim that perceptions about President Obama are associated with support for the Tea Party remains valid. Still, we need to conduct a more rigorous analysis of the relationship between support for the Tea Party and all of the factors that appear to explain it. Recall that our chief claim in this chapter is that the perceived threat associated with change the president and his policies represent helps to drive support for the Tea Party. More important, this helps explain Tea Party support over and above well-known sources such as political orientations and out-group hostility, including racism. But we cannot be sure of this until we account for alternative explanations.

For instance, people who are sympathetic to the Tea Party argue that their support for it is really nothing more than adherence to conservative ideological beliefs in small government, fiscal responsibility, and low taxes. Others argue that the Tea Party is really the base of the Republican Party. If partisanship is ultimately a function of who people are (i.e., part of one's identity), and their perception of party performance, support for the Tea Party is likely an expression of both. In sum, this set of explanations suggests that once we account for partisanship and ideology, the connection between the threat associated with the president and his polices, and what the Tea Party represents, will disappear.

Another set of explanations centers on group-based intolerance, even bigotry. People who oppose the Tea Party, in other words, believe that antipathy toward the president and his policies has everything to do with racism, or a need to keep subordinate groups in their place. Followed to its logical conclusion, once these explanations are taken into account, beliefs about the president and his policies should fail to inform what people think about the Tea Party.

If, however, beliefs about the president remain associated with support of the Tea Party, even after accounting for these alternative explanations, it suggests a few things. For instance, if the relationship survives upon consideration of ideology, belief in limited government, and partisanship, it's safe to say that the relationship is not about politics or ideology. If the relationship remains intact after we account for racism and social dominance orientation, and ethnocentrism, we can say that out-group hostility, directed at African Americans specifically or at any subordinate groups, fails to influence the relationship in general. In sum, if perceptions of Obama and his policies remain associated with Tea Party support after accounting for all of these competing

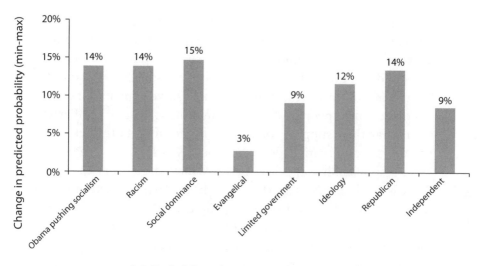

2.8. Probability of supporting the Tea Party
Note: All predictors shown are significant at $p < 0.05$, one-tailed

explanations, it supports our claim that there is something sui generis about Obama that worries Tea Partiers and their supporters.

A more rigorous test of our claim entails the use of a methodology that affords us the ability to account for all of the alternative explanations for Tea Party support and permits us to isolate the association between it and the perception of whether or not Obama is attempting to implement socialist policies.[45] Figure 2.8 displays the results. To facilitate presentation, we showcase the results only for the most theoretically relevant alternative explanations.

After accounting for several alternative explanations, concerns about the president and his agenda increases the likelihood of being a believer by 14 percent, confirming our claim. This may not sound like much, but when one considers all of the alternative explanations we include, it's almost shocking that the association between perceptions of Obama and support for the Tea Party remains intact. Having said this, we can also report that several other factors inform sympathy for the

Tea Party, including partisanship and ideology. Republicans are 14 percent more likely than Democrats, and Independents are 9 percent more likely than Democrats, to be true believers. Likewise, self-identified conservatives are 12 percent more likely than self-identified liberals to connect with the Tea Party, and people who believe that government should do less are 12 percent more likely than those who don't believe this to sympathize with the party. Racism and social dominance orientation also matter. Racial resentment reserved for blacks increases by 14 percent the likelihood that one is a believer, and the more people subscribe to the belief that some groups are superior to others (social dominance orientation), the likelihood that they support the Tea Party increases by 15 percent.[46]

■ ■ ■

The results confirm our claim that concerns about the president and perceptions of his agenda play a part in whether or not people feel connected to the Tea Party. The fact that our claim sticks, even as we account for all manner of alternative explanations, suggests we are onto something. It does, in fact, seem that there is something unique about Obama, something that transcends politics, ideology, or race. As we have argued, we believe that, as president, as the face of the country and its commander in chief, Obama represents a threat to the American way of life that Tea Party sympathizers have come to know and cherish. This finding further supports a claim we made in chapter 1 in which we argued that if members of out-groups hold positions of power, members of the in-group are likely to perceive the powerful out-group members' goals to be antagonistic to those of the less powerful in-group. Based on the power and authority the president wields, it's no surprise that people who support the Tea Party, most of whom are white, feel a loss of control. Recent work in social psychology indicates that when people perceive a loss of control over events in their lives, they tend to see things that aren't there, a symptom of conspiratorial thinking.[47] Seeing things that aren't really there may include the production of all-powerful imagined enemies, something that's used as a means of coping with perceived powerlessness.[48]

Moreover, it seems as though the two conventional explanations of why people support the Tea Party are valid. For people who say they support the Tea Party for reasons associated with their ideological beliefs or partisan loyalty, we supply evidence to support these claims. A preference for limited government also matters. This is an important finding insofar as Tea Party activists, elites, and supporters often claim that this is a big part of what they're about. Moreover, the fact that it registers an independent impact, one beyond a more general commitment to conservative principles, is even more impressive, validating the Tea Party's sincerity. While there's no doubt that the Tea Party is on the ideological right, we'd like to stress that they appear to be on the Far Right, beyond mainstream conservatism.[49]

In addition to our findings on the Tea Party, our results also have something to say about right-wing movements in general. We believe this to be the case for at least two reasons. First, the demographic makeup of Tea Party supporters is strikingly similar to that of earlier right-wing movements. Second, as in earlier treatments of such movements, politics, ideology, religion, and out-group hostility all influence support for the Far Right. We are also able to account for the agent of change that so often spurs right-wing movements. Still, the results of our study depart from those of our predecessors in that we are able to incorporate measures of out-group hostility no other researchers have taken into account. Even in the absence of President Obama, adding social dominance, for instance, to explain support for right-wing movements, represents an advance. It shows that support for the American right wing is something more than partisan allegiance or ideological beliefs. However, under the present circumstances, out-group hostility is especially important since the source of change, and threat, is a powerful person from a "subordinate" group.

It's worth noting other factors that explain support for the Tea Party, and ones that ultimately don't. Thanks to Skocpol and Williamson's work on the Tea Party in *The Tea Party and the Remaking of Republican Conservatism*, we also included a variable that assesses the extent to which people rely on Fox News as their principal source of information.[50] Since they argue that Fox News bears at least partial responsibility for the rise of the Tea Party, we thought it prudent to account for it in our analysis. Sure enough, it affects support for the Tea Party, increasing by 14 percent the likelihood that someone will become a true believer over people who draw on other sources for news.[51]

But as we stepped up the rigor of our analysis, it appears that the respondents' race no longer influences support for the Tea Party, as it did in our descriptive analysis. A separate analysis reveals that social dominance orientation mediates the relationship between racial group membership and support for the Tea Party. This doesn't surprise us since race helps determine one's social dominance orientation.[52] In other words, it's very difficult to separate social dominance orientation cleanly from race itself. At 84 percent (shown in figure 2.5), our descriptive findings demonstrate that Tea Party supporters are overwhelmingly white, something that is supported by other recent work on Tea Party supporters.[53] Furthermore, our efforts to clarify the relationship between Tea Party support and economic insecurity, desire for conformity, and ethnocentrism, by holding constant several important alternative explanations, failed to disconfirm what we found earlier. In short, none of these have anything meaningful to say about who supports the Tea Party and who doesn't.

CONCLUDING THOUGHTS

This chapter sought to get a handle on Tea Party supporters by examining who they are and what motivates them to support the movement. In the end, we validated our core claim that Tea Party supporters are concerned with the emergence of Obama. More to the point, we argue that true believers are concerned that Obama as president of the United States, and everything that the position represents, is subverting the social prestige they have come to enjoy. In other words, the subculture that is most closely aligned with "real" America likely believes that Obama's election signals the erosion of their position in America.

Even so, critics may assert that the effect we observe for Obama is really about expressing dislike for what they see as Obama's socialist agenda, not fear of subversion per se. We can even see some charging us with exaggerating the threat as it relates to Obama. In other words, perhaps this so-called fear of subversion is really just about partisanship, ideology, or maybe even race. That would be a credible claim had we not controlled for ideology, preference for small government, and partisanship. We know it's not about race, either, because we dealt with that issue, too. For good measure, we also added social dominance orientation, authoritarianism, and ethnocentrism. Still, what people think about Obama continues to matter. After going through all of these competing explanations, our interpretation that anxiety associated with Obama (including his perceived foreign origins and the perceived subversive content of his policies) pushes some people toward the Tea Party appears reasonable.

As this chapter closes, we'd like to take the opportunity to highlight what becomes an important claim as we move forward: emphasizing our use of Tea Party support as a proxy for reactionary conservatism. This chapter examined the *sources* of Tea Party support. We needed to assess our claim that support for the Tea Party is, among other factors, driven by the perceived threat posed by Obama and his polices. Our results clearly support this claim. We now need to assess the *consequences* of Tea Party support, something that we do in the balance of the book.

As we move forward, we will argue that, similar to ethnocentrism, social dominance orientation, authoritarianism, and racism, reactionary conservatism (indexed by Tea Party support) should also be considered a predisposition. That is, reactionary conservatism is similar to all of the above in that, conceptually, it promotes "inclinations to judge an object in a particular way,"[54] a way guided by the social learning to which the individual is exposed in childhood. Since we treat reactionary conservatism as a major theoretical intervention, we follow convention. To elaborate, this chapter took the first conventional step as it pertains to examining a new theoretical approach: we assessed the *sources* of reactionary conservatism (support for the Tea Party). Beginning with chapter 3, we take the next step: assessing the *consequences* of reactionary conservatism disguised as Tea Party support.[55] Long story short, for the remainder of the book, we explore the extent to which it influences policy-related attitudes and behavior, independent of more conventional explanations. We now turn to this task.

3

Exploring the Tea Party's Commitment to Freedom and Patriotism

IN CHAPTER TWO, we witnessed an array of factors that were associated with support for the Tea Party. We confirmed what many historians have suggested in their accounts of the Far Right, including that conservative principles, as well as partisanship, affects the extent to which Americans support the Tea Party. This is consistent with earlier work on right-wing movements. Skeptics of the Tea Party have long suspected that it is at least in part motivated by antiblack racism, as well as more general group-based antipathy. This, too, was confirmed in chapter 2. More important, our claim about the fear associated with the perceived subversive intentions of Obama holds fast, even after accounting for various and sundry competing explanations for why people support the Tea Party.

This suggests that there is something sui generis about Obama, something that cannot be reduced to whether one is a loyal Democrat or Republican, a committed conservative or liberal, whether one believes blacks are always asking for a handout or not (racial resentment), and whether one is a devoted egalitarian or not (social dominance orientation). Our evidence suggests that the connection between Obama and the Tea Party has to do with what he represents as the president, the face of the country, and the commander in chief, among many other hats the president wears.[1]

We now have a firm grasp on what *informs* support for the Tea Party. For the balance of the book we explore *consequences* associated with sympathy toward the movement. As we shift gears to make an assessment of the consequences of Tea Party support, however, we'd like to remind the reader that support for the Tea Party indexes reactionary conservatism. Ultimately, we argue that reactionary conservatism, for which support for the Tea Party functions as a proxy, is what has come to be known as a "predisposition."

By *predisposition* we refer to a preexisting, fairly fixed tendency to respond to seemingly disparate objects and events in a uniform way. Political predispositions are generally the products of early childhood socialization, personal experiences, or political ideals passed down from one's parents. Often, these are precursors to a set of values and group attachments that ultimately structure the way in which people react to things in the political environment. Based on these criteria, party identification, ethnocentrism, social dominance orientation, and authoritarianism are predispositions insofar as each is a product of socialization, experience, or values.[2] Reactionary conservatives, indexed by support for the Tea Party, represent the real Americans who perceive the emergence of Obama as the president of the United States as an assault on their place in America.

As such, we begin with the relationship between Tea Party support and two themes on which the movement frequently draws: freedom and patriotism. If its retronym (Taxed Enough Already) and mission statements on many of its websites are true, the Tea Party is principally concerned with shrinking government and broadening individual freedoms or liberties. We've already witnessed the extent to which the desire for small government promotes support for the movement among the masses, but to what extent does support for the group push one to embrace civil liberties?

If its rank-and-file followers are any indication, the Tea Party is really about freedom from too much government, and this preference should extend to all spheres of life, including, say, freedom of speech. Freedom, in this sense, is about the absence of governmental constraints on freedom of expression. Indeed, as their resistance to the Patriot Act attests, longtime Texas congressman Ron Paul, and his son, the freshman senator from Kentucky and founder of the Tea Party caucus, Rand Paul, are both steadfast supporters of civil liberties, expressed as freedom from constraints imposed by government.[3]

These issues, as we detail below, remain relevant in the aftermath of the January 8, 2011, shootings of Congresswoman Gabrielle Giffords in Tucson, Arizona, and the recent flood of legislation concerning illegal immigration. The absence of such liberties threatens American democracy as we know it, something that clashes with the notion of American identity.[4]

Further, Tea Party websites and rallies are often rife with patriotic imagery, including the American (Stars and Stripes) and Gadsden ("Don't Tread on Me") flags, and there is rarely an event at which at least a few people don't break out the retro tricornered hats and knee-length breeches. While it's true that people who call themselves patriots take pride in wearing and displaying the flag (in America), more authentic patriotism, as we argue below, transcends simple displays of patriotic symbols. Patriotism instead, is more about putting the interests of the community or country before self.[5]

In what follows, we explore how support for the Tea Party informs patriotism and civil liberties, but we do so with a specific purpose in mind. We'd like to know what Tea Party supporters really think about patriotism and civil liberties, but we cannot ask standard questions. To ask how much people love America (patriotism) and, in the case of civil liberties, how much they support free speech, produces overwhelming consensus, with at least seven in ten Americans saying they have both strong affection for the country and support free speech.[6] Yet, in both cases, people aren't forced to make hard choices; nothing tangible is at stake. We need a way to make people think in more concrete ways about patriotism and freedom.

Since the Tea Party—and candidates with which it is associated—often declare a love of freedom, as well as patriotism, we propose to test their commitment to both. Like Darren Davis in his book *Negative Liberty*,[7] we use civil liberties as a proxy for freedom. We feel comfortable in doing so since freedom, as far as we're concerned, is generally thought to be commensurate with the absence of constraints.[8] As we move forward, freedom is to be understood as the absence of governmental impediments. As such, we force a trade-off between civil liberty (freedom) and security, both of which are important values. From there we will move on to patriotism.

We use patriotism as a means of forcing a trade-off of a different kind: freedom versus equality. Or, as we will make clear, this trade-off can also be viewed as one between a patriotism more consistent with prioritizing one's self-interest over the interests of the nation versus one in which the national interest is prioritized over self-interest. Some may take issue with the way in which we operationalize patriotism as a trade-off between freedom and equality. Indeed, some might say that to cherish both is patriotic. This is true. Still, many of the Founding Fathers, to whom the Tea Party often turn for guiding principles, emphasized the importance of civic virtue,[9] and placed the common good over self-interest, something that entails sacrifice. In the present context, insuring that people are treated more equally imposes a greater burden on the public. Doing so, however, is in the interest of the common national good, more so than individual freedom, something that's more about self-interest.

At the end of the day, we will put our claim—that support for the Tea Party is a predisposition that represents reactionary conservatism—to the test. As with other right-wing movements, we believe that support for the Tea Party represents a reaction to the perceived loss of social prestige of those who see themselves as "real" Americans. As we have already illustrated, similar reactions were present with the Klan of the 1920s and the John Birch Society in the 1960s.

We begin with an overview of the framework on which we draw in analyzing the connection between Tea Party sympathy and civil liberties and patriotism. We then inspect the relationship between freedom and support for the Tea Party with our public opinion data. This is followed by our examination of the connection between patriotism as we have described it and sympathy for the Tea Party movement. By turning to the individual level survey data, we can empirically establish the views of Tea Party supporters instead of trying to infer them from signs at rallies or press releases on their websites. The data gives voice to the larger swath of movement sympathizers and allows us to draw some conclusions about what supporters actually believe. We wrap up the chapter with a few concluding thoughts.

Values and Value Conflict

Before proceeding to investigate our claims, we think it is wise to first offer a description of what we mean when we refer to *values* and *value conflict*. The literature suggests that values possess the following properties: they're concepts that index preferred end states or behavior, they transcend specific situations, serve as guidelines for the evaluation of behavior or events, and vary in their relative importance.[10] In this way, values depart from attitudes in their relative abstraction (attitudes are more specific) and in how their priority varies according to the individual or even across society.[11]

Drawing on perhaps the most widely used approach to the study of values, one sketched by psychologist Shalom Schwartz, our approach views values, and the goals and behavior they represent, as ultimately animated by the "three universal requirements of existence to which all individuals and societies must be responsive: needs of individuals as biological organisms, requisites of coordinated social action, and survival of the welfare needs of groups." From this, ten value types that anchor more discrete values emerge. For instance, *freedom*, as a value, is tethered to the more general value type *self-direction*, as "independent thought and action—choosing, creating, exploring." Self-direction, Schwartz argues, "was derived from organismic needs for control and mastery." Hence, values represent goals and behavior driven by human needs.[12]

With this thumbnail sketch of values in mind, we turn to two of the ones with which America is often identified. According to political scientists Herbert McClosky and John Zaller, freedom is the primary value with which Americans identify, and for good reason. Freedom permits us, among other things, to say whatever we wish, associate with whomever we choose, engage in occupations of our own choosing, and worship how we see fit. For McClosky and Zaller, the pursuit of freedom originated within the British politics in which the nobility and middle class sought to limit the power of the monarch, using the rule of law to do so. Eventually, colonists in the New World appropriated this framework, directing it at the English monarch, King George III. Indeed, as the U.S. Constitution and Bill of Rights make clear, keeping centralized power in check, through *individual* rights, was a priority for the fledgling nation, and the principal raison d'être for the American Revolution.[13] In the absence of the ability of people to make contracts with whomever one pleased, the ability to freely compete, and the freedom to acquire wealth, it's unlikely capitalism would have survived, much less thrived.

While equality doesn't resonate as much with some Americans as liberty, according to McClosky and Zaller, it remains an important value. Even Alexis de Tocqueville, the celebrated early-nineteenth-century French visitor to the United States, noted relative equality of condition among Americans (African Americans, of course, notwithstanding). However, equality—at least in the American context—is more about equality of opportunity than equality of outcomes.

Individualism—the belief that people are to rely on their own talents and ingenuity to succeed—represents another value deeply embedded in the American political psyche. In this account, the central government was to have a minimal role. Too much help from central authority, the Founding Fathers believed, would rob Americans of their drive to succeed and diminish the desire to work hard, a belief that continues to resonate today.[14]

As many have noted, some values may conflict with others. Even if we start with the values just mentioned, potential conflict abounds. Consider the conflict between freedom and equality in the context of an urban, industrial democracy.[15] Using the welfare state as an example, because it so easily reveals the value conflict between freedom and equality, McClosky and Zaller illustrate the ensuing tension that resides within the American public: "The conservative defenders of capitalism contend that government, in trying to guarantee the welfare of its citizens, will undermine self-reliance and individual initiative, stifle the private economy, and destroy such cherished American values as competition and the desire for achievement."

At the same time, liberals "argue with equal conviction that the promise of American democracy cannot be realized without the assistance of the welfare state. How, they ask, can a genuine democracy be achieved when powerful private interests dominate the society and millions of citizens lack the necessities for a decent and fulfilling life?"[16] A more sustained look at values, at a theoretical level, makes clear why freedom and equality conflict.

Schwartz, as we mentioned, employs a framework in which human needs and desires drive values. His ten value types fall into two broad categories: individual interests and collective interests. Freedom (especially the type referred to in the above-mentioned quote from Schwartz), as it turns out, is associated with a value type commensurate with individual interests: achievement. (Another type of freedom is discussed below.) Within this domain, a premium is placed upon success and ambition, among other values.

Equality is associated with a value type more conducive to the realization of collective interests: universalism. In this domain, tolerance and the welfare of everyone are among the top priorities. As we have suggested, freedom and equality conflict because the associated value types, achievement and universalism, are hard to reconcile. For instance, where the former is about "acceptance of *others as equals* and concern for their welfare" the latter promotes "the pursuit of *one's own* relative success . . . over others" (emphasis ours).[17]

How do people ultimately resolve instances in which values conflict? This resolution comes generally by way of a trade-off between the conflicting values.[18] In other words, after some consideration, people will ultimately choose one value over another as they think about issues. Psychologist Philip Tetlock's work suggests that people engage in trade-offs when survival in the real world demands decisions in which values conflict, the competing values are roughly equal to each other, the trade-off is culturally acceptable, there is no socially acceptable way to avoid the decision, and there's accountability to others.[19] Moreover, trade-offs must be considered in context, in specific situations, such that the value selected depends on the issue at hand.

As Darren Davis points out, this is more about framing than anything else.[20] He suggests that framing the competition between values in more concrete ways—yanking it from an abstraction in which it's possible that some may see no conflict—makes the conflict more realistic, permitting the analyst to glean what's really important to the individual. In the end, once it's clear what values are at stake, the value in which people place the highest priority generally carries the day.

To summarize, we now know that values emerge from human needs. They also represent ideals, preferred ends that inform behavior and serve as guidelines by which social behavior is judged. We also know that some values are in conflict—including freedom and equality, two of the core values often associated with America. As we shall see below, value conflict in America isn't restricted to the concepts of freedom and equality. Indeed, security is also an important, if not necessarily a core, American value. In cases where core values collide, though, often the value that enjoys the highest priority with the individual ultimately wins out. We'd like to stress, however, that it's not a static process. The value that ultimately prevails should shift according to context, and the way in which the issue is framed. If, as we suspect, the Tea Party movement represents the most recent representation of the Far Right, we anticipate that it will affect how Americans view freedom and patriotism. We begin with civil liberties.

Freedom, Civil Liberties, and the Tea Party

The history of civil liberties can be traced to what has come to be known as the Bill of Rights, itself a product of the constitutional ratification process. A faction of the Founding Fathers, one that had little faith in a strong central government, insisted on safeguards capable of protecting the individual freedoms over which the American Revolution was waged. More to the point, this faction of the founders, led by Thomas Jefferson, Patrick Henry, and George Mason, believed the aristocratic composition of the federal government, including the representatives, to be incompatible with tending to local issues and sensitivity to local custom. They feared that representatives might dismiss the interests of ordinary citizens in favor of those with power and influence, something that would alienate the people from their representatives and the central government. This, in turn, could result in resistance to central government, an event that would force it to resort to antidemocratic methods in order to force compliance. Consequently, Jefferson and his colleagues insisted on the explicit inclusion of protections that would become the Bill of Rights. They did so because they feared that the absence of explicit guidelines for the government could cause arbitrary encroachment upon the citizens' newfound freedom.[21] Hence, the Bill of Rights and the civil liberties it generated were motivated by the preservation of freedom.

Since the time of Samuel Stouffer's pioneering study conducted in the middle of the twentieth century, *Communism, Conformity, and Civil Liberties*, scholars have often sought to understand the real-world application of abstract democratic procedural norms. Stouffer's study, undertaken in the infancy of the Cold War but near the height of Senator Joseph McCarthy's hunt for "communist sympathizers," probed—among other things—Americans' willingness to furnish the procedural rights, to which Americans had become accustomed, to suspected communists and their sympathizers. Put differently, he sought to discover whether or not Americans practiced what they preached about toleration. As it turned out, they didn't.[22]

The key is that Stouffer forced Americans to think hard about how far they were willing to go to permit a widely despised group—one that purportedly aimed to subvert America and everything for which it stood—the benefit of American fairness. Eventually, more scholars followed Stouffer's path, producing work in which Americans were forced to apply relatively abstract principles, such as freedom of speech, to social groups and organizations they detested. Some of political scientist James Gibson's work is illustrative in this sense. In one study, completed in the 1970s, Gibson and Richard Bingham undertook the exploration of how far a primarily Jewish community in Skokie, Illinois—many of whose members had survived the Holocaust—would go to accommodate the desires of the National Socialist Party of America (aka the American Nazi Party) to conduct a march in that city.

In another study, undertaken in the 1980s, Gibson examined the reaction of gays and lesbians to a march planned by the Ku Klux Klan—to protest homosexuality—that would take place in a Houston neighborhood in which many of the former group lived. At issue in both cases was the right of unpopular organizations to publicly express their beliefs—in close proximity to the very communities who felt most threatened by their presence. These communities were forced to choose between observing the rights of bigoted, violent organizations who might have

brought harm to them, and refusing to recognize those organizations' freedom of expression and assembly. Ultimately, in
both cases, the Nazis and the Klan asserted their First Amendment rights to free speech and freedom of assembly. And, in
each case, the threat provoked intolerant responses from the
aggrieved communities. In the end, though, each community observed the law—by compulsion in Skokie and through negotia-
tion in Houston.[23]

More recently, political scientist Darren Davis adopted a similar approach to explore civil liberties in the aftermath of the
terrorist attacks on America on September 11, 2001, though his
work returns us to a more classical account, one the Founding
Fathers would surely appreciate. How far are Americans willing
to let the government encroach upon their civil liberties in order
to ensure collective safety? His results suggest that support
for civil liberties is contingent upon perceived threat. Indeed,
as Davis illustrates, even political liberals—a group that under
normal circumstances zealously defends civil liberties—made
concessions in the interest of security in the wake of 9/11.[24] Yet,
as the perception of threat receded, so too did Americans' willingness to forfeit freedom. Even so, the point is that citizens
were forced to think not in the abstract but in very real, concrete
ways about balancing civil liberties with freedom.

From Stouffer through Davis, this approach spans almost
fifty years and has been applied in several contexts, anchored
by real disputes. It's a way in which scholars have been able
to conquer the "abstract versus concrete" issue in which it is
common to achieve consensus when people are asked whether
or not they support, say, free speech. Because many Americans
recognize this as a norm of American democracy, and they don't
often confront these issues, they don't give them much thought.
So, more often than not, Americans tend to offer the socially
desirable answer in support of free speech: toleration. But when
asked to apply the principle to a more tangible issue or group,
consensus typically breaks down.

Why does the application of civil liberties seem to melt consensus? We believe at least one answer is that making the issue more material, bringing it closer to home, often forces a value conflict. It makes one choose, for instance, between freedom and security—both of which are important values.[25] Indeed, if we reconsider the studies mentioned thus far, each one is an attempt, in some way, to balance freedom and security of some kind.[26]

So, to get more meaningful answers to our civil liberties questions, ones not likely to be affected by social desirability, we, too, will force people to choose between important, competing values: freedom and security. We combine this with the current context to get a fix on whether support for the Tea Party makes a difference in the values it ultimately selects. By current context, we refer to the increased salience of race since the election of President Obama,[27] in addition to the fear and outrage that occurred in the wake of the January 2011 shootings in Tucson. We begin with an examination of racial profiling, followed by free speech, and indefinite detainment.

Racial Profiling

If racial profiling is an "act of investigating a particular racial group because of a belief that members of the group are more likely to commit certain crimes [than other groups],"[28] it has been around a long time in America, beginning in colonial America when African Americans were believed more likely to participate in criminal activity.[29] A similar rationale was used to "justify" the internment of 120,000 Japanese Americans during World War II. Yet, the term (racial profiling) avoided common usage until 1987, when it entered public discourse, largely in the context of drug interdiction during America's "war on drugs." Here, the term is commensurate with the practice of using traffic stops as a pretext for drug busts targeting black and Latino motorists. Beyond the issue of the legality of the practice, one that violates the Fourth Amendment (i.e., using race as the *sole* criteria for searches and seizures) and the Fourteenth Amendment (i.e., violating the equal protection clause if it's found that profiling is based on discriminatory treatment beyond the Fourth Amendment), racial profiling is questionable on several grounds.

For one thing, insofar as the practice is justified in the name of the efficient allocation of law enforcement given scarce resources, it's not at all clear that it yields tangible results. In fact, research suggests that African Americans and Latinos are no more likely than whites to possess illicit drugs.[30] Indeed, if it's about maximizing the dollar amount of drug busts, racial profiling is a failure. Beyond the affront to individual innocents subjected to harassment because of their race, effectively paying a "tax" based on the color of their skin, there are the social costs associated with racial profiling. These include increased incarceration rates, felony disenfranchisement, neighborhood instability, and further crystallization of the perceived relationship between race and crime.[31]

Of course, all of this was prior to the terrorist attacks on September 11, 2001, after which racial profiling was, for the most part, accepted as a means of combating terrorism.[32] This represented an about-face from just six months earlier, when, in March 2011, Attorney General John Ashcroft rejected racial profiling as a tactic. Since then, however, racial profiling has returned to the public agenda. Consider recent immigration legislation in several states, beginning with Arizona's Support Our Law Enforcement and Safe Neighborhoods Act (SB 1070), which triggered similar legislation in Alabama, Georgia, South Carolina, Indiana, and Utah. Though many of the original statutes have recently been struck down following the Supreme Court ruling in *Arizona v. United States*, "show me your papers" remains in effect in all states to which it applies. This statute permits what critics view as racial profiling, granting local and state law enforcement agencies latitude to check a suspect's immigration status in the event they find probable cause that the suspect has committed a crime.[33] We used the following question on our survey to capture sentiments on racial profiling:

Some people say that law enforcement should be able to stop or detain people of certain racial backgrounds if these groups are thought to be more likely to commit crimes. This is called racial profiling. Others think that racial profiling should not be done because it harasses many innocent people on account of their race. Which of these opinions do you agree with most?

Free Speech

Another civil liberty worthy of scrutiny is free speech. Like racial profiling, the last time this emerged as a contentious issue was in the aftermath of the 9/11 terrorist attacks. In that context, as Darren Davis reveals in his book *Negative Liberty*, 62 percent of Americans were willing to permit the government to curb the ability of teachers to criticize "America's policies toward terrorism," trading freedom for a perception of increased security. In the present context, controversy swirled in the wake of Jared Loughner's rampage in Arizona on January 8, 2011, an act of violence that resulted in the death of six people, and that critically wounded a sitting member of the U.S. Congress, Representative Gabrielle Giffords.

In the immediate aftermath of the event, the airwaves crackled with charges that rancorous political discourse might have played a role in the shooting. In the run-up to the midterm elections in 2010, political figures on the right often drew on violent imagery and metaphors as a means to convey their determination to prevail in the November elections. Consider Sarah Palin's use of crosshairs to "target" twenty congressional seats. Believing them vulnerable, she "targeted" districts in which the sitting representative supported health care reform.[34] We cannot forget Sharron Angle, then candidate for a seat in the Senate, who proposed "Second Amendment remedies" to deal with what she claimed was a "tyrannical" government and as a means of dealing with her competition in the 2010 election, Majority

Leader Harry Reid. Or consider the actions of Jesse Kelly, Giffords's Republican opponent in Arizona. In an ad crafted for a campaign event, he invited supporters to "Get on target for victory. Help remove Gabrielle Giffords from office. Shoot a fully automatic M16 with Jesse Kelly."

In response, Keith Olbermann, late of MSNBC (and Current TV) shot back that Palin, Angle, and Kelly, among others, needed to acknowledge what he saw as their contribution to the violence that occurred in Tucson. Whatever one thinks of the snarky delivery of his comments, we think they conveyed the sentiments of many on the left and in the center. For that reason, Olbermann's comments are worth quoting at length:

> We need to put the guns down. Just as importantly, we need to put the gun metaphors away permanently. . . . It is essential . . . to insist not upon payback against those politicians and commentators who have irresponsibly brought us to this time of domestic terrorism, but to work to change the minds of them and their supporters—or if the minds of them and their supporters are too closed, or . . . too triumphant, to make sure by peaceful means that those politicians and commentators . . . have no further place in our system of government. If Sarah Palin . . . does not repudiate her own part in amplifying violence and violent imagery in politics, she must be dismissed from politics. . . . If Jesse Kelly, whose campaign against Congresswoman Giffords included an event in which he encouraged his supporters to join him firing machine guns, does not repudiate this, and [how] . . . it contributed to the black cloud of violence that has enveloped our politics, he must be repudiated by Arizona's Republican Party. . . . Violence, or the threat of violence, has no place in our Democracy.[35]

Shortly after the shooting, Representative Robert Brady (D-PA) even discussed introducing a bill that would make it a federal crime to use language or symbols that may threaten the safety of federal officials. With this in mind, our survey included the following question:

> Some people say that media professionals should be able to say whatever they wish even if what they say intentionally misleads people or may even ultimately result in violence of some kind. Others say that media professionals should be prevented from saying things that are intentionally misleading or may ultimately result in violence. Which of these comes closest to your opinion?

Indefinite Detainment

The issue of whether or not people—especially those who are accused of terrible crimes—should be held in detention indefinitely has been around for some time. Because the Founding Fathers were all too familiar with the arbitrary nature with which those in power were able to confiscate one's property and liberty, something they wished to avoid in the future, they hedged against this threat as part of the Fifth Amendment, later modified as part of the Fourteenth Amendment, as part of the "Due Process Clause" of the Constitution. In other words, neither federal nor state governments are allowed to deal with suspects as they wish; government must adhere to the rule of law. Indefinite detainment also violates the Sixth Amendment guarantees of a speedy trial and one's ability to confront witnesses.[36] Unlike racial profiling or free speech, there is no immediate proximate event that permits this issue to be seen as one in which something tangible is at stake. We used this as a check against the other two, a baseline question if you will. Our survey included the following question:

> Some people say law enforcement should be able to arrest and detain anyone indefinitely if that person is suspected of belonging to a terrorist organization or in the process of committing a terrorist attack. Others say that no one should be held for a long period of time without being formally

charged with a crime. Which of these options do you agree with most?

We believe exploring the relationship between civil liberties and support for the Tea Party is important in that it permits an assessment of the extent to which the Tea Party promotes freedom in context: in tangible, real situations. In light of recent immigration laws passed in several states, ones that critics equate with racial profiling, racial profiling is one area believed to be important to investigate. Another is free speech in the aftermath of the Tucson shootings. Indefinite detainment, again, is our baseline since nothing much has happened on that front in some time.

Mapping the Relationship between Freedom and Tea Party Support

Before we settle whether or not differences exist between Tea Party sympathizers and the rest of the public, we must first grasp how the public views these issues as a whole. As figure 3.1 suggests, it's pretty clear that with one exception, the public insists on keeping the government at bay, recognizing civil liberties. For instance, with racial profiling, only 22 percent of Americans are willing to permit police to stop and possibly detain someone because of their racial background. Likewise, when it comes to detaining someone who may be a terrorist, or is suspected of belonging to a terrorist organization, less than half of the public (42 percent) are willing to sanction it. Yet, when it comes to free speech, the public is less inclined to go along. Indeed, 73 percent of Americans believe that media professionals (journalists) should be stopped from saying things that are factually untrue, or making statements that may lead to violence of some kind. While it may seem shocking to some that so many prefer security to civil liberties when it comes to free speech, our results corroborate Davis's findings on free speech. In the context of the aftermath of 9/11, he found that almost two-thirds of his respondents preferred security instead of civil liberties.[37]

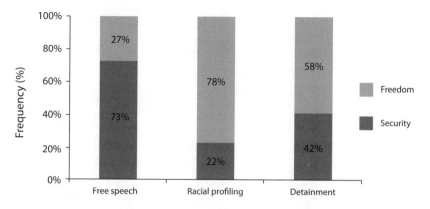

3.1. Support for freedom versus security
Note: Total $N = 1188$, with 308 true believers, 488 middle of the road, and 392 true skeptics; relationship significant at $\chi^2 \; p < 0.000$

For the most part, the data indicates that Americans take civil liberties seriously. The lone exception was free speech, but given the context in which the questions were asked (shortly after Congresswoman Giffords's shooting), we think it shouldn't be too alarming that the public was open to possibly restricting the speech of journalists who either play loose with the facts or whose rhetoric may incite violence.

Now we turn to the question of whether or not strong support for the Tea Party drives a wedge between true believers, those who strongly support the aims of the Tea Party, and those opposed to its goals, true skeptics. Let's return to racial profiling in figure 3.2. Here, we observe a 38-point gap separating believers and skeptics, where 47 percent of the former is in favor of racial profiling versus only 9 percent of the latter. Moving to figure 3.3, the results are similar for detainment, if less extreme. Here, a 19-point gap emerges between the groups that like and dislike the Tea Party: 52 percent of believers support the idea of government detaining someone indefinitely in contrast to 33 percent of skeptics.

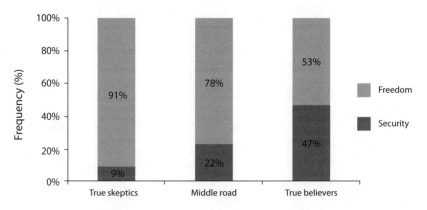

3.2. Support for racial profiling, by Tea Party support
Note: Total $N = 1188$, with 308 true believers, 488 middle of the road, and
392 true skeptics; relationship significant at χ^2 $p < 0.000$

The relationships flip as our analysis moves to free speech. Here, in figure 3.4, it appears that believers assume the mantle of civil libertarians *relative* to folks who are skeptical of the Tea Party along with those who are in the middle—that is, those who either somewhat support or somewhat disapprove of the Tea Party. Indeed, 42 percent of the believers are willing to permit journalists freedom to say whatever they please versus 19 percent of skeptics, and 26 percent of those in the middle.

We have provided tentative validation of our claim that various levels of support for the Tea Party encourage people to take divergent positions on civil liberties. Instead of asking people questions on which consensus normally forms, we pushed them to make a choice between security and civil liberties as a means of testing their commitment to freedom. Our first cut at the findings, ones that examined the pattern of responses to our trade-off questions, square with prior work. For instance, whether or not the public senses a threat, as they did in the aftermath of 9/11, or now, when terrorist threat is relatively lower, racial profiling is roundly rejected by most of the public. In like fashion, our findings that the public's support for freedom over se-

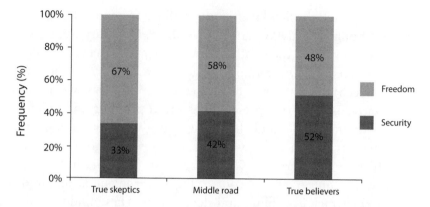

3.3. Support for indefinite detainment, by Tea Party support
Note: Total $N = 1188$, with 308 true believers, 488 middle of the road, and
392 true skeptics; relationship significant at χ^2 $p < 0.000$

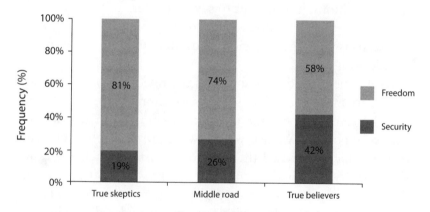

3.4. Support for free speech, by Tea Party support
Note: Total $N = 1188$, with 308 true believers, 488 middle of the road, and
392 true skeptics; relationship significant at χ^2 $p < 0.000$

curity follows earlier work, in which the prospect of indefinite
detention based on suspicion of terrorist activities or associations
is rejected. Our results shadow similar work, confirming that the
Sturm und Drang associated with recent national trauma pushes
people to prefer censorship over freedom of speech.[38]

We expected the first layer of our findings to align with earlier work, though it's always good to confirm. Our purpose, however, is to examine the depth of Tea Party supporters' commitment to freedom. Our findings suggest that, with one exception (free speech) the commitment isn't very deep—at least when the alternative is security represented as racial profiling and indefinite detainment. We find this a bit odd given our findings in the analysis of Tea Party websites we presented in chapter 1 in which "big government" was clearly something with which they were concerned. Of course, big government is required to conduct racial profiling and detainment. These findings are more easily understood, however, when framed in light of the general suspicion and anxiety right-wing movements, and their sympathizers, harbor for members of "Other" groups.[39] Under these conditions, it seems fair to say that when forced to choose, believers' fear of racialized out-groups taking over the country (security) trumps suspicion associated with big government (freedom).

As we mentioned, free speech is the one issue on which believers are more likely than skeptics to embrace freedom. As the data indicate, support for free speech—framed in this way— isn't very popular. We ask you, however, to remember the context in which we posed the question: shortly after the Tucson shootings. So, it's understandable why less than 30 percent of the public supports free speech. Still, the percentage of Tea Party supporters that are okay with free speech under these circumstances is more than double the percentage of those who don't like the Tea Party. Why is their commitment to freedom present here, especially under these circumstances, and not with the other two examples of civil liberties?

Perhaps it's the case that the other two imply breaches of law and order, whereas irresponsible journalism is more a matter of taste. Another possibility is that, by way of the heated rhetoric surrounding the political contest in which Giffords was engaged, the Tea Party was implicated in the violence.[40] In this case, support for freedom of speech among Tea Party supporters is really about circling the wagons, a way of protecting the in-group members. We realize that if one sees Tea Party supporters as conservatives that these results don't make any sense because conservatives normally reject free speech.[41]

Recall, however, our contention that true believers aren't conservatives per se, but *reactionary* conservatives. The above analysis fails to discriminate between the two types of conservatives. We confront this challenge by narrowing the analysis to all self-identified conservatives and comparing among conservatives, separating Tea Party conservatives from non–Tea Party conservatives. Further, we don't limit the analysis to free speech: we extend it to the other expressions of freedom as well. If we are correct, we expect a repeat of the results we observed in chapter 1, and daylight should emerge between Tea Party conservatives and non–Tea Party conservatives.

As figure 3.5 illustrates, sharp differences emerge between conservatives who are true believers and conservatives who aren't sold on the Tea Party, suggesting that the differences observed between Tea Party sympathizers and non–Tea Party sympathizers isn't about whether or not one is conservative. To be sure, the differences between the two conservative groups in their support of indefinite detainment for those suspected of terrorist affiliation or plotting terrorist acts is negligible: 54 and 56 percent, respectively. The similarities end there. For instance, there is a 19-point gap separating who we think are reactionary conservatives from more mainstream conservatives on free speech in which 46 percent of Tea Party conservatives favor it under these circumstances, and 27 percent of non–Tea Party conservatives support it. An even larger gulf emerges over the issue of racial profiling in which a 27-point gap separates the respective conservative camps where 55 percent of Tea Party conservatives support racial profiling versus 28 percent of non–Tea Party conservatives.

These results effectively rule out ideology as a cleavage that separates believers from everyone else. We must hunt elsewhere if we are to account for differences between believers and skeptics.

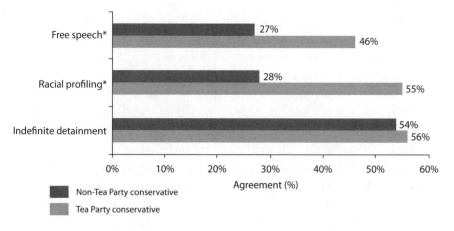

3.5. Support for civil liberties, by type of conservatism
Note: Total conservative $N = 407$, with 204 true believers in the Tea Party;
*significant at $\chi^2 p < 0.000$

It's entirely possible that factors for which we have yet to account go a long way toward explaining the relationships we have observed. For instance, when it comes to civil liberties, it may well be the case that Tea Party sympathizers are simply more authoritarian than people who remain unpersuaded by the Tea Party's message. If this is something we ultimately find, it suggests that, at least where civil liberties are concerned, the difference between believers and skeptics is really about how both groups see social order, not any intrinsic differences between believers and skeptics. Perhaps this accounts for the differences we have so far observed. We now turn to the task of untangling this knot.

Can Support for the Tea Party Say Something New about Civil Liberties?

Until now, our claim that believers depart from the rest of the public remains intact. It seems as though sympathy for the objectives of the Tea Party, one way or another, inform peoples' views on civil liberties. But we can't afford to become too comfortable with our findings because there are alternative explanations for which we must account. Indeed, it's possible that some third factor lurking in the background is responsible for the connection we've observed between sentiment for the Tea Party and freedom, and we just haven't accounted for it yet. It could be the case, for instance, that support for the Tea Party and support for racial profiling may actually be connected through people's belief that members of subordinate groups need to remain in their subordinate position in American society (social dominance). Likewise, as we've already mentioned, the relationship between freedom of speech and one's orientation toward the Tea Party may be compromised by authoritarianism: allowing too much freedom interferes with the social order preferred by authoritarians.

So what are the predispositions that would typically be associated with views on civil liberties? We reviewed many in the prior chapter. First, we need to consider political predispositions such as ideology and partisanship. Conservatives believe that rights are earned; they aren't beyond revocation. Liberals, on the other hand, believe rights are natural, unassailable. By virtue of the connection between ideology and partisanship, we should anticipate that many Republicans, similar to conservatives, would place less emphasis on civil liberties in post-9/11 America than will Democrats.[42]

Second, we also need to account for less manifestly political predispositions, ones that political psychologist David Sears calls *motivational predispositions* because they fulfill individuals' needs in some way. Perhaps the most powerful one, as we have already seen, is social dominance orientation (SDO), a concept that explains the need for people to support group-based domination. As SDO increases, so, too, should support for laws and policies that maintain the social position of dominant groups. As we focus on civil liberties, we should find that SDO

dampens support for them. Another motivational predisposition, the need for social cohesion and conformity captured by
authoritarianism, suggests that these people also prefer to deny
civil liberties. We believe this to be the case since authoritarianism is generally accompanied by a relatively rigid way of thinking, one not conducive to weighing the pros and cons associated
with the way democracy is supposed to work.[43] Thus, those who
are seen as challenging authority and, therefore, social cohesion,
are viewed as out of bounds. Ethnocentrism is relevant to the
extent that society is reduced to "us versus them." In this case,
it's the law-abiding "us" versus the law-breaking "them."

These are plausible scenarios, very good reasons why supporting the Tea Party should make no difference when it comes
to civil liberties, or freedom, if you will. After all, what differences we have observed so far in this chapter may simply be
attributed to the fact that believers are more conservative than
everyone else, or that they believe some groups should simply
stay in their respective places. These are all reasonable alternative explanations for the relationship we have observed so far in
the tables and charts discussed just a few pages earlier.

Even so, we believe that support for the Tea Party captures
the perceived existential threat to the mainly white, middle-
aged, middle-class, largely male slice of America represented
by the Obama presidency. Support for the Tea Party, in short,
represents reactionary conservatism. Reactionary conservatism
is a predisposition motivated by the anxiety associated with
the perception that real Americans are losing their country. Recall our study in Washington State noted in chapter 1 in which
we found 75 percent of Tea Party sympathizers are "very concerned" that the country they know is slipping away and changing too fast, while an additional 17 percent are "somewhat"
concerned. Likewise, we found that 78 percent of true believers
are "very concerned" that there are forces in American society
that may be changing the country for the worse, and 13 percent
are "somewhat" concerned about this.[44] Obviously, this moti-

vation departs from ones already mentioned, and serves as the basis of our expectation that support for the Tea Party will continue to impact the way people feel about freedom.

To summarize, if we find that support for the Tea Party continues to affect the way people think about civil liberties after accounting for the aforementioned alternatives, it supports our claim that reactionary conservatism is sui generis. If not, and what we observed in the more simple analysis undertaken above fails to hold, then we can say that the relationship between support for the Tea Party and civil liberties is really about something else, including a desire for social conformity (authoritarianism, for instance). If we take the Tea Party at face value, we should expect its supporters to champion civil liberties. By this we mean the extent to which civil liberties are a means of keeping the state at arm's length, and the Tea Party is about small government, we can see how Tea Party sympathizers may support civil liberties.

We explore free speech first, in figure 3.6. Do the results we observed when we examined the relationship between support for the Tea Party and free speech remain valid once we include manifold competing explanations? They do. It seems that believers are indeed 27 percent more likely than skeptics to stand behind journalists having the right to say whatever they wish, regardless of the consequences. In other words, as they claim, Tea Party supporters do in fact side with freedom more so than do true skeptics, who opt instead for security when it comes to the rights of journalists. There are other factors that inform Americans' opinion on free speech framed in this way: ideology and authoritarianism. We thought it likely that those with relatively authoritarian dispositions would probably prefer an outcome more consistent with conformity, which in this context should push them to reject free speech. Indeed, people who are relatively strong authoritarians are 19 percent less likely than those less concerned with conformity to back free speech. Likewise, conservatives are 8 percent less likely than liberals to

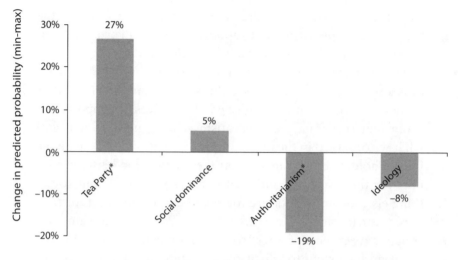

3.6. Probability of supporting free speech
*Significant at $p < 0.05$, one-tailed

support the right of journalists to say what they please, regardless of the consequences.[45]

What happens when we consider racial profiling? Does level of support for the Tea Party affect how people view it? Figure 3.7 provides some answers. As we did with free speech, we must account for competing explanations, ones that can also explain Americans' opinions on racial profiling.[46] Only after doing so are we confident in our findings. As it turns out—even after accounting for various explanations, some of which were indeed important—believers are 14 percent more likely than skeptics to condone racial profiling. In addition to true believers, people who are comfortable with some groups in society dominating others—those with a high degree of social dominance orientation—are 40 percent more likely to endorse racial profiling than those who fail to subscribe to group-based inequality. Ideological preference, partisanship, authoritarianism, and ethnocentrism have no real impact on whether or not people

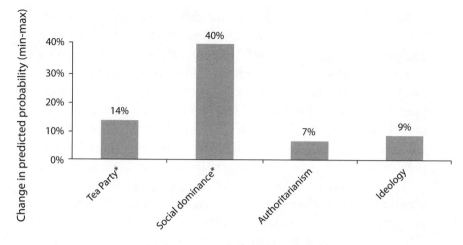

3.7. Probability of supporting racial profiling
*Significant at $p < 0.05$, one-tailed

support or oppose racial profiling. In other words, critics cannot say that support for the Tea Party, and how it informs citizens' views on racial profiling, is tied to any of these explanations.

In addition to these rival explanations—most of which wash out—some of the controls (not depicted in figure 3.7 but available in table A3.1 in the appendix) have a real impact on the ways in which Americans view racial profiling. Another surprise is that relative political sophisticates are 10 percent more likely to permit racial profiling than those less sophisticated in politics. Likewise, older versus younger folk, and the wealthy versus the not so well-off, choose security over freedom in this context. More specifically, older Americans are 9 percent more likely than younger generations to support racial profiling, and the wealthy are 14 percent more likely to support it than those who aren't so well-off. Race is important, too: African Americans are 13 percent less likely than all other races to accept racial profiling; no surprise here.

So far, our claim that support for the Tea Party promotes attitudes apart from well-known predispositions, such as ideology and partisanship, remains valid. Apparently, at least in the cases in which freedom of speech and racial profiling are at issue, we can say that reactionary conservatism is driving Tea Party support. Does the importance of Tea Party–related sentiment spill over to the issue of indefinite detainment? How about more specific threats to the existing social order, ones represented by the president and his policies? In the preliminary analysis above, we revealed varying levels of support for illegal detention, but these differences fail to survive a more rigorous analysis. After we account for other explanations, as figure 3.8 reveals, we find no differences accruing to support for the Tea Party. This suggests the possibility that the relationship between sympathy for the Tea Party and detention is really accounted for by something else.[47]

In the meantime, there are several other factors that explain support for indefinite detention. Among them, social dominance orientation is the most robust, with people who are comfortable with the permanence of inequality being 38 percent more likely to agree with indefinite detainment than those who prefer a more egalitarian social order. Similarly, self-identified conservatives are 24 percent more likely than liberals, and people who are driven by conformity (authoritarians) are 30 percent more likely than those not so driven to reject the civil libertarian option, instead embracing the necessity of locking someone up indefinitely.[48]

Taking a step back, we see that real differences have emerged between believers and skeptics. In the end, support for the Tea Party matters. Ideology, social dominance orientation, and authoritarianism are all strong competing explanations. Still, even after accounting for various and sundry alternative explanations for why Americans weighed their decision to choose perceived security over freedom, or vice versa, one's attachment to the Tea Party continues to matter. Since we are careful to include both political and motivational predispositions as explanations in

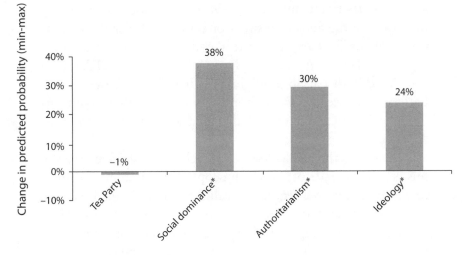

3.8. Probability of supporting indefinite detainment
*Significant at $p < 0.05$, one-tailed

our analysis, it strengthens our claim that the movement forges a collective identity among people who feel their country slipping away from them. In this regard, our findings are similar to Davis's in that situational forces, in addition to those associated with predisposition, condition how people think about trade-offs between perceived security and freedom.

Of at least equal importance, we think, is what these findings suggest: responses to the value conflicts presented to people is in part driven by the fear that the American way of life is disappearing for "true" Americans—Tea Party supporters. Some might say that believers are simply concerned about law and order. However, if this were the case, sympathy toward the Tea Party should have no impact, because a preference for law and order is more closely tied to conservatism than anything else. Support for the Tea Party, as we've argued all along, reflects *reactionary* conservatism. With the racialized discourse around the recent immigration measures in the South and Southwest, how Latinos are often perceived as social and criminal deviants,[49] and Tea Party ties to anti-immigrant organizations, it's probably the case that the perceived situational threat of illegal immigration explains Tea Party supporters' endorsement of racial profiling. Beyond concern with perceived social and political deviance associated with Latino immigrants is fear of being overrun by Latinos numerically and culturally, something that could undermine American identity, challenging what it means to be an American.[50]

Reconciling the results for free speech is a bit trickier. We say this because a trade-off in which people are placed in a position to choose between a legitimate value and one deemed morally wrong is called a "taboo trade-off." A taboo trade-off, according to psychologist Philip Tetlock, is "a comparison [of values] that people deemed illegitimate because the comparison subvert[s] or destroy[s] a culturally cherished value."[51] In this case, the value that's subverted is security: a desired state of "safety, harmony, and stability of society."[52] Even in this context, one in which some attempted to link the Tea Party to the violence in Tucson by way of the hostile discourse surrounding races in "targeted" congressional districts, it's possible to fashion an explanation for why believers were more willing than skeptics to support freedom over security.

Perhaps it's the case that, when forced to choose, believers opt for freedom because, as we mentioned earlier, they felt under siege from the political left. However, that was before we had taken ethnocentrism into account, something that should dissolve the association between believers and free speech were it really about in-group protection. But ethnocentrism accounts for just a small part of what may be perceived as an attack from the left. Conservatism, rooted in its demand for law and order, should take up some of the explanatory slack, as should a preference of conformity (authoritarianism). To be sure, conservative principles matter, but in the *opposite* direction of Tea Party support: conservatives don't support free speech.[53] No surprise here in that they're typically for order and security. The same can be said for authoritarianism. In the end, holding constant ethnocentrism, conservatism, and authoritarianism permits us to speculate that embracing free speech, especially in this context, is more about a refusal to yield to a government run by Obama.[54] After all, as we have pointed out, the president is the government personified. More specifically, he's the chief law enforcement officer. Of course, our observation that conservatism and Tea Party support cut in opposite directions—one in support of free speech, the other security—suggests that Tea Party support really is a proxy for reactionary conservatism, departing from more conventional conservatism.

The one case in which support for the Tea Party failed to furnish any additional explanatory leverage is when we consider the issue of indefinite detainment. In this particular case, we ultimately found in a separate analysis that the association we observed earlier between support for the Tea Party and the people's preference, pro or con, on indefinite detainment, was masked by social dominance orientation, an orientation to intergroup relations in which egalitarian treatment isn't much of a priority. Before accounting for social dominance orientation, support for the Tea Party performs consistently with what we observed in earlier analysis, in which we investigated the relationship between indefinite detainment and attachment to the Tea Party: believers opted for security over freedom.

In hindsight we're not surprised that upon accounting for social dominance orientation, the relationship between support for the Tea Party and indefinite detainment vanishes. Since social dominance orientation boils down to the maintenance of group-based inequality, it makes sense to us that Tea Party support is actually working through social dominance orientation to affect the views of its supporters on detainment. Why should these people (presumed terrorists), who are already presumed guilty, benefit from due process? From the perspective of a Tea Party supporter, these are the people from whom they wish to recover their country.

Other explanations for the trade-off were as expected. For
instance, preference for group dominance (SDO) depressed support for freedom across the board. (Recall that SDO was a non-
factor on the issue of free speech.) No surprise here. Similarly,
we would expect conservatives to lean more toward security
than freedom. Finally, a desire for conformity (authoritarianism) also militates against a preference for freedom over security. Again, we expected as much.

We'd like to note a possible objection to our findings in this
section. The question that attempts to tap free speech in context
failed to designate who (or what), exactly, stood to prevent journalists from saying misleading things or discussing content that
might lead to violence. It was a conscious choice on our part to
avoid invoking the federal government as the principal threat
to free speech in our question. We did so because we were concerned with priming Tea Party types who, as we have witnessed
in their discourse, have no use for the federal government, especially one captained by Barack Obama. Hence, framing the
question as we did probably underestimates the degree to which
believers disagree with skeptics on free speech—at least in the
context in which we posed the question. It's also worth noting that differences between moderate and reactionary conservatives are also underestimated. We now shift our focus to
patriotism.

PATRIOTISM AND THE TEA PARTY

Patriotism, as a general concept, indexes one's love for his or
her country. That's simple enough, but what does it mean? It
goes beyond simple affection for one's country. Patriotism is
also about a commitment to, and critical understanding of, a
set of political principles and ideals, not the simple conformity
and reactionary jingoism with which the term is often con-
fused.[55] More to the point, patriotism is commensurate with
one's commitment to doing what one can to force a society to

honor the values on which it is based. Hence, when necessary, patriotism furnishes a language for reform, one that provides an intellectual framework for the opposition of domination and oppression. As political philosopher Maurizio Viroli maintains, oppression, domination, and discrimination are anathema to patriots because, among other things, they violate the principal goal of patriotism: the ability to maintain a free society in which political, civil, and social rights are enjoyed by all.[56]

To make this work, however, citizens must remain vigilant in defense of their freedom, something that requires unselfishness, a willingness to sacrifice. They must prioritize the common good over self-interested pursuits, especially if they wish to remain free of both external domination (in the case of losing a war) and internal domination (the product of corrupt public officials). As the logic goes, individual freedom is bound to maintaining a free society, and a free society can only be maintained if its citizens are willing to sacrifice a measure of autonomy to ensure such freedom, including military service or active participation in public life.[57] This view of patriotism squares with sociologist Morris Janowitz's concept of civic consciousness, in which he calls for more balance between rights and obligations rather than overemphasizing rights.[58] Janowitz believes democratic citizenship to be more than the protection of narrow economic self-interest. Instead, he posits, citizens are obligated to actively participate in the maintenance of their own freedom. Part of more civic-minded patriotism is the willingness to criticize the faults of political authorities; failing to do so will result in the erosion of liberty.

Ultimately, patriotism is more about promoting the common good and the general welfare of the community than it is about the promotion of narrow, self-interested motives.[59] Moreover, as we have already mentioned, the language of patriotism is congruent with reform. Consider, for instance, the ways in which an activist, civic-minded patriotism helped to reform the South in postwar America. As political scientist Christopher Parker shows, black men, through their willingness to serve in the military of a country that treated them at best as second-class citizens, drew on the language of patriotism to motivate their push for reforms. Their sacrifice on behalf of the black community, and the national political community, was a source of pride for African American veterans and furnished them with the wherewithal to oppose white supremacy. In the end, they were a major part of the success of the civil rights movement.[60]

History suggests that the civic-minded behavior inspired by military service, and how it contributed to social change in the South, wasn't limited to black veterans. As historian Jennifer Brooks points out, some Southern white veterans, because of their shared sacrifice with the black soldiers with whom they interacted during World War II, returned to the South to fight side by side with their counterparts for political and economic equality on behalf of black Southerners and the working class. Many were motivated to take such a stand by the contradiction of waging war against "a racially intolerant enemy" while "defending a discriminatory nation."[61] This kind of cooperation in service of contesting injustice doesn't happen in the absence of self-sacrifice.

Yet, when it comes to the practice of American patriotism in recent history, the evidence indicates that the country has turned away from its (mostly) proud past. In fact, some scholars, referring to American patriotism, feel the country has lost its way—in part because Americans fail to prioritize the needs of the nation over the pursuit of more individual, self-interested goals. For instance, political theorist Mary Dietz laments the loss of a more classical understanding of patriotism in which patriots defend the constitution and *equal* liberty while condemning corruption, among other things. As she suggests, this version of patriotism is all but forgotten, lost with the drift of American patriotism to the right, a move that squelches constitution-based criticism of the state and its policies.[62]

Several psychologists have successfully adapted the normative insights associated with patriotism, and subjected them to empirical tests. They show that departing from classical, more civic-minded patriotism isn't without real, tangible consequences. For instance, they show that right-leaning, more self-interested patriotism, in which unquestioned deference to political authorities and an unwillingness to criticize national policies takes root, dampens prospects for maintaining a free society. It is commensurate with the "my country, right or wrong" sentiment, one that hovers dangerously close to nationalism, in which fairness and equality are jettisoned in favor of *individual* freedom and national power.[63] These patriots tend to prefer the Republican Party, and support the military.[64] They also fail to support social and political tolerance insofar as they believe cultural "Others" threaten American cultural homogeneity, and don't believe that people of different political beliefs have the right to express them in America.[65] Finally, the more they see America as flawless, the less likely they are to actively engage in politics; they tend not to pay much attention to politics and aren't too interested in participating in the political process.[66]

This is in contrast to a more classical form of patriotism, one laden with neither partisan nor ideological baggage. This type of national attachment promotes the unselfishness for which a more classical, civic-minded patriotism—outlined above by Morris Janowitz—calls. As political psychologists Leonie Huddy and Nadia Khatib have shown, more civic-minded patriotism encourages people to become increasingly attentive to politics. They have also shown that it generates active participation in the political process by way of voting.[67] Moreover, this patriotism pushes Americans to help their compatriots through charitable donations and participation in volunteer organizations.[68] Furthermore, the unselfishness of more civic-minded patriots permits them to disavow violating the civil rights of Arabs and Muslims insofar as they refused to support racial profiling in the aftermath of 9/11.[69]

In what follows, we seek to capture the differences in the types of patriotism just discussed and how support for the Tea

Party affects the ways in which people see each type. One question in our survey, as a baseline if you will, simply asked about the extent to which Americans should criticize their country:

> Some people say that patriotism is about supporting your country, right or wrong. In other words, Americans shouldn't criticize their country, even if they disagree with its policies. Others say that criticism is necessary, and that true patriots must challenge America to live up to its values. Which comes closest to your opinion?

This question was designed to tap into the "my country, right or wrong" type of jingoistic patriotism. We then introduced patriotism framed as value conflict. Here we juxtaposed classical patriotism (in which citizens' obligation to nation overrides self-interest) to what's come to be known as *pseudo* patriotism in which self-interest trumps national interest.[70] The questions on which our survey draws map well theoretically onto Schwartz's framework outlined earlier in that freedom and equality are in opposition:

> Some people say that it's our patriotic duty to help subsidize an education for those without access to good schools, something that will ultimately strengthen the United States. Others say that redistributing the money of hardworking Americans is wrong because it takes money away from the people who earned it and gives it to people who didn't work for it. Which comes closest to your opinion?

> Some people say that true patriotism is about pushing America to realize its promise of equality, even if it means enacting new laws to ensure that everyone is treated equally. Others think it is unnecessary to enact new laws to prevent discrimination, especially if these laws are already in place. Which comes closest to your opinion?

In addition to pitting classical, civic patriotism against a more right-wing version, in which freedom is in conflict with equality, one question taps into redistribution for the benefit of the country. Of course, this suggests a zero-sum game in which the citizen is forced to think about money coming out of her pocket. The other question is designed to gauge the extent to which people support state intervention in an effort to bring values in line with social practice. Also, stepping back even farther, we'd like to probe the principle/policy disconnect. That is, it's relatively painless to endorse a principle. But to endorse policy designed to implement the principle is altogether different because now something tangible is at stake.[71]

The Tea Party and Patriotism: A Preliminary Analysis

We now put the relationship between support for the Tea Party and patriotism to the test. To simplify matters, we'd like to borrow an old, but still fitting, way in which to distinguish between the more classical, civic-minded patriotism we have described, and the type of patriotism fixed on more individual pursuits. Adorno and his colleagues, in the *Authoritarian Personality*, coined the terms *pseudo* patriotism and *genuine* patriotism. The former, which is based on "blind attachment to certain national cultural values, uncritical conformity with prevailing group ways, and rejection of other nations as outgroups," is juxtaposed with the latter, a concept consistent with a "love of country and attachment to national values based on critical understanding."[72] Hopefully, these labels will make plain the differences we seek to explore, for they seem to capture much of the discussion we've had so far. As the reader will soon see, it appears that believers are more likely than skeptics to opt for pseudo patriotism. However, before we examine such differences, we must first consider the distribution of patriotism without regard to one's orientation to the Tea Party. If the following results are any indication, America and its policies aren't beyond criticism.

In fact, as figure 3.9 indicates, 83 percent of Americans believe that it's one's patriotic duty to criticize the country if it's not living up to its values. Only 17 percent believe it wrong to criticize

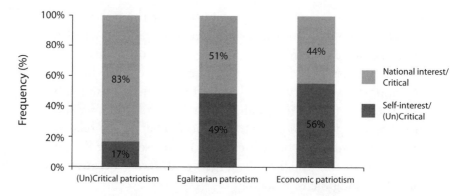

3.9. Support for national- versus self-interested patriotism
Note: Total $N = 1188$, with 308 true believers, 488 middle of the road, and
392 true skeptics; relationship significant at $\chi^2\ p < 0.000$

the country. Framing it as a question of "patriotic duty," we asked people to essentially choose between egalitarianism and freedom, national interest or self-interest. We wanted to push the limits of patriotism: How far would Americans go to put country first? When patriotism is framed in such a manner, the responses are more evenly distributed. At 56 percent, most Americans put their country first, believing it their patriotic duty to increase access to a quality education for those who don't currently have it, so long as it will strengthen the country. In contrast, 44 percent of Americans don't like the idea of subsidizing education for the less fortunate, even if it'll ultimately improve the country.

The results are mixed to this point. On the one hand, when patriotism is defined by the willingness of Americans to criticize the country, there is overwhelming consensus. Yet when patriotism is framed as an assessment of Americans' willingness to entertain paying higher taxes in the interest of strengthening the country through more equal access to education, yawning gaps in opinion emerge. So what will happen when patriotism is framed in terms of embracing equality more directly, rejecting discrimination, even if it means passing more legislation to accomplish this? The results mirror the ones we witnessed with subsidizing more equal access to education. In fact, there's an almost even split in the public over the issue: 51 percent to 49 percent. These results suggest that slightly more than half of Americans believe, as a country, we've done enough to combat the invidiousness of discrimination: we don't need additional laws. America's done enough to ensure equality.

What happens when we bring support for the Tea Party into the mix? If prior work is any indication, we expect that Tea Party sympathizers are loath to criticize America. But since they are likely to see a threat from more civic-minded patriotism, in which other nonwhite groups may dislodge their position in the age of Obama, we think they'll resolve their value conflict in favor of a more individualist patriotism.

As we turn to investigate the extent to which support for the Tea Party makes any difference, figure 3.10 indicates no difference across levels of Tea Party support—at least when patriotism is framed as one's willingness to criticize. The numbers are practically the same insofar as 89 percent of skeptics agree with the proposition that patriotism requires one to criticize the country when necessary versus 84 percent of believers who support this position.

However, in figures 3.11 and 3.12, real differences begin to emerge once patriotism is framed as a choice between freedom and equality, where freedom is about self-interest and equality is about national interest. Here, almost 45 percentage points separate the two groups: where 33 percent of true believers put country first, indicating their willingness to help subsidize a better education for Americans if it'll help strengthen the country. However, among skeptics, this number more than doubles to almost 80 percent (78 percent). Finally, when patriotism is framed as a clash between freedom from big government and equality as equal treatment of one's compatriots, we observe another pronounced gap in opinion: almost 40 points. Where only 26 percent of true believers endorse stopping at nothing to promote equal treatment, this jumps to 65 percent among those who are less persuaded by the Tea Party's message.

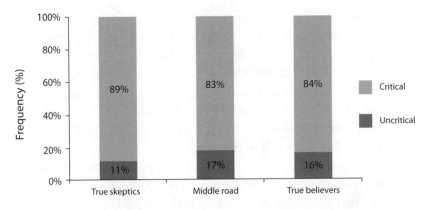

3.10. Support for (un)critical patriotism, by Tea Party support
Note: Total *N* = 1188, with 308 true believers, 488 middle
of the road, and 392 true skeptics

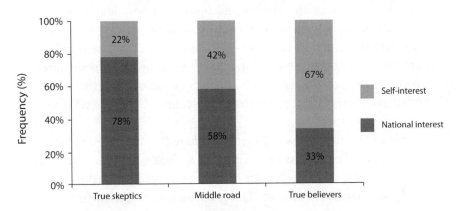

3.11. Support for economic patriotism, by Tea Party support
Note: Total *N* = 1188, with 308 true believers, 488 middle of the road, and
392 true skeptics; relationship significant at χ^2 $p < 0.000$

Now that we have examined the differences between true believers and true skeptics, we turn to a more challenging comparison, one in which we attempt to peel away reactionary
conservatives from the more moderate conservatives. As we did
in our analysis of freedom, we confine our comparison to self-

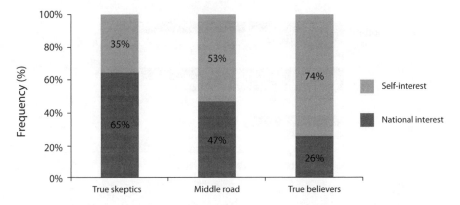

3.12. Support for egalitarian patriotism, by Tea Party support
Note: Total $N = 1188$, with 308 true believers, 488 middle of the road, and
392 true skeptics; relationship significant at $\chi^2\ p < 0.000$

identified conservatives, allowing us to neutralize the effect of
ideology. If Tea Party supporters are just conservatives, then *all*
self-described conservatives will give fairly similar answers.

As figure 3.13 makes clear, similar results obtain for patriotism as for civil liberties. While there is an almost negligible five-
point gap separating Tea Party and non–Tea Party conservatives
on the issue of whether or not patriots should criticize America,
more daylight separates the two groups on the other ways of
understanding American patriotism. When patriotism is framed
as a choice between strengthening the country through subsidizing education versus not doing so, 47 percent of non–Tea
Party conservatives opt to do so versus 26 percent of Tea Party
conservatives. An even wider gap emerges when framing patriotism as a choice between more or less egalitarianism in America.
Where 39 percent of more mainstream conservatives prefer to
continue trying to guarantee more equal treatment for all, only
12 percent of reactionaries think likewise.

What are we to make of these preliminary findings? Why,
in other words, do our findings reveal such consensus on one
question but divisions on the last two? The principal difference,

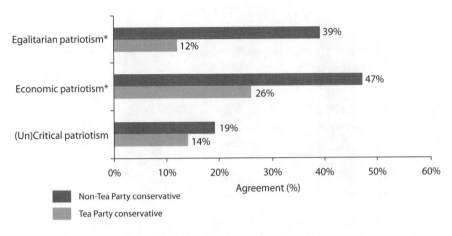

3.13. Patriotism, by type of conservatism
Note: Total conservative $N = 407$, with 204 true believers in the Tea Party;
*significant at χ^2 $p < 0.000$

we think, rests upon the absence of value conflict in the first question and the presence of it in the last two. Again, the first patriotism question we examined was framed in terms of one's willingness to criticize the country. Because American patriotism originated as dissent, rooted in core values that Americans have defended for almost 240 years, we shouldn't be surprised by consensus here. More to the point, there's no real, tangible conflict of values; there's nothing at stake.

However, we cannot say that about the other two questions, those that use patriotism as a means of pitting egalitarianism against freedom. This, we believe, is the principal explanation for the observed results. Tea Party sympathizers, in this case, are more in favor of freedom than equality, where the relationship even holds after we account for ideology, revealing a rift among self-identified conservatives. Still, there's a possibility that these results will fail to hold under more rigorous examination. Indeed, it's possible that once we account for other factors such as party loyalty, one's opposition to egalitarianism (social dominance orientation), and authoritarianism, the differences we have observed may disappear. We attend to this issue below.

Does Support for the Tea Party Really Affect How People View Patriotism?

In order to have any confidence in our preliminary findings that support for the Tea Party affects the kind of patriotism to which one is drawn, we must entertain alternative explanations. Fortunately for us, many of the explanations that applied to civil liberties apply here and will help us tease out suspected differences between sympathy for the Tea Party and political ideology, that is, whether or not one identifies as a liberal or a conservative, among other factors. Our expectations are that political predispositions, such as partisanship and whether one sees himself or herself as a liberal or conservative, matter.[73] We imagine that conservatives and Republicans will likely resolve their value conflict in favor of a more individualist, less than civic form of patriotism. Since more civic-minded patriotism ultimately results in more social leveling, we also include SDO, i.e., one's preference for group dominance. Because of the social-leveling effect of civic patriotism, and because this flies in the face of established social norms, we need to account for authoritarians' need for conformity. To round things out, we also control for in-group favoritism—that is, ethnocentrism. We can imagine a scenario in which "we" hardworking Americans refuse to pave the way for "them," the too-lazy-to-improve themselves, even if it strengthens the country.

We start a more rigorous analysis of the relationship between patriotism and Tea Party sentiment with patriotism framed, again, in the guise of Americans who are willing to criticize the country versus those who believe their country is always correct. Looking back to our preliminary analysis, regardless of Tea Party sentiment, Americans overwhelmingly rejected jingoistic patriotism, the type consistent with "my country, right or

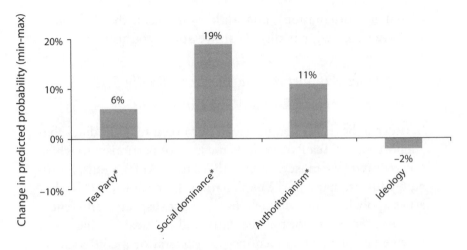

3.14. Probability of supporting (un)critical patriotism
*Significant at $p < 0.05$, one-tailed

wrong" sentiment. Consequently, the gap between believers and skeptics was shockingly small. Yet, there's always the possibility that this gap is actually larger, masked by a third factor, one that we didn't consider in our first stab at the relationship. An equally likely outcome is one in which the existing disparity between the groups—tiny as it is—will vanish entirely.

As figure 3.14 reveals, our results indicate that believers are 6 percent more likely than skeptics to subscribe to the proposition that America is beyond criticism. The effects are even greater for people who are proponents of group dominance (SDO), where they are 19 percent more likely than people who subscribe to a more egalitarian social order to believe that the United States is beyond criticism. To no one's surprise, authoritarianism decreases the probability that one will criticize the country by 11 percent relative to those who aren't comfortable with social conformity.[74]

Our analysis now turns from patriotism framed in a manner that gave way to a broad consensus—one in which cleavages were hard to find—to one that's more contentious. When pa-

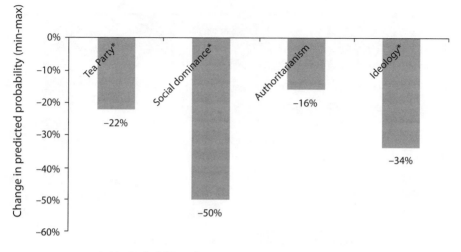

3.15. Probability of supporting economic patriotism
*Significant at $p < 0.05$, one-tailed

triotism is framed as an issue that forces Americans to make a choice between putting oneself first or one's country first, we find that sentiment associated with the Tea Party drives a wedge through public opinion. The question is whether or not the division we observed in the preliminary assessment persists once we account for competing explanations. Since this question asks Americans to consider subsidizing public education, for instance, we think it plausible—even probable—that political ideology may account for the differences we've observed so far.[75]

Further, since the object was to first get a handle on the degree to which sentiment associated with the Tea Party and patriotism framed a choice between self-interest and national interest, such alternative explanations were excluded. In the interest of a more rigorous analysis, one that will permit us to have more confidence in our findings, we now include them.

We turn now to figure 3.15. As it turns out, accounting for ideology has no bearing on the extent to which Tea Party–related sentiment affects Americans' calculus on whether they

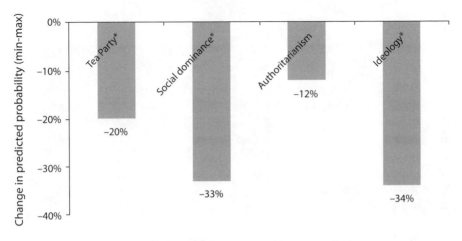

3.16. Probability of supporting egalitarian patriotism
*Significant at $p < 0.05$, one-tailed

should consider self or country first. Still, believers are 22 percent less likely than skeptics to put national interest ahead of self-interest. Similar patterns emerge among people who prefer group dominance, those who are ideologically conservative, and folks who desire social conformity. In short, those who prefer social dominance are 50 percent less likely than folks who are uncomfortable with group domination, conservatives are 34 percent less likely than liberals, and people with a desire for conformity (authoritarians) are 16 percent less likely than those who can do without it, to put country first.[76]

Our final crack at patriotism—this time an effort designed to force Americans to make a trade-off between ensuring a more egalitarian social order through legal channels, if necessary, and freedom—yielded results similar to our first two analyses. By this we mean to say that Tea Party–related sentiment, as figure 3.16 illustrates, continues to inform the ways in which Americans express their love of country, even as we account for every conceivable competing explanation. Consider the following: among the competing explanations, social dominance orientation, authoritarianism, and ideology, each has a significant impact on patriotism framed as a trade-off between freedom and equality. For instance, as we move from people who are repulsed by social dominance to those who embrace it, and as the transition is made from self-identified liberals to conservatives, the probability that Americans support the proposition that we should stop at nothing to realize equality decreases by 33 percent and 34 percent, respectively. Still, even with the impressive impact on opinion of competing explanations and controls (full model results are located in table A3.2 in the appendix), Tea Party–related sentiment manages to carry some weight. Indeed, true believers are 20 percent less likely than true skeptics to pursue equality by any means necessary.[77]

Once again, we did everything we could to falsify our claim that sentiments associated with the Tea Party matter. And once again, after accounting for all manner of competing explanations, our claim that support for the Tea Party is related to patriotism holds. To be sure, explanations related to both political and motivational predispositions inform how one resolves value conflicts associated with patriotism.[78] Still, the impact of whether or not one is a believer or skeptic remains associated with the version of patriotism people support. This suggests that the association between Tea Party sentiment and patriotism isn't masked by predispositions of any kind. This strengthens our contention that support for the Tea Party is consistent with a long-standing trend in right-wing movements in which its constituents are concerned that the America they know is slipping away. As we have illustrated, this line of thinking is typical with the episodic nature of national, right-wing mass movements, ones that don't come along very often.

In this light, one that casts support for the Tea Party as an expression of anxiety borne of concern with subversion of the American way of life, we can better understand our findings. Those who support the Tea Party are likely to believe America is beyond criticism, a position with which even Walter Berns, a conservative political philosopher, disagrees.[79] Yet this finding does not surprise us, since uncritical patriotism is often tied to a preference for the status quo.[80] Of course, one can argue that what we're tapping into is merely conservatism. At this point, however, we're careful to remind the reader that we've already accounted for conservatism. Indeed, in the more basic analysis we conducted above, we revealed daylight between Tea Party conservatives and non–Tea Party conservatives. What we have observed, then, is something different. We can, therefore, tie the remaining results, ones associated with the imposition of value conflict, to anxiety associated with concern of subversion of some kind. Tea Party supporters are also more likely than everyone else to prioritize self-interest over what's best for the country, and to resist efforts to guarantee equality for their compatriots. Both of these positions are unsustainable—at least if one wishes to practice patriotism of the more classical kind, in which a willingness to sacrifice narrow self-interest for the good of the country is the norm.

Concluding Thoughts

In this chapter we sought to explore two things. First, we needed to establish that support for the Tea Party makes a difference on concepts of importance to the Tea Party and its followers: freedom and patriotism. More to the point, we needed to show how increases (or decreases) in Americans' support for the Tea Party inform how they resolve their value conflicts. Second, we needed to test our claim that support for the Tea Party stands apart from more conventional explanations for right-wing preferences, including conservatism, social dominance orientation, and authoritarianism. We succeeded on both counts.

Corroboration of our substantive claims, that various levels of support for the Tea Party affect American public opinion, is important. Perhaps most important, however, is that we took a step toward validating our central theoretical claim. In the process of accounting for the many competing explanations, this chapter advances the claim that support for the Tea Party represents a reaction to the perception that America is slipping away from the Tea Party's constituents—perhaps a paranoid reaction, not accounted for by more conventional explanations of civil liberties and patriotism. In short, reactionary conservatism.

We worked hard to tease out the differences we observed. We thought it best to examine the values to which Tea Party sympathizers adhered in context by adjusting how they're framed. Both racial profiling and free speech were included in our survey, for the most part, because of our desire to explore civil liberties in a concrete setting, in which something tangible is at stake. It paid off. While security isn't something actively promoted by the Tea Party, it remains an important value. The fact that Tea Party supporters, if forced to choose, preferred freedom only once is telling. It suggests that perhaps their commitment to freedom is qualified, not unconditional. This is not to say that believers aren't necessarily committed to freedom. Rather, our findings indicate that, with the exception of free speech, believers place a premium on security, not individual liberty. Since adherence to conservative principles, among many other factors, cannot account for our outcome, we draw the only remaining plausible conclusion: believers don't want to yield autonomy to Obama as the American president, the face of the government.

Likewise, we had hoped that framing patriotism as a trade-off between freedom and equality would make patriotism more concrete and move it closer to its more classical meaning: prioritizing the national common good over individual self-interest. Our results suggest that upon framing patriotism as a choice between freedom (and the associated self-interest) and equality, which is more consistent with the classical version of patriotism, Tea Party supporters continue to opt for the more individualistic version of "patriotism."

We are in no way saying that Tea Party supporters aren't patriotic. For the most part, this turns on how one defines patriotism. If one defines patriotism as unfettered pursuit of self-interested goals, one can say believers are patriotic. If, however, one defines patriotism along more classical lines, more consistent with putting the interest of the community before self-interest—an interpretation commensurate with a more egalitarian society— one may question believers' commitment to patriotism.

So far, it seems as if support for the Tea Party enjoys a tangible impact on opinion. Nevertheless, our findings in this chapter represent only a small step in our exploration of what we believe to be the Tea Party's broader impact on American politics. In the following chapters, we extend our investigation to the ways in which the Tea Party helps to shape views on President Obama, as well as the way in which identification with it affects political activism. First, though, we turn to how, if at all, support for the Tea Party affects intergroup relations.

4

Does the Tea Party Really
Want Their Country Back?

I N CHAPTER THREE we examined Tea Party supporters' commitment to freedom and patriotism. Among the other themes
that emerged in our analysis is that true believers appeared
reluctant to protect the freedom of racial minorities insofar as
they seem willing to permit racial profiling. Likewise, as we
examined patriotism, we found Tea Party sympathizers don't
appear interested in ensuring that everyone is treated equally,
something for which minorities of all types have always striven.
Indeed, freedom and equality, as we pointed out, are hallmarks
of American identity. How can Tea Party sympathizers consider
themselves real Americans but fail to adhere to American values?

Our findings in chapter 3, along with the general tendency
of right-wing movements to oppose change of any kind, rec-
ommends that we take a closer look at what Tea Party sympathizers think about minority groups of all kinds. There is some
evidence that suggests the Tea Party is hostile to groups that

fail to conform to the American stereotype we have discussed in prior chapters. Still, it is almost always anecdotal. We depart from this trend in the present chapter. Here, our purpose is to undertake a more systematic examination of the ways in which support for the Tea Party influences how people view minorities, something we believe is important for the following reason.

Over the past few decades America has experienced many social, demographic, and political changes. In particular, the minority and immigrant population has grown dramatically, eventually leading to the election of many prominent African American, Latino, and Asian American candidates to office. At the same time, minority groups have continued to promote equal rights, especially civil rights for a range of groups, including racial/ethnic minorities, women, and sexual minorities. In the late 1960s, a shock reverberated through the American political system when millions of Americans participated in antiwar, civil rights, and counterculture protests. In doing so, myriad modes of inequalities were exposed, leading to calls for more social, political, and economic inclusion. Yet, during this period of social change, some Americans were suspicious of—even opposed to—the groups that were demanding America bring its practices into better alignment with its values. As we have already demonstrated, American history is filled with periods during which increasing visibility and calls for equal treatment among out-groups was repeatedly met with opposition from dominant groups.

The question is whether or not support for the Tea Party adds anything to existing explanations for why some Americans resist extending equal treatment to groups deemed to fall beyond the American normative ideal we discussed in prior chapters. Most explanations revolve around commitment to conservative principles. In the 1960s, conservatives contested both the Civil Rights Act and the Voting Rights Act on what, they argued, boiled down to an insistence on states' rights: local custom should prevail over federal intervention.[1] From this perspective, the federal government had no business ordering states around.

In the 1970s, conservatives resisted women's rights, reproductive and otherwise (the Equal Rights Amendment), and gay rights on the basis of social conservatism: political ideology that focuses on the preservation of "traditional values" and morality. To do otherwise, and grant these groups' claims, according to the Far Right, courted calamity and threatened everything from the nuclear family to American national security.[2]

Even so, political scientists Pamela Conover and Virginia Gray suggested that resistance to women's rights, as well as gay rights, *really* revolved around the perception that the preferred lifestyle of the Far Right, in which traditional gender roles prevailed, as well as traditional economic arrangements in which white males were at the top, was slipping away, under attack from left-leaning forces.[3] Likewise, as we discuss in some detail later, Robert Welch and the John Birch Society believed the Civil Rights Movement to be part of a communist plot to subvert "the American way" of life. Today, we see similar reactions by the Tea Party movement toward several minorities, but we still don't know what motivates their apparent reaction to marginalized groups.

At issue in this chapter is whether or not Tea Party supporters see all Americans as equal members of society entitled to the same access to the American dream. Put differently, do Tea Party supporters believe in the extension of equal rights to minorities of all types? Or do they think certain groups are less deserving? High-profile interested parties support each point of view. For example, the NAACP famously issued a report in the summer of 2010 denouncing many Tea Party supporters as racist.[4] In response, many Tea Party organizers denied the charge of prejudice, insisting that the Tea Party is a color-blind movement dedicated to reducing government spending. If this is true, it's quite possible that a commitment to conservative principles motivated their resistance to policy simply because they believed government was too involved in American life.

We freely acknowledge that out-group antipathy and politics, as conventional explanations, may both explain the way in which Americans understand members of minority groups. However, our contention is that they don't explain how Tea Party supporters see these groups. With this in mind, we investigate our claim that support for the Tea Party represents a reactionary impulse in which "Others," including the president, are perceived as trying to pry the country away from "real" Americans. However, as we did in chapter 3, we must reckon with alternative explanations for Tea Party support (as proxy for reactionary conservatism) to help explain hostility toward policies designed to assist out-groups in achieving some measure of the American dream. Beyond commitment to conservatism, we confront other important social and political predispositions like authoritarianism, ethnocentrism, social dominance orientation, and partisanship. Only after considering these competing explanations can we have confidence in our findings that support for the Tea Party represents a new way of thinking about out-group antipathy, one motivated by reactionary conservatism.

Foreshadowing our findings, our stated position, that sympathy for the Tea Party represents a reaction to the perception that their country is becoming lost to real Americans, is supported. If sympathy for the Tea Party were simply about conservatism, or even about being a loyal partisan of the Republican Party, the attitudes of believers should be indistinguishable from more mainstream conservatives and Republicans as it pertains to whether or not they support egalitarian policies benefiting minorities. Yet, as our results indicate, one's orientation toward the Tea Party continues to help shape how people view policies designed to assist minorities of all types. These views remain independent of political predispositions, such as ideology and party identification, as well as motivational predispositions, such as social dominance orientation, ethnocentrism, and authoritarianism. In sum, after accounting for a host of alternative explanations, our central claim is validated: support for the Tea Party represents the reaction of its constituents to their perception that America no longer belongs to them. Indeed, as our interviews, content on Tea Party–related websites, and experimental results indicate, Tea Party sympathizers are reacting to the perception that the America they know is slipping away.

In what follows, we first outline the ways in which the diversification of America appears to coincide with the emergence of the Tea Party. We follow this with a preliminary analysis in which we explore the relationship between Tea Party sympathy and selected minorities. We then conduct a brief discussion of competing theoretical approaches to the study of out-groups. Next, we proceed to test our claim that support for the Tea Party represents something unique to the study of intergroup relations. We close the chapter with a few concluding thoughts.

A CHANGING AMERICA AND THE EMERGENCE OF THE TEA PARTY

Since the civil rights era, America continues to experience demographic change. Some believe America's shifting demography is at least partially responsible for the election of Barack Obama. For instance, Tom Tancredo, a conservative former five-term congressman from Colorado's sixth district, announced to thunderous applause at the 2010 National Tea Party convention in Tennessee, "Obama's election represents multiculturalism run amuck." However, as chapter 2 suggests, the emergence of the Tea Party movement, at least if support for the Tea Party is any indication, cannot be reduced to perceptions of President Obama alone, even if his presidency helped catalyze the movement. Several other factors are also important in helping to explain Tea Party sympathy, including racism and the belief that subordinate groups should remain in their respective places.

In 1970, 83 percent of the U.S. population was white (non-Hispanic). By 2010, the white share of the U.S. populace declined to 63 percent—a 20 percentage-point decline in one generation.[5] Accompanying this change has been an increase in African American, Hispanic, and Asian populations in the United States, and a vigorous debate about civil rights and immigration. For example, Latinos grew from 35 to 50 million over the previous decade, Asians went from 10 to 15 million, and African Americans stood at 39 million by 2010.[6] Finally, approximately 4 percent of the adult population identifies as part of the LGBT community.[7] In raw numbers, this figure represents approximately 9 million Americans, or roughly the size of New Jersey's population.

With the increasing prevalence of minorities in the United States, the untutored may be inclined to believe that the putative leader of global democracy wouldn't hesitate to fully include this group as members of the polity. Recent history suggests he'd be wrong. In Texas, where the state added four U.S. House districts entirely as a result of Latino population growth, the Republican-controlled state legislature adopted a plan that only created one new Latino district, resulting in months of lawsuits and challenges.[8] In California a coalition of African American groups sought to maintain black representation when early redistricting maps suggested their seats would be cut or consolidated.[9] Along with other impediments to voting rights and representation pursued by the Right, the Supreme Court will soon rule on these cases. In the struggle for same-sex rights, the repeal of Don't Ask, Don't Tell was achieved, permitting gays and lesbians to openly serve their country. Likewise, lower courts overruled California's anti-same-sex marriage measure, Proposition 8, in 2010.[10] In fact, as we write, same-sex marriage is permitted in eight states: California, Connecticut, Iowa, Maryland, Massachusetts, New Hampshire, New York, and Washington State. However, as was the case with voting rights, the Right has successfully pressed the Supreme Court to rule on whether or not same-sex couples are permitted to legally marry.

What does the Tea Party want? What are some of its goals? From at least one account, the Tea Party believes in a reduced role for the federal government, more fiscal responsibility, lower taxes, a free market, and a commitment to states' rights.[11] Indeed, these are core conservative, even libertarian, principles, very much in keeping with traditional American political culture.[12] Yet, as we have already mentioned, supporters of the Tea Party seem to want something beyond limited government and free markets. We think it likely that the election, and subsequent presidency of Barack Obama and the change it symbolizes, represents a threat to the social, economic, and political hegemony to which supporters of the Tea Party have become accustomed.[13] Moreover, as we have already demonstrated, Tea Party supporters believe the president is out to destroy the country through what they perceive as his "socialist" policies.

Still, as some suggest, these feelings of anxiety and anger were hardly confined to conservative Republicans. Indeed, as some scholars show, working-class whites were quickly swept up by the Tea Party.[14] Our results in chapter 2 indicate that middle-class whites agree with the Tea Party's message. Scholars have recently highlighted Democrats' failure to gain the political support of some middle- and working-class whites, and, at times, progressive politicians have even added to their discontent. In fact, many white Democrats felt under attack when Barack Obama suggested that bitter working-class Americans "cling to their guns and religion" during the 2008 Democratic primary elections.[15] The lack of attention working-class whites received from Democrats became central to Howard Dean's fifty-state strategy, which attempted to garner the support of all Americans across many different walks of life.[16] Specifically, former presidential candidate and Democratic National Convention chairman Howard Dean argued that while the economic policies of the Democratic Party were in line with many midwestern and southern whites, the Republican Party had done a better job of reaching out to this group by promoting a religious, moral, and value-based agenda that oftentimes emphasized antiminority views.

The politically correct and progressive rhetoric of many Democrats led them to avoid scapegoating immigrants for unemployment, sexual minorities for a perceived decline in values, or blacks for urban decay. As Democrats avoided blaming out-groups, conservative activists increasingly emphasized reprehending these same groups. In many cases, Democrats left the door open for Republicans, and subsequently the Tea Party, to court working-class whites, despite the fact that Republican economic policy is sometimes at odds with working-class economic interests. Beyond economic motivation, working-class whites are sometimes swayed by conservative stances on "moral" social policies, at the expense of their economic self-interest.[17] The need for an expanded and energized Republican base, alongside Democrats' inability to relate to working-class whites, created an opportunity for a new movement to form, in part based on cultural anxiety of a changing America.

Returning to the question of Tea Party aims, we have reviewed a full content analysis of the posts on official Tea Party websites across the country, and found a tendency to promote conspiratorial views and antiminority sentiment, relative to the mainstream conservative website and blog, the *National Review Online* (NRO). Beyond just counting the number of posts on different topics, which we report in chapter 1, we also read each post and article carefully for the tone, language, and rhetoric on which citizen activists drew. A few examples here of statements made in posts on Tea Party websites will shed some additional light on the views that Tea Party sympathizers hold toward minority groups today.[18] The following statements were pulled only from actual posts by people officially affiliated with each website, as opposed to the comment section, which is open to anyone. Thus, we can be confident that these statements reflect those who consider themselves strong supporters of the Tea Party: Tea Party activists.

Regarding immigration, one statement read: "Our porous borders are endangering citizens and draining our coffers, as we provide for a growing number of illegals who do not even pay taxes."[19] Another statement referred to Mexican immigrants as "invaders" and called for people to arm themselves: "We must stand in strong defiance of those who support amnesty to illegal invaders and virtually open up our borders, and we must instead stand arm in arm with Arizona and draw a line in the sand on the banks of the Rio Grande. The only good carjacker or rapist is a dead carjacker or rapist. Case closed. It's so simple only stupid people could find fault with that. A polite society is an armed society."[20]

As opposition to Latino immigration increased among the Tea Party, it was routinely argued that even U.S. citizen Latino children were not entitled to government spending, as one statement declared: "Twelve billion dollars a year is spent on primary and secondary school education for children here illegally and they cannot speak a word of English! Seventeen billion dollars a year is spent for education for the American-born children of illegal aliens, known as anchor babies. The dark side of illegal immigration: nearly one million sex crimes committed by illegal immigrants in the United States."[21]

Regarding blacks, one statement read: "Those that voted for Obama just because he is black, and not based on whether he was qualified to do the job, is not the dream that Dr. King had in mind. As far as I am concerned, it was nothing more than affirmative action that got him his job. I am also appalled at the idea that we have to lower test standards for African Americans because they can't compete with their Caucasian counterparts."[22]

Moving to values, religion, and homosexuality, one statement read: "We have removed God from every aspect of life because we don't want to insult or offend anyone and now we have a generation of youth that refuses to believe in God and won't even think about going to church. Now our kids come home from school and talk about who says they are gay. Now our kids are having sex earlier and earlier. They have no innocence anymore. They are indoctrinated at early ages and inundated constantly by sex and homosexuality."[23] Elsewhere, Tea Party bloggers have specifically endorsed the notion that a changing society is dangerous: "I tried to explain that we don't know what the long-term effects of homosexual child-rearing will be. Societally, we've been trending toward stripping definition from all things of meaning as we descend further and further into a sea of relativist gray, where liberalizing attitudes are incrementally breaking down the practices and institutions that bind the individuals of a society together."[24]

Anti-gay comments aren't limited to values. Returning to the conspiratorial discourse discussed in chapter 1, many posts emphasize a gay-agenda set determined to take over America: "The 'problem' with the Homosexual agenda is that it is not only about Homosexuality. In fact, the 'Gay Agenda' is far-reaching and encompasses every other liberal agenda there is. Liberals traditionally support other Liberals, even if their agendas are entirely different. Therefore, Sexual minorities are far more likely to support Obama-Care, Cap-and-Trade, Government takeovers of the Banking, Automotive and other industries, Global Warming threats, environmentalism, Trans-gender, Bi-Sexual and Homosexuals in the military and in governmental leadership positions, and even Marxism in our government."[25]

We use each of these examples to illustrate that an out-group sentiment exists on many of the major Tea Party websites. However, it could be the case that just a small handful of folks within the Tea Party are writing such things, and this is not reflective of most Tea Party supporters. Thus, we turn to the quantitative evidence from our national telephone survey to assess to what extent Tea Party sympathizers are more likely to hold negative attitudes toward minority groups today. If the Tea Party beliefs are mainstream, as Juan Williams suggests,[26] then we will not see any differences in the percentage of Tea Party supporters who are anti-gay or anti-immigrant, relative to the overall population. However, the continuation and proliferation of such antiminority statements on Tea Party websites in 2011 leads us to expect it reflects a larger attitude among the roughly 45 million or so Americans who call themselves Tea Party sympathizers.

TEA PARTY SYMPATHIZERS AND ATTITUDES TOWARD MINORITY GROUPS

Despite similarities with the Far Right, some who are sympathetic to the Tea Party think it's squarely in the mainstream, or insist that Tea Party supporters are simply more conservative,[27] but no more or less bigoted than anyone else.[28] In our 2011 Multi-State Survey of Race and Politics, we probed a variety of attitudes and beliefs, as we have reviewed in earlier chapters. By turning to the public opinion data, we can test whether or not Tea Party supporters bear similarities to the Far Right movements of the twentieth century. As we outline in our review of the Klan of the 1920s and the JBS in chapter 1, out-group hostility was part and parcel of what such right-wing movements were all about. In the case of the Klan, out-group hostility was explicit in their opposition to blacks, and almost any other minority group that did not fit their ideal of white, Protestant, American society. With the Birchers, they stood behind claims of communism and socialism but painted with a broad brush those who aided minorities or supported civil rights. They called the unanimous decision in *Brown v. Board*, to overturn racial segregation, a communist plot and actively campaigned against racial "mixing" of public schools, even calling for the impeachment of Supreme Court chief justice Earl Warren.[29]

The link between the Tea Party and the Far Right of the past isn't limited to theory. At least in one case, the link is also hereditary. Fred Koch, founder of Koch Industries and father of Tea Party financiers Charles and David Koch, played an integral role in the formation, funding, and ideology of the John Birch Society in the late 1950s and early 1960s.[30] Not only was the elder Koch taken with the conspiratorial ideas of the JBS, that is, the complicity of "eastern elites" in a communist plot to take over America, but he singled out blacks and other minorities as the accomplices, writing that "the colored man looms large in the Communist plan to take over America."[31] However, are the Koches—father and sons—elite outliers, or are these viewpoints also held by the mass public who consider themselves supporters of the Tea Party? Below, we return to our survey to provide answers.

First, we wish to examine whether or not people in the mass public who sympathize with the Tea Party differ in their attitudes and behavior from the public. Second, we wish to also

account for competing explanations of why Tea Party sympathizers are motivated by intolerant attitudes. In other words, we
need to move beyond assaying the simple relationship between
Tea Party support and bigoted attitudes. We can only be confident that support for the Tea Party informs bigoted attitudes
if we adopt a more rigorous approach in which we rule out
the possibility that authoritarianism, racial resentment (racism), ethnocentrism, or social dominance orientation are really responsible for the relationship we observe. As in previous
chapters, we begin our analysis through an exploration of how
orientation toward the Tea Party shapes relevant attitudes. In
this case, we compare the way(s) in which Tea Party sympathizers differ from everyone else in the American public, including
those who have no use for the Tea Party, when it comes to attitudes toward different minority groups. We explore a variety of
topics, including how people feel about selected groups through
feeling thermometer ratings, racial attitudes toward illegal immigrants, and opinions on gay and lesbian equality.

After examining these results, we move on to provide a more
rigorous test to determine whether or not the relationships we
observe, when we're looking at just support for the Tea Party
and out-group sentiments, hold after we include competing explanations. In other words, it's possible that once we make adjustments for established explanations of the ways in which
people see out-groups, like commitment to conservatism, ethnocentrism, authoritarianism, and social dominance orientation,
identifying with the Tea Party may no longer be a relevant explanation for negative out-group attitudes.

THE TEA PARTY AND ATTITUDES
TOWARD MINORITIES

Beyond the general findings we explore above, we wish to gauge
more specific attitudes toward prominent minority groups in
America today: Latino immigrants and the gay and lesbian community. As the 2010 census made clear, minority population

growth is driving the new multicultural and diverse America. Hispanic, African American, and Asian American populations grew at rates fifteen to fifty times faster than the white population.[32] From 2000 to 2010, the white, non-Hispanic population grew by 1 percent while the black population grew by 15 percent. The Hispanic population grew by 43 percent and the Asian population by 46 percent. Furthermore, the 2010 census provided estimates of gay and lesbian households and demonstrated the tremendous increase in the number of Americans willing to self-identify as gay or lesbian just in the last decade, with large lesbian, gay, bisexual, and transgender (LGBT) communities now prominent across all fifty states.[33]

We focus specifically on these groups because much of the recent public debate over public policy encompasses constituents of these communities: same-sex marriage, Don't Ask, Don't Tell, and debates over immigration reform. Another reason is that the growth of Latinos, and the increasing political demands of the gay and lesbian community, may become a cause for concern with many who affiliate with the Tea Party. The data suggests that supporters of the Tea Party are statistically more likely to hold negative attitudes toward immigrants and sexual minorities across a range of different issues and topics, and are firmly opposed to the idea of group equality.

Anti-Immigrant Attitudes

The ratification of Arizona's SB 1070 marked the return of immigration to center stage in American politics after a brief period out of the limelight.[34] The law, which allows for the racial profiling of Latinos based on the suspicion that they could be undocumented immigrants, was defended by Arizona governor Jan Brewer by charging that the federal government was not doing its job to control undocumented immigration, and that the state had the right to take steps to do so. Moreover, Tea Party supporters, many of whom are states' rights advocates, made immigration restriction one of the central issues in the 2010 election. Ultimately, the Supreme Court struck down much of SB 1070. Still, suspected illegal immigrants may be asked to prove their citizenship (the "Papers, please" provision) if they're stopped for another violation.[35]

Statements about immigration from Tea Party politicians and groups largely portray immigration as a threat to Americans or American culture, validating a claim we have made about the Tea Party and its supporters from the beginning: the Tea Party fears their country is slipping away. One glaring example of this is Sharron Angle's 2010 campaign ad "Best Friend," which features a voice-over that ominously states, "Illegals [are] sneaking across our borders putting Americans' jobs and safety at risk," while showing video of dark-skinned actors sneaking around a chain-link fence.[36] Angle was a darling of the Tea Party movement in Nevada and attacked Harry Reid on immigration in both the "Best Friend" ad and a second ad called "At Your Expense," which charged that Reid supported special college tuition rates for undocumented immigrants paid for by Nevada taxpayers.[37] Both ads juxtaposed the dark-skinned actors portraying illegal immigrants with white Americans working, or with their families as part of the image.

Sharron Angle was not the only Tea Party candidate who tried to use the threat of Latino immigration to capture votes in the 2010 election. In Arizona, J. D. Hayworth, John McCain's Republican primary challenger, made immigration one of the central themes of his campaign. To no one's shock, Hayworth authored a book on the subject of undocumented immigration in 2005 called *Whatever It Takes*. In his book, he argues for increased immigration enforcement and notes that while immigration is clearly good for the country, the proportion of immigrants coming from Mexico is too high, and may lead to America becoming a bicultural nation. In Hayworth's own words, "bicultural societies are among the least stable in the world."[38] Hayworth was a strong supporter of Arizona's SB 1070 but believed that even more steps had to be taken against undocumented immigrants, stating at a 2010 rally in Mesa, Arizona, that "there is a whole new term: birth tourism. In the jet age there are people who time their gestation period so they give birth on American soil."[39] To prevent this, Hayworth argues, the state of Arizona should stop birthright citizenship, a view echoed by Russell Pearce, a state senator from Arizona and the architect of SB 1070.

From the beginning, the Tea Party movement absorbed much of the residual nativist sentiment in the wake of the decline of the Federal Immigration and Enforcement coalition (FIRE) and the Federation for American Immigration Reform (FAIR).[40] Tea Party organizations also sought to portray immigration as a threat to America in the lead-up to the 2010 general election, continuing through a tactical shift to state and local politics in 2011. Tea Party Nation, one of the six major national factions of the Tea Party, e-mailed its roughly 35,000 members in August and asked them to post stories highlighting the victimization of Americans by illegal immigrants. The group specifically asked for stories about undocumented immigrants taking the jobs of members, committing crimes, or undermining business by providing cheap labor to competitors.[41] The Americans for Legal Immigration PAC (ALIPAC) assisted two Tea Party groups, Voice of the People USA and Tea Party Patriots Live, in coordinating rallies in support of Arizona's SB 1070. The ALIPAC mission statement points out that, "Our state and federal budgets are being overwhelmed. Schools, hospitals, law enforcement, and public services are being strained while the taxpayers incur more costs and debt. Our nation's very survival and identity are being threatened along with our national security."[42] ALIPAC is supported by FAIR, an organization designated as a hate group by the Southern Poverty Law Center because of its links to white supremacist organizations.[43]

Of course, nativism isn't confined to organizations and their officials. It's likely the case that people who aren't members of the Tea Party, but identify with it, harbor similar attitudes. In fact, recent work illustrates that perceived threats from immigrant groups inform peoples' opinion toward immigrants, as well as policy prescriptions intended to level the playing field.[44] Interviews with Tea Party supporters suggest these attitudes are real. When Tea Party supporters were asked how immigrants made them feel, one respondent said, "I don't know really, but maybe nervous. I see what they have done. Here they come, they have no insurance. They are draining state governments. We have to provide for them because they are here." Other people conflated illegal immigrants, legal immigrants, and Hispanics while explaining their cultural deficiencies. For instance, one man says, "Nevada has grown to be heavily Hispanic in the last 15 years. And Good Lord, education reflects that. You know, the education standards they are just plummeting because—yeah, I mean, the Hispanic children—everybody needs to be educated, but if they weren't here illegally, our kids would be in better shape. It's wrong for the American people." Still others suggested an actual criminal threat from immigrants, saying, "They make me nervous. I have relatives down in Tucson; one is a law enforcement officer. You never know if they are going to get killed."

Given this context, we examined views toward immigrants in America today in our Multi-State Survey of Race and Politics. While the Tea Party has not been shy about taking a clear stand against illegal immigration, as the above-cited quote suggests, we find that some movement supporters have equally negative views toward immigrants in general, that is, regardless of the legal status they may enjoy. Are Tea Party supporters against all immigrants, regardless of legal status? Or, are their objections really about law and order? After all, it could be the case that Tea Party supporters simply object to the fact that illegal immigrants broke the law to get here, or illegally overstayed their visas. In an effort to gauge the extent to which Tea Party supporters discriminate between legal and illegal immigrants, we asked a battery of questions in which we made clear distinctions between the two classes of immigrants. For the purposes of the present chapter, we use four questions from our survey: two solicit opinions on immigrants, the other two mention illegal immigrants specifically. If Tea Party sympathizers are not "anti-immigrant" in general, we shouldn't find that they hold negative attitudes toward legal immigrants. Instead, they should oppose illegal immigrants.

We begin with how the public views illegal immigrants, after which we investigate attitudes reserved for legal immigrants. As of December 2010, a Gallup poll reported that 54 percent of Americans supported the DREAM Act, a policy proposal in which the government grants legal status to illegal immigrant youth who came to the United States at a very young age, if they attended college or enlisted in the armed forces.[45] Our survey, conducted three months later, amplifies these results. Overall, 62 percent of Americans support the DREAM Act. However, once we investigate further and scrutinize the data by the extent to which people support the Tea Party, patterns begin to emerge. Consider the contents of figure 4.1. Among parts of the mass public who aren't persuaded by the Tea Party's message, support for the DREAM Act never falls below 68 percent (middle of the road), and tops out at 83 percent for skeptics. Among believers, however, support for the DREAM Act falls to 46 percent.

Another question in which illegal immigrants were invoked involves the Constitution, specifically, the Fourteenth Amendment. Indeed, Section 1 of the Fourteenth Amendment says that anyone born in the United States shall be considered a citizen. In January 2011, Republicans introduced a bill to repeal Section 1 of the Fourteenth Amendment. They argued that since birthright citizenship is an incentive for "illegals to race for the border," perhaps it should be repealed.[46] The Tea Party threw its support behind this measure.[47] Even so, we don't know how rank-and-file Tea Party supporters in the mass public feel about repealing birthright citizenship. If our findings are correct, a healthy swath of them do. Among supporters of the Tea Party, 56 percent support repealing birthright citizenship of U.S.-born children of illegal immigrant parents, a right protected by the

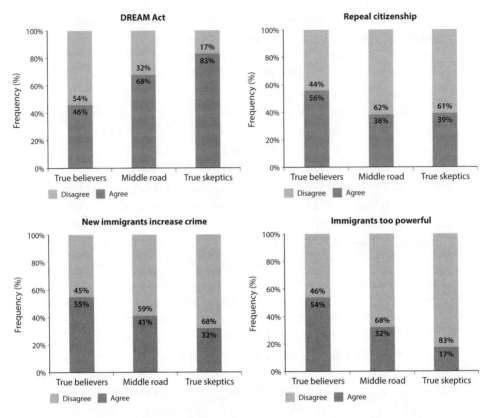

4.1. Attitudes toward immigrants, by degree of Tea Party support
Note: Total $N = 1188$, with 308 true believers, 488 middle of the road, and
392 true skeptics; relationships significant at χ^2 $p < 0.000$

Fourteenth Amendment of the Constitution. Support for the repeal of the Fourteenth Amendment declines to 38 and 39 percent among people lukewarm to the Tea Party and skeptics,
respectively. (For the record, 44 percent of the entire sample
favors repealing birthright citizenship.)

Do such differences emerge when *legal* immigrants are the
target of inquiry? To explore this, we asked two questions that
should permit us to assess what the public thinks about immigrants in general, with no reference to their legal status. In one

question, we probed public perception about whether or not "new immigrants increase crime in America." Among those who have a strong distaste for the Tea Party, 32 percent agreed with the statement, a figure that rises to 41 percent among people who are relatively indifferent to the Tea Party. For true believers, though, the results indicate that 55 percent believe that new immigrants cause the crime rate to increase. Finally, we asked people to report on whether or not they believed their political power to be in decline as a consequence of immigration. To gauge this, we asked whether or not they agreed with the following statement: "the more influence that immigrants have in politics the less influence people like me have in politics." Among Tea Party supporters, 54 percent agreed with the statement, compared to just 17 percent of Tea Party skeptics and 32 percent of folks with no strong feelings about the Tea Party.

We expected big differences to separate true believers from true skeptics, and that's exactly what we found. For questions covering illegal immigrants, that is, the questions touching on the DREAM Act and repealing the portion of the Fourteenth Amendment concerning birthright citizenship, we witnessed 17- and 37-point differences between groups who are attracted to the Tea Party and those who reject it. For questions tapping attitudes toward immigrants in general (whether or not new immigrants affect the crime rate and whether or not immigrants are too powerful), we see differences of 23 and 37 percentage points, respectively, between believers and skeptics.

Now that we have examined differences between believers and supporters, we repeat the exercise conducted in chapter 3 in which we successfully peeled off reactionary conservatives from more moderate conservatives. Again, we argue that Tea Party conservatives are really reactionary conservatives in disguise. As before, we limit this part of the analysis to all self-identified conservatives. Again, our suspicions are confirmed: there are tangible differences between Tea Party conservatives and non–Tea Party conservatives, suggesting that conservatism—on its own—cannot account for Tea Party supporters' attitudes. The comparison between Tea Party and more mainstream conservatives is least striking when we consider perceptions of immigrants without discriminating between legal and illegal aliens. In fact, differences are negligible when the focus is on perceptions of immigrants' power. Still, when we assess the perceived criminality of immigrants as a whole, among conservatives, 9 percentage points separate the conservative camps (see figure 4.2).

When the focus shifts to the questions we ask about illegal immigrants, however, the daylight separating Tea Party and non–Tea Party conservatives widens considerably. For both questions, the one asking about whether or not the Fourteenth Amendment should be repealed, and whether or not the DREAM Act should be passed, 20-point gaps emerge between Tea Party and non–Tea Party conservatives. Indeed, two-thirds of Tea Party conservatives favor repealing at least part of the Fourteenth Amendment, and only 30 percent support the DREAM Act. These figures are hard to reconcile with those of their conservative brethren, 46 percent of whom favor repealing part of the Constitution and 50 percent of whom support the DREAM Act. These findings confirm our narrative in which Tea Party conservatives are reactionary, and non–Tea Party conservatives are more mainstream. The former are more concerned that immigrants are taking over their country; the latter are more preoccupied with law and order.

Homophobia and the Tea Party

We now turn to explore a minority of another kind: sexual minorities. Many individual Tea Party sympathizers have denied that social issues, including rights for lesbian, gay, bisexual, and transgendered people, have played a large role in the Tea Party movement.[48] The movement, they claim, is fundamentally built on principled conservatism, limited government, and lower taxes. Others have claimed that gay men and lesbians should flock to the Tea Party because its libertarianism will result in greater political freedom for LGBT people. The campaign web-

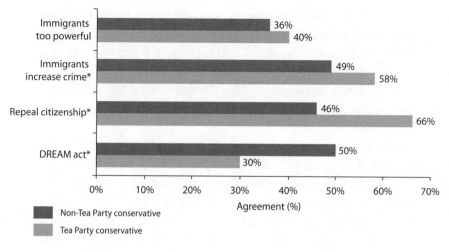

4.2. Support for immigrant equality, by type of conservatism
Note: Total conservative $N = 407$, with 204 true believers in the Tea Party;
*significant at χ^2 $p < 0.000$

sites of two major 2010 Tea Party candidates, Rand Paul and Christine O'Donnell, failed to mention lesbian or gay issues at all, while Sharron Angle mentioned opposition to same-sex marriage only in passing.

Despite the limited mention of sexuality on the front pages of the Tea Party movement, subsequent campaigning frequently promoted anti-gay positions in these three major campaigns. In addition to opposing same-sex marriage, Angle took stands against adoption by lesbians and gay men, as well as extending antidiscrimination laws to cover sexual orientation and gender expression.[49] She also declared in a candidate questionnaire that she would not take campaign money from any group that supported homosexuality.[50] Previous comments about sexual minorities were among the many sound clips that plagued O'Donnell during election season. She claimed that being gay was "an identity disorder" and also worked with ex-gay ministries that claim to change sexual orientation, and with the Concerned Women for America, which espouses very conservative views regarding sexuality.[51] In stating his disapproval of the 1964 Civil Rights Act and the Americans with Disabilities Act, Rand Paul signaled that he would disapprove of similar proposed legislation, including the Employment Non-Discrimination Act (ENDA), a law designed to prohibit workplace discrimination against lesbians and gay men.

Libertarianism and these anti-gay, socially conservative impulses create great tension in the Tea Party, tension that is evident both in the above examples from campaign websites and Tea Party message boards. The tension further reveals itself in long interviews with Tea Party supporters who frequently claim nominal tolerance of gay men or lesbians while categorically deeming their lifestyle unacceptable, beyond the pale of full inclusion in the American polity. A Tea Party supporter from our 2010 MSSRP study illustrates the conflict to which we refer: "I think they've got a right to exist," he explains, "but I don't particularly want them around me." To be sure, this tension— between libertarianism and grudging acceptance on the one hand and social conservatism and condemnation on the other— identifies a possible fissure in the Tea Party movement. Still, such disagreement between the libertarian wing of the conservative movement and the socially conservative wing has been around since the 1950s. After all, one prioritizes the individual; the other places a premium on conformity and social cohesion.

Overall, the open-ended interviews seem to confirm that many Tea Party members' anti-gay attitudes can be classified as more resentful than old-fashioned, or what has come to be known as "traditional heteronormative," a way of viewing American social life in which heterosexuality is the sexual orientation that Americans should prefer. Anything else is believed deviant.[52] These Tea Party supporters protest gay men and lesbians' inability or unwillingness to adopt community norms by "flaunting" their sexuality publically. They avoid expressing anti-gay sentiment violently, and few claim to want to arrest or physically harm members of the LGBT community. Some do express anti-gay sentiments in terms of "old-fashioned" heterosexism and the language of sin, such as the North Carolina respondent who said, "I just pity them . . . because I know where they are going at the end of time." Still, many anti-gay views will be expressed in more subtle ways that clearly mark gay men and lesbians' subordinate role in American public life.

People voice this more subtle form of homophobia by expressing tolerance toward gay men and lesbians, as long as they stay in their "place." Few will deny the right of queer people to exist in the abstract, and many, on the basis of claims toward limited government, will oppose policies that actively seek out gay men and lesbians for punishment, such as military policies prior to Don't Ask, Don't Tell. This does not mean that folks view lesbians and gay men as equal members of the polity. Indeed, the logic of Don't Ask, Don't Tell,[53] a policy adopted by the armed forces in the early 1990s as a first step to recognizing the same-sex lifestyle, appears to guide many members' beliefs of the normative role for lesbians and gay men in American life. For them, the ideal gay or lesbian citizen is one who never "flaunts" his/her sexuality. Practically speaking, this is difficult for any individual gay man or lesbian to attain because the respondents expansively define "sexuality." Many actions whose sexuality is erased for heterosexuals are defined as explicitly sexual for homosexuals. These can include holding hands with a partner, discussing a relationship, or otherwise visibly embodying gender difference.

Membership in political movements and groups that protest for gay rights also have the potential to end nominal Tea Party support for lesbians and gay men. By both denying that systemic discrimination against sexual minorities exists, and by claiming any governmental remedy for discrimination is reverse discrimination or "special rights,"[54] this rhetoric denies political agency to sexual minorities.

Ultimately, the rhetoric of the Tea Party appears to follow a logic in which gay men and lesbians are identified on the basis of their behavior. A good or "respectable" gay man believes in the American Creed and avoids the identity politics of the main-stream gay rights movement. His demeanor is assimilated to heterosexual norms, and he does not challenge anyone's "right to disagree" with his lifestyle. On the contrary, a bad or un-acceptable lesbian is one who has politicized her sexual orienta-tion, either by challenging the "right to disagree" or by pushing for legislation such as the repeal of Don't Ask, Don't Tell or the passage of the Employment Non-Discrimination Act (ENDA). She may also reject heteronormativity and dress in a way that defies gendered norms or is flamboyant. A survey participant from California best sums up this distinction: "I have it in my family; and as individuals, I feel positive. As a group, I feel nega-tive, because I think that when your child is being taught by a teacher . . . you're going to be very unhappy when they're teach-ing a five-year-old child how to be a good little lesbian or homo-sexual." Likewise, a participant from Nevada distinguished be-tween not caring "what they [gay men and lesbians] do amongst themselves" and having an unfavorable view of them "if they try to push marriage." This characterization is not unique to sexual minorities. Similar shifts in public opinion have been observed between favorability of black Americans in general compared to black nationalists on the American National Election Study.[55]

While some arguments have been made in the past by Tea Party supporters to clarify their views toward immigrants as financially motivated—that is, they claim to be concerned about the burden on the economy placed by social welfare programs to benefit racial or ethnic minorities—there is no reasonable way to construe an argument that negative attitudes toward sexual minorities is financially motivated in the same way. Thus, if we continue to find significantly different attitudes toward sexual minorities among Tea Party supporters, as we did in their atti-tudes toward immigrants, it increases the odds that their hostil-ity is associated with cultural disapproval of the group and their lifestyle. Recall that earlier we reviewed statements made by of-ficial Tea Party blog posts in which authors argued that sexual minorities were "indoctrinating" children today and corrupting society—clearly not a "rein-in spending or reduce taxes" mentality. When we turn to the quantitative evidence from the national public opinion survey to which we refer, we corroborate what we have already observed in the interviews.

Figure 4.3 displays the results of four questions about attitudes toward sexual minorities in our society today. We begin with the most prominent topic during recent years, whether sexual minorities should be allowed to serve openly in the U.S. military. In a separate analysis, overall, we find 62 percent of the middle in our sample agrees that sexual minorities should be able to serve openly in the military, a finding that confirms robust levels of support reported in other public opinion polls taken during the December 2010 debate over repealing Don't Ask, Don't Tell.[56] However, once we separate true believers, people in the middle, and true skeptics, stark differences emerge. Only 48 percent of Tea Party sympathizers agree that sexual minorities should be able to serve in the military openly, compared to 76 percent of those opposing the Tea Party.

Beyond these two contemporary public policy issues, we queried attitudes toward the acceptance and position of sexual minorities today. We asked, "is society better when it encourages gay men and lesbians to be open and talk about their sexual orientation publicly or when it encourages them to keep their sexual orientation to themselves?" Responses to this question reveal another instance in which we observe anti-gay attitudes among supporters of the Tea Party. While 63 percent of Tea Party opponents favor sexual minorities talking publicly about their sexuality, only 28 percent of Tea Party sympathizers agree. Not only do Tea Party supporters wish to limit the rights of gays and lesbians, they don't want gays and lesbians airing their grievances or life experiences in public—an interesting contrast to their support for free speech in chapter 3.

Finally, we asked a question about perceptions of political power, somewhat similar to the question referenced above

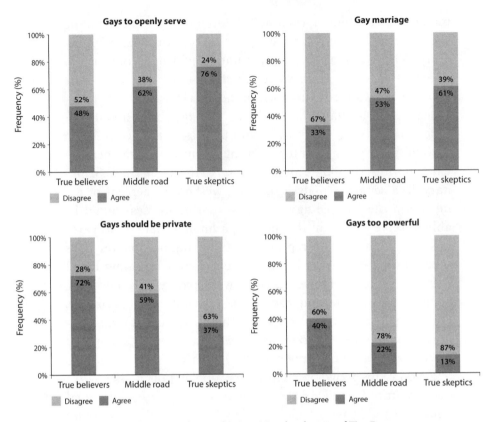

4.3. Attitudes toward sexual minorities, by degree of Tea Party support
Note: Total *N* = 1188, with 308 true believers, 488 middle of the road, and 392 true skeptics; relationships significant at χ^2 p < 0.000

about immigrants and political influence. Here, 22 percent of the people we surveyed, who don't have strong feelings about the Tea Party, believe sexual minorities have too much political power today. When we canvass opinions of believers and skeptics, however, differences, once again, emerge. Where 40 percent of believers think sexual minorities have too much political clout, that figure drops to 13 percent among skeptics.

So far, the distance separating believers and skeptics is significant, never getting any smaller than 25 percentage points.

Based on what we've heard from Tea Party supporters in our interviews, this is no shock. We expected as much. Critics, however, can charge that the differences can be attributed to conservatism; that believers are simply more conservative than anyone else. This is relevant because conservatives, as we have already outlined in prior chapters, are about traditionalism, among other things. Traditionalism rejects "alternative lifestyles," including homosexuality. This is a valid objection.

To remedy this, we continue with our practice of limiting our analysis to self-identified conservatives as we attempt to pry Tea Party conservatives away from other conservatives. If our claim that Tea Party conservatives are in fact reactionary is true, we should see differences emerge between them and non–Tea Party conservatives. This is precisely what happens as is evident by our results in figure 4.4. It's worth noting that the Tea Party conservatives and non–Tea Party conservatives remain in lockstep on the issue of whether or not sexual minorities should keep their lifestyle to themselves. Still, on every other question, we see a familiar pattern take shape in that Tea Party conservatives are less tolerant than their non–Tea Party brethren.

So far, from what we've witnessed, people who believe in the Tea Party tend to harbor some degree of hostility toward immigrants—legal and otherwise, and members of the gay and lesbian community, more so than other Americans, and more so than mainstream conservatives. Returning to chapter 1, we think it has something to do with their perception that the country is slipping away from them, giving rise to what we believe is reactionary conservatism. However, we can't say this for sure until we account for other possible explanations for out-group hostility.

It could be the case, for instance, that Tea Partiers' commitment to conservative principles is the real reason why we see the differences we observed. Another explanation is that Tea Party sympathizers favor people like themselves more than they dislike out-groups. For the negative attitudes we observed regarding

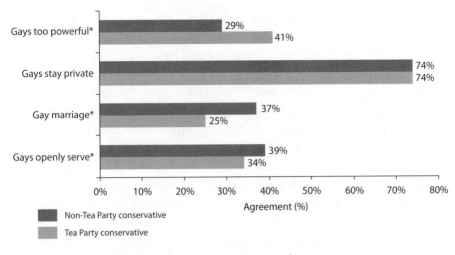

4.4. Support for gay rights, by type of conservatism
Note: Total conservative $N = 407$, with 204 true believers in the Tea Party;
*significant at χ^2 $p < 0.000$

gay rights, it might simply be a matter of a perceived violation of a moral code, or that evangelicals think homosexuality is a sin. In any case, we won't have confidence in our preliminary findings, that attachment to the Tea Party has something to say about intergroup attitudes, and the willingness (or lack thereof) of Americans to extend more equal treatment to out-groups, until we rule out competing explanations and account for these other factors in our analysis. We now turn to that task.

CAN ORIENTATION TO THE TEA PARTY TELL US ANYTHING NEW ABOUT MINORITY RIGHTS?

So far, the results reviewed in this chapter are very clear—Tea Party sympathizers hold relatively negative views toward minority groups in the United States compared to people who aren't as persuaded by the Tea Party. To solidify our findings, as we have said, we need to consider alternative explanations. Conservatism is an obvious alternative explanation. For illegal immigrants, it's simply a matter of law and order: they're committing a crime. For gay rights, the practice of homosexuality is morally wrong. It's against the Bible. Political explanations are also important: partisan politics are almost always implicated in immigration reform. With the exception of libertarians, Republicans are generally dead set against gay rights relative to Democrats. People who draw on myths that legitimate arrangements in which dominants rule over subordinate groups (social dominance orientation) are likely to believe that sexual minorities and illegal immigrants should remain in relatively subordinate positions because both groups are believed to be inferior. People that prefer their in-group, in the following cases, the native-born and heterosexuals, will likely reject policies geared to promoting the welfare of illegal immigrants and the lesbian and gay community.

To the extent that illegal immigrants and the LGBT community are perceived in violation of social norms in some kind of way, authoritarians are likely to oppose policies designed to help them. Our view is that support for the Tea Party is a proxy for the paranoid fear of subversion typically associated with the Far Right: reactionary conservatism. As such, we believe that it will have an independent effect on policies designed to make America a more perfect union. From the historical record, and what we've already seen, we continue to entertain the possibility that the Tea Party and its supporters, if they're anything akin to the Far Right, believe the country is being stolen from them. At this point, though, this is little more than informed conjecture.

For us to draw more firm conclusions, we must make sure that the results we observed earlier aren't really a function of one of the above-outlined alternative explanations. As we've done in chapters 2 and 3, we turn to regression analysis, a statistical tool that permits us to test our claim that support for the Tea Party ceteris paribus dampens the enthusiasm for measures that promise to pave the way for marginalized groups to receive more equal treatment. Again, it's possible that our observation

of Tea Party websites, in which citizen activists said a host of
negative things about illegal immigrants and homosexuals, may
be limited to a few fringe members. It's also possible that ultimately support for the Tea Party has nothing to do with negative
attitudes toward these groups. Rather, these attitudes may really
be more about social dominance or authoritarianism. Using the
same questions we featured in the prior section as outcomes, we
now turn to the models in which we attempt to assess the independent impact of Tea Party support.[57]

Tea Party Support and Immigrants

We begin with attitudes held toward immigrants. We use the
same topic cluster explored in figure 4.1 above.[58] Even after considering all of the alternative explanations, our claim that the believers are less likely than skeptics to embrace illegal immigrants,
and their *legal* children, is supported. That is to say, believers
are more likely to harbor anti-immigrant attitudes than skeptics.
As figure 4.5 illustrates, supporting the Tea Party *decreases* the
probability of supporting the DREAM Act by 13 percent. Moreover, sympathizing with the Tea Party increases the probability
of supporting the repeal of birthright *citizenship* by 10 percent,
and increases the probability of agreeing that immigrants are too
politically powerful by 5 percent. Similar results obtain where
support for the Tea Party increases the probability by 10 percent
that sympathizers believe new immigrants increase crime upon
arriving.

   As one might expect, some of the competing explanations are
also important. Social dominance orientation is the most consistent one. Across the board, as figure 4.5 shows, anti-immigrant
attitudes are more likely among people who tend to reject egalitarianism than those who believe in a more egalitarian order
(social dominance orientation). Self-identified conservatives are
more likely than liberals to reject the proposal for the DREAM
Act, and to believe that new immigrants aren't trying as hard
as older immigrants to assimilate. A desire for conformity, that

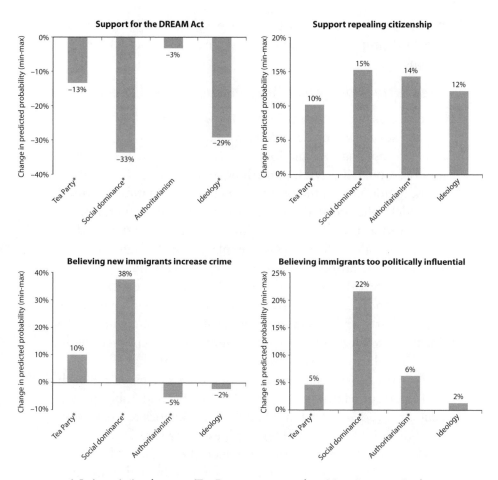

4.5. Association between Tea Party support and anti-immigrant attitudes
*Significant at $p < 0.05$, one-tailed

is, authoritarianism, registers in half of the models: repealing birthright citizenship and the perceived decline of their political power. This suggests that continuing birthright citizenship, and the rising political influence of immigrants, threatens American society. Otherwise, it makes no difference. Partisan (not shown) differences register only for attitudes on the DREAM Act, where

Republicans are less likely than Independents and Democrats to favor the proposal. (For full results, please see table A4.1 in the appendix.)

Tea Party Support and Perceptions of Sexual Minorities

Next, we use the same method to inspect the range of attitudes toward sexual minorities. Here, we must account for an additional competing explanation: the ways in which people view nontraditional lifestyles, something that taps into morality.[59] Thus, in addition to the other competing explanations we used to model policy-related attitudes toward illegal immigrants, we added moral traditionalism. With this, we have attempted to account for all of the competing explanations thought to be associated with attitudes toward the LGBT community. Yet, as figure 4.6 reveals, beyond these more established explanations, we find, once again, that the relationship between support for the Tea Party and several anti-gay attitudes remains intact. To illustrate, when it comes to sexual minorities openly serving in the U.S. military and same-sex marriage, the probability of Tea Party sympathizers supporting these issues decreases for each by 14 percent relative to skeptics. Moving beyond public policy, believers are 13 percent more likely than skeptics to prefer sexual minorities keep their choice of lifestyle private.

There is only one situation in which the empirical bond between Tea Party support and anti-gay and lesbian attitudes dissolves: on whether or not the LGBT community has too much political influence. Here, we find that the relationship between Tea Party support and anti-gay and lesbian issues, in this case, the perception of having too much political influence, is really about social dominance orientation. In other words, the data suggests that Tea Partiers and their followers' concern that their losing political power to the LGBT community isn't ultimately rooted in anxiety related to losing America. Instead, Tea Partiers and their followers reject the political empowerment of sexual minorities because they feel like this community shouldn't have political influence; they don't deserve it. They should remain in

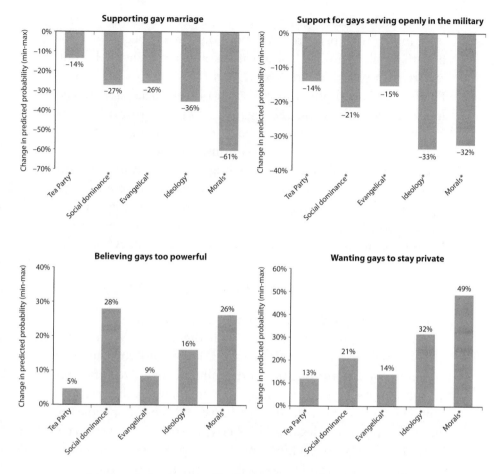

4.6. Association between Tea Party support and anti-gay attitudes
*Significant at $p < 0.05$, one-tailed

their subordinate political position on account of the lifestyle the LGBT community lives.

As our results in figure 4.6 make abundantly clear, there are additional attitudes and dispositions associated with gay rights; chief among them is the way in which people view morality. The more one takes issue with, say, alternative lifestyles, the more they're likely to reject gay rights and the gay community. Moreover, in line with prior research, and our own expectations, we find that self-identified conservatives and evangelicals harbor negative attitudes toward sexual minorities—across the board. Finally, we find those who rate high on the social dominance index are very likely to have negative viewpoints toward sexual minorities. As we mentioned above, our interpretation here is that people who reject egalitarianism also reject the idea that sexual minorities should have equal rights. For authoritarianism (not shown), the results reveal that preference for conformity registered only with same-sex marriage. The results suggest that these people believe permitting sexual minorities to wed threatens the social order. (For full results, please see table A4.2 in the appendix.)

■   ■   ■

The results in this chapter are strikingly consistent. The bottom line is that people who identify with the Tea Party are more likely than those who don't to take a less-than-flattering view of out-groups. Returning to our overall narrative, even after accounting for a myriad of competing explanations, the relationship between support for the Tea Party and the way people see illegal immigrants—legal and otherwise—remains intact. This indicates that we're picking up something separate from conservatism, party identification, ethnocentrism, and social dominance orientation. We submit that support for the Tea Party is picking up the anxiety and anger associated with the perception, harbored by believers, that they're losing their country. The Tea Party rallies in Arizona over the contentious SB 1070 suggested this directly through their signs and slogans. This sort of reactionary conservatism is driven, at least in part, by the paranoid social cognition that we discussed in chapter 1, which may explain why support for the Tea Party stands apart from competing explanations when evaluating attitudes toward immigrants and sexual minorities.

Critics may charge that our findings are relatively small. Indeed, there were other factors that had a more significant impact on the way people think about minorities and whether or not they should be treated more equally. This we cannot deny; there are many well-known factors that are associated with negative attitudes toward out-groups, those beyond what people identify as "American," either in appearance or practice. Even so, we accounted for every conceivable alternative explanation, something exceedingly rare in the social sciences, and our independent effects of Tea Party support remain valid. In short, based on what we were up against, we should have found no validation for our claim that support for the Tea Party matters. But we did. In other words, there's "a there, there," one that goes beyond one or two "bad apples" or isolated racist signs at the movements rallies. The data indicates quite clearly that as a whole, Tea Party supporters are far more likely to report anti-immigrant and anti-gay sentiments than those who dismiss the movement.

Concluding Thoughts

Over the past few decades America has experienced many social, demographic, and political changes. In particular, the minority and immigrant population has grown dramatically, something that's culminated in the election of many prominent African American, Latino, and Asian American candidates to office. At the same time, minority groups have continued to push for equal rights, especially civil rights, for a range of groups, including racial/ethnic minorities, but also women and sexual minorities. To a degree, the shock of these social changes to the dominant in group was absorbed by the previous eight years of the Republican presidency of George W. Bush. Even as society and demographics changed, calling into question the perceived social order of yesteryear, political control of the country rested in the hands of a Republican administration.

In 2008 everything changed, with Barack Obama's election and subsequent presidency. While this alone was not the sole inspiration of the Tea Party movement, the election of Obama provided an opening for many of his critics to reach out to those disaffected by the social change in America, and to perhaps question, "What happened to my country?" Not only did the social and demographic landscape of America look different in 2008 than it did a generation before, but so too did the office of the president of the United States.

In this chapter, we set out to assess the extent to which supporters of the Tea Party harbor negative attitudes toward minority groups in America. Along the way, we discovered that the Tea Party is beginning to look more and more like the contemporary representation of the Far Right. Like the Klan and JBS, it too shares an aversion to social change. Critics may charge that it's really not a fear of subversion that accounts for the Tea Party supporters' rejection of policies intended to make marginalized groups more equal in America. Instead, it's really more about conservatism. Or, in the case of gay rights, it's really about a religious or moral disagreement with the gay lifestyle. However, on both counts, Tea Party sympathizers are on shaky ground, because we accounted for all of these factors (and more), and support for the Tea Party still registers. This suggests that their opposition to these policies and groups has more to do with their reactionary disposition than anything else.

Many sympathetic to the Tea Party claim they're simply die-hard conservatives, not reactionaries. If this were the case, it would have been evident in the data gathered and reviewed in this chapter. Yet, as we make plain, the conversations that take place on the Tea Party websites have very few positive things to say about minorities. Furthermore, our in-depth interviews with Tea Party sympathizers suggest a connection to the rhetoric used online. Those who strongly supported the Tea Party avoided any explicit racist language during our telephone interviews. Still, they conveyed a general antipathy for minority groups and questioned whether groups like immigrants or sexual minorities should have equal opportunity in America. How far does this line of antipathy extend? We plan to find out in chapter 5, for we follow this trail of inquiry all the way to the White House.

5

The Tea Party and Obamaphobia: Is the Hostility Real or Imagined?

HAPTER FOUR DEMONSTRATED that Tea Party sympathizers harbor strong, negative views toward minority groups of all types. Believers, as we have come to identify them, seem reluctant to acknowledge claims to equality made by other groups that deviate in some way from the perceived American norm represented by the Tea Party, or what we have referred to as out-groups. Moreover, it's worth noting that believers' rejection of these groups isn't completely tied to politics, ideology, desire for conformity, or even their preference for antiegalitarian practices. Instead, we argue, and the evidence suggests, that the rejection of these minorities rests on a foundation of fear and anxiety: Tea Party supporters believe their country is rapidly escaping their grasp. We now apply this framework to President Obama, who we believe is the Tea Party's chief antagonist and target.

It is now passé to restate that the 2008 election was historic.

The election of Barack Obama as the first black president was indeed historic, and with it marked an important change in American political history. In chapter 2, we demonstrated that support for the Tea Party is at least in part a reaction to the presidency of Barack Obama. It's no surprise that those on the right frequently lament presidents who are Democrats. Nonetheless, it's hard to find another time during which a social and political movement of comparable size formed so quickly and held such deep-seated anger toward the person holding the highest office in the land. Barack Obama was in office no more than three months into his term before well-attended "Tax Day" Tea Party events were staged in more than 750 cities across the country to protest the stimulus, among other things.[1]

We think it likely that the election of Barack Obama, and the change it symbolized, represented a clear threat to the social, economic, and political hegemony to which supporters of the Tea Party had become accustomed. More to the point, as our evidence indicates, Obama's ascendance to the White House, and his subsequent presidency, triggered anxiety, fear, and anger among those who support the Tea Party because of what he represented: tangible evidence that "their" America is rapidly becoming unrecognizable. This is what we call Obamaphobia.

Even as Tea Party supporters railed against government spending, and an expanding federal government, it seemed their underlying frustration was with Barack Obama himself, who they called Kenyan, Muslim, and un-American, among other things. Any president is sure to face challenging criticism over policy disputes. However, response to Obama and his policies appears to transcend simple policy disagreement, with many Tea Party supporters openly questioning the president's patriotism, and his American citizenship on several occasions. Such emotional responses, we believe, are ultimately driven by the belief, held by many Tea Party supporters, that Barack Obama is out to destroy the country, the reactionary impulse we originally observed in chapter 1.

Earlier, we demonstrated that opposition to Obama, and what his policies are perceived to represent, is associated with Tea Party sympathy. In this chapter we explore in more detail the extent to which Tea Party sympathizers express anti-Obama attitudes. While the reader may not be surprised that Tea Party supporters hold strong negative views toward the president, our analysis suggests that their viewpoints go well beyond what parties on both sides believe animate attitudes toward the president.

Tea Party sympathizers say it's all about politics and ideology; that attitudes concerning Obama are simply a function of partisanship and commitment to conservatism. If this is true, the hostility observed by Tea Party critics who say it's all about racism is imagined. Critics argue that Tea Party sentiment, as it relates to Obama, is driven more by racism and out-group hostility than anything else. Given their deep roots in American social and political history, we think it's likely that both are sources on which people draw to shape their views about Obama. Still, if out-group antipathy—driven by racism, ethnocentrism, or social dominance orientation—explains believers' hostility to the president, Obamaphobia remains elusive. Put differently, it's quite possible that the hostility directed toward the president by Tea Party supporters may really be a function of the way believers feel about out-groups, not anxiety associated with the perception that they're losing America. Our claim is that Obama-related attitudes are also shaped by factors that go beyond predispositions driven by conservative principles, partisanship, and out-group hostility broadly defined. If this is true, the relationship between support for the Tea Party and Obamaphobia is real.

To summarize, we examine three competing theoretical claims with respect to presidential approval. First, one may argue that reactions to President Obama are based on political predispositions, including ideology, partisanship, and economic evaluations. Second, viewpoints toward Obama are based on motivational predispositions related to out-group hostility: ra-

cial resentment, authoritarianism, or social dominance orientation. A third theoretical claim, one we maintain with respect
to the Tea Party, is that attitudes toward President Obama are
motivated by what the Tea Party and its supporters perceive as
the president's malign intent. Here, we examine whether or not
Tea Party support does indeed have its own independent effect
on presidential evaluations. We also explore attitudes related
specifically to President Obama, ones that mark him as an alien
of some kind.

In the end, Tea Party sympathizers and their critics are both
wrong. It's true that conservatism and Republican partisanship
are associated with anti-Obama sentiments. Tea Party critics'
beliefs are also valid in that antipathy toward the president
is also related to out-group hostility of both general and specific kinds: social dominance orientation and antiblack racism.
Still, the issue is whether or not the association between support for the Tea Party and anti-Obama sentiment may be explained in terms of conservative principles and politics or out-
group hostility of any kind. On this count, they're both wrong,
because Tea Party sympathy remains tethered to anti-Obama
attitudes, even after accounting for these other important alternative explanations. As we will see, anti-Obama sentiment
covers a range of issues. When asked about Obama's intelligence, morality, American citizenship, and Christianity, Tea
Party sympathizers are far and away the most negative toward
the president.

In what follows, we take a hard look at several facets of the
ways in which the Tea Party and its supporters relate to Obama.
We open with evidence confirming our argument: the Tea Party
is likely a reaction to the election of Barack Obama and his developing presidency. We then introduce the reader to standard
ways in which scholars have explained presidential approval,
stressing the importance of perceptions of the economy and
partisanship. We wrap up the chapter with a few concluding
thoughts.

THE EMERGENCE OF THE TEA PARTY AND
THE OBAMA PRESIDENCY

The roots of this movement can be traced to the December 2007 anniversary of the Boston Tea Party, when Ron Paul supporters held a "money bomb" to raise funds for Paul's 2008 presidential run.[2] Paul, while campaigning for the Republican nomination, was not considered a mainstream Republican based on his Libertarian beliefs, and the money bomb reflected this. Organized by a thirty-seven-year-old rock promoter, the money bomb relied on the enthusiasm and donations of online supporters, many of whom were first-time donors. Paul's Campaign for Liberty (CFL) went on to play a significant role in the growth of the Tea Party, according to a recent NAACP report, though there is little crossover in membership.[3] Paul has embraced the Tea Party, speaking at a number of rallies around the country since the birth of the movement.

Though Paul's candidacy may have provided some of the initial impetus, the Tea Party itself did not emerge during the 2008 campaign. Rather, it was following the election of Barack Obama that the term "Tea Party" began to be used to describe a political movement. Below, figure 5.1 charts the prominence of the term "Tea Party" as measured by searches on Google among U.S. Internet users from 2007 to 2011. As the graph makes clear, a relatively small and steady number of searches were conducted on the term "Tea Party" from January 2007 to January 2009. The term peaked at its highest point in April 2009, followed by several notable increases surrounding key Tea Party rallies in 2009 and 2010, suggesting the Google search data is an accurate reflection of the group's monthly popularity in American politics. For example, we observe a significant increase in April 2010 immediately following the signing of Obama's health care bill, the Affordable Care Act, and then again in October–November 2010 during the contested midterm elections. The point here is that the Tea Party was formed as a political move-

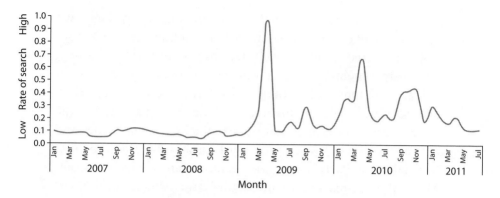

5.1. Popularity of search term "Tea Party" on Google among
US Internet users, by month, 2007–2011

ment not long after Obama had been sworn in as the forty-
fourth president of the United States.

While April 2009 marks the Tea Party's coming-out party, its
foundation was laid in the immediate aftermath of Obama's victory over John McCain. The Libertarian Party of Illinois formed
the Boston Tea Party of Chicago in December 2008 to promote
lower taxes and reduced government spending. Its founder,
Dave Brady, later claimed he gave Rick Santelli the idea for the
Tax Day Tea Parties that marked the real explosion of the movement onto the national political scene in April 2009.[4] Santelli,
a CNBC on-air editor, delivered a speech from the floor of the
Chicago stock exchange on February 19, 2009, that was largely
credited with popularizing the concept of the Tax Day Tea Parties.[5] Following Santelli's broadcast, the character of the Tea
Party movement shifted toward a more organized entity.

Crucial in the transition of the movement from localized anti-
tax, antistimulus protests to something more organized and
national in character, was Brendan Steinhauser and the D.C.
lobby and training organization FreedomWorks. After Santelli's on-air diatribe, Steinhauser wrote a ten-step instructional

document to assist interested parties in organizing their own Tea Party rallies to protest the Obama administration's policies and posted it on his website. Shortly after the document was posted, Steinhauser's website saw a significant increase in traffic.[6] FreedomWorks, founded by former congressman Dick Armey, quickly became involved, calling supporters across the country and asking them to organize their own Tea Parties and announcing a nationwide tour. On February 27, 2009, the first "official" Tea Party event was held, organized by Freedom-Works, the free-market-oriented Sam Adams Alliance, and Americans for Prosperity.

FreedomWorks was just one of six national Tea Party factions that arose in February 2009. FreedomWorks, ResistNet, and Our Country Deserves Better PAC existed prior to Santelli's speech, but three more formed in its wake: 1776 Tea Party, Tea Party Patriots, and Tea Party Nation. On tax day, April 15, 2009, just as Obama was enjoying his highest job approval numbers ever, on the anniversary of his first one hundred days in office, anti-Obama Tea Party rallies were held in Washington, D.C., and in hundreds of cities across the country.[7] An ABC/ *Washington Post* poll reported Obama had a 69 percent job approval rating in mid-April 2009, and when asked about the man, a Fox News poll reported that 68 percent had a favorable view of Obama one week after tax day.[8] So, before any real anti-Obama sentiment materialized, just three months into his first term, Tea Party organizers had already organized major protest rallies denouncing the president.

According to the *New York Times*, these rallies began to associate Obama with socialism, an attack against the president that was later extended to portray him as un-American. In an account of the Tea Party protest in Texas on April 15, 2009, the *Times* described the scene this way: "Paul Sommer, 41, of Humble, Tex., said he came out because he feared the country was drifting toward socialism under President Obama. 'I don't agree with them taking my money,' he said. 'I'm a small-business owner. I don't want them taking everything.'"[9]

So, even though Obama had been in office barely three months, and a majority of the American public approved of his job performance, the record suggests that Tea Party supporters were beginning to yoke him to socialism and peg him as un-American. More protest followed in the summer of 2009, and by September 12, 2009, FreedomWorks organized a large rally in Washington, D.C., marking the first large-scale national rally and the emergence of the Tea Party as a national movement.

Still, the Tea Party movement operated on the fringes of U.S. politics for much of 2009. However, they became a nationally known entity following President Obama's signing of the Affordable Care Act on March 30, 2010. The Tea Party Patriots, one of the six major Tea Party factions, led protests across the country. During a march on the nation's capitol, allegations were made that Tea Partiers spit on members of Congress, shouted racial epithets, and threw bricks through windows of members of Congress.[10] Apparently, Tea Party sympathizers perceived the increased influence of African Americans, Hispanics, and the LGBT community in national politics, indicated by many signs at Tea Party rallies in which antiminority slogans were emphasized.[11]

Tea Party supporters voiced opposition to a wide range of policy reforms ranging from the Trouble Asset Relief Program (TARP), the stimulus package, and health care, to immigration reform and the formal acceptance of gays in the military. While the targets of these policies varied considerably, Obama was the common denominator. Tea Party sympathizers not only opposed policy reforms, as did most self-described conservatives, they also opposed Barack Obama the person. Independent of his policy agenda, Tea Party websites are littered with rumors that Obama was a secret Muslim, that he had no valid American birth certificate, that he was anti-Christian, that he was a secret socialist or communist, and above all, he was not a real American.

All the above suggests that the rancor directed at the president, among Tea Party types, went beyond simple ideological or partisan differences. For instance, non–Tea Party conservatives often called for an end to questions about Obama's birth certificate.[12] They preferred to engage the president on policy, avoiding ad hominem attacks. In response, Tea Party conservatives continued pushing their conspiratorial rhetoric, including a Tea Party–sponsored book published in 2011 claiming to prove that Obama wasn't qualified for the presidency. The book claimed that the president wasn't born in the United States, insisted on his allegiance to Kenya, and stressed his upbringing in a Muslim environment in Indonesia.[13] These assertions led many to conclude that Obama wasn't an American citizen.

While many of the rumors and attacks about Obama had surfaced during the 2008 primary or general election, they quickly decreased, only to resurface after the rise of the Tea Party movement in April 2009. For example, in the Google search index in figure 5.2, we find a relatively low interest in the search term "socialism" in 2007 and 2008, until October 2008 when the first charges that Obama would promote socialism apparently began to resonate. However, the interest in the term waned following Obama's victory, only to resurface with notable and steady peaks in 2009–2010 after the emergence of the Tea Party.

As we make clear in content analysis in chapter 1, the conspiratorial attacks on Obama were unique to the Tea Party, failing to emerge on mainstream conservative websites like the *National Review Online (NRO)*. While the Tea Party claimed to be concerned primarily with government spending and states' rights, a considerable portion of their official blog posts concerned topics such as whether or not Obama actually had a valid U.S. birth certificate, or whether he had a secret agenda to make America a socialist welfare state, or whether he secretly prayed from the Qur'an in the West Wing. It is worth repeating the statistics reported in chapter 1—these conspiratorial attacks on Obama accounted for 33 percent of all official blog posts on Tea Party websites compared to just 5 percent of entries on the *NRO*: more than a sixfold difference.

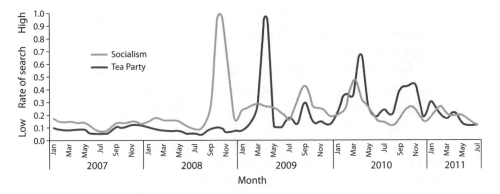

5.2. Popularity of search terms on Google among
US Internet users, by month, 2007–2011

While the percentages reported above show a distinct difference with respect to anti-Obama attitudes, they don't show the
depth of the viewpoints raised by Tea Party supporters. If we
look in more detail at the official blog posts on Tea Party websites, we find just how convinced they were that Obama was not
an American citizen. For example, with the launch of the Tea
Party in April 2009, one Tea Party website proclaimed:

> Barack Hussein Obama is a fraud on the American people!
> The lunatic left helped him get elected and is using him
> in a power grab to rapidly replace our capitalist system
> with far-left socialism that will ruin our country. We can
> stop this power grab because we are convinced that Barack
> Hussein Obama is not a natural-born citizen of the U.S.
> and therefore is not qualified to be President of the U.S.A.
> It is our intent to offer the kind of reward that will mo-
> tivate someone to produce Barack Hussein Obama's real
> birth certificate that can be proven to be valid![14]

Speaking at a Tea Party convention in 2010, former Colorado
congressman and Tea Party favorite Tom Tancredo continued to

use the "birther" issue to portray Obama as un-American. Tancredo told the crowd of Tea Party supporters, "if his wife says Kenya is his homeland, why don't we just send him back?" This was followed by an interview on Fox News radio in which he said, "whether she was talking about his, the physical homeland, the place where he was born or she was just talking about his 'home country' being that's where his heart is—it's not America . . . I do not believe Barack Obama loves the same America that I do, the one that the Founders put together. I do not believe that. I think that he wants that changed."[15]

Finally, even after the release of Obama's official Hawaiian birth certificate in April 2011, Tea Party supporters continued to question his American citizenship. Three full months later, in July 2011, three Tea Party groups in Arizona debated and passed motions at meetings asking their member of Congress to call for an official investigation into Obama's citizenship and eligibility to be president, stating, "Is Barack Obama a natural born citizen eligible to hold the office of President per the terms and historical meaning of Article II, Section I, Clause 5 of the United States Constitution?" and further questioned, "Is the recently released long form birth certificate which he personally endorsed on April 27, 2011 from the White House Press Room legitimate and identical to an original held by the Department of Health in Hawaii or was it a forged document and therefore a felony under U.S. Criminal codes?"[16]

We use each of these examples to illustrate that a conspiratorial, anti-Obama sentiment exists on some of the major Tea Party websites, and among their most prominent supporters. However, it could be the case that only a small minority within the Tea Party is espousing such views, and this is not typical of most Tea Party sympathizers. Thus, we return to our survey to examine whether or not Tea Party sympathizers are more likely to hold negative attitudes toward President Obama than do skeptics of the movement. If the Tea Party represents an authentic slice of American sentiment, then we will not see any differences between Tea Party supporters who believe Obama is Muslim, has no birth certificate, and has a socialist agenda, relative to the rest of the population. If, however, prior chapters are in any way indicative, we think it likely that the views of Tea Party supporters—the true believers—will prove out of step with both Tea Party skeptics and mainstream conservatives.

EXPLAINING PRESIDENTIAL APPROVAL

Since the advent of survey research, scholars of American politics have been fascinated with understanding, explaining, and predicting presidential approval. Indeed, models exploring the factors that explain presidential approval are among the most common across time in the study of American politics.[17] Of course, partisanship and ideology are important considerations, with partisanship leading the way: Democrats tend to like Democratic presidents, and, not surprisingly, Republicans really like Republicans. As it turns out, there's another factor associated with the evaluation of presidents, one that rivals even partisanship.

The leading explanation for why Americans either like or dislike the president is the state of the economy. Michael MacKuen, Robert Erikson, and James Stimson have marshaled the clearest evidence that evaluations of the economy is an important factor to consider if we wish to better understand the criteria by which Americans evaluate the president.[18] For some time, scholars have debated the relative importance of retrospective or prospective economic evaluations,[19] that is, whether or not people look to the past to evaluate the economy, or look forward. Regardless of one's approach, there can be no doubt that the ways in which Americans perceive the economy is important to evaluations of the president. Certainly, other issues can matter as well, and as they become salient, the public often judges the president on a host of other factors, including foreign policy, social or moral issues, trade policy, and the deficit, especially as the media intervenes to draw more attention to these issues.[20] Still, "other issues" are wrapped up so tightly in partisanship and ideology that it is difficult to disentangle them from the ways in which Americans judge their president.

As Obama took the stage in January 2009 to be sworn in as the forty-fourth president of the United States, and the first African American to hold that office, even cable news commentators seemed to know that our models of understanding presidential approval were about to change. In the immediate aftermath of Obama's victory, news stories alerted us that gun sales had increased dramatically throughout the southern United States. The FBI reportedly foiled a potential assassination plot against Obama. While many Americans embraced their newfound respect for multiculturalism, for many, the political correctness was superficial.

While the economy, partisanship, and ideology will never cease to inform how Americans view the presidency, the Obama presidency may have exposed a host of new variables as a means of understanding what Americans think about their president. During academic conferences, concepts such as racial resentment and ethnocentrism are now frequently deployed as a means of exploring attitudes toward Obama.[21] We argue that even beyond these concepts—and beyond partisanship, ideology, and the economy—support for the Tea Party will produce its own effect on presidential approval in addition to the aforementioned standard factors associated with evaluations of the president.[22]

As we discussed above, and as the evidence suggests so far, Tea Party anti-Obama sentiments appear to transcend partisanship and ideology. They attacked his name, they attacked his relatives, and they questioned his patriotism and the extent to which he can be considered American. Others may simply point to the partisan rancor and ideological extremism that characterize Washington, D.C., today as a means of explaining the anti-Obama sentiment we have observed. Tea Party critics would say that the Tea Party movement and its followers reject Obama on the basis of his race. As we have already argued, we think Obamaphobia is about something else. We think it's about the threat he represents as president to the existing order, to which Tea Partiers and their followers have become accustomed.

Tea Party Sympathizers and Presidential Approval

Despite such similarities to the Far Right, many who are sympathetic to the Tea Party think it's squarely in the mainstream,[23] or insist that the Tea Party is simply more conservative but harbors no negative racial views toward Obama.[24] As we have in prior chapters, we now turn to our 2011 Multi-State Survey of Race and Politics, in which we probe a variety of attitudes and beliefs, including what people think about President Obama. First, we wish to examine whether or not people in the mass public who sympathize with the Tea Party differ in their attitudes and behavior from the public at large. Second, we wish to account for competing explanations of why Tea Party sympathizers retain such hostile attitudes toward President Obama.

Overall, the data suggests that supporters of the Tea Party are statistically more likely to hold negative attitudes toward Obama across a variety of different issues and topics, going beyond the expected range of simple Republican opposition to a Democratic president. If it were just partisanship and ideology at play, we'd expect Tea Party supporters to be frustrated with President Obama and his policies. However, as we turn to our analysis, in which we are able to account for the alternative explanations of perceptions of the president, our findings indicate they are more than frustrated. Taken together with the interviews we reviewed in chapter 1, as well as the content of the Tea Party websites we examined, it's clear that Tea Party sympathizers believe the president is on a mission to destroy the country.

As in prior chapters, we begin our analysis with results comparing how Tea Party sympathizers and Tea Party opponents differ from the overall American public when it comes to attitudes and approval of President Obama. We explore a variety of topics, including beliefs that the president is knowledgeable, moral, or a strong leader. We also ask respondents questions about Obama's personal biography, such as his place of birth and his religion. After examining these results, we move on to provide a much more rigorous statistical test to determine if there is a lasting association between support for the Tea Party and holding anti-Obama attitudes, or rather if the effect for the Tea Party diminishes once we account for things like an individual's ideology, partisanship, racism, economic evaluations, and more.

Presidential Traits

There are a variety of dimensions on which the public can, and does, evaluate the president. The most commonly known is job approval, as reported for more than fifty years in the Gallup tracking poll. However, beyond simple job approval, the public often reflects on other qualities and characteristics of the president, such as their leadership ability, knowledge, and degree to which they empathize with average Americans.[25] Scholars of the presidency have long studied questions assessing these traits, for they provide very important shortcuts for the public to evaluate the competence of the American chief executive. As Donald Kinder writes, "judgments of character offer citizens a familiar and convenient way to manage the avalanche of information made available to them each day about public affairs."[26] He concludes, observing that "judgments of a president's character may also reflect an interest in the maintenance of public standards and the very special place of the president in public life."

Needless to say, this takes us back to chapter 1, in which we elaborated on the centrality of the presidency to the American way of life, and his ability to provide a sense of stability to Americans in tough times. So while the public may ultimately support a particular policy, it may still oppose the president as a person, and vice versa. Examining presidential traits gets to this deeper understanding of whether or not the public sees the president, in this case Barack Obama, as fit to lead the country.

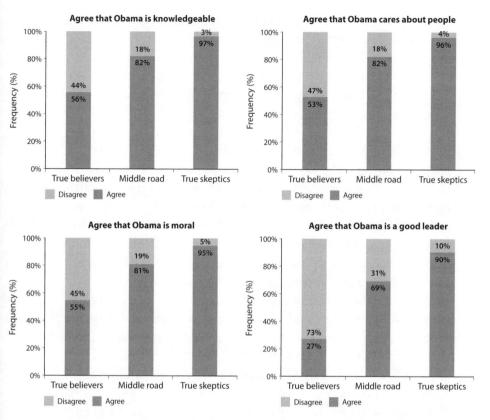

5.3. Attitudes toward Obama's traits by degree of Tea Party support
Note: Total *N* = 1188, with 308 true believers, 488 middle of the road,
and 392 true skeptics; relationships significant at χ^2 *p* < 0.000

Our first sets of results are contained in figure 5.3, in which
we probe the public's attitude toward presidential characteristics or traits by degree of Tea Party support. Presidential traits
have long been an important component of understanding presidential approval, and most scholars agree that partisanship,
ideology, and evaluations of the economy are the key factors
to understanding such things as whether or not the president
demonstrates strong leadership.[27]

Here, we examine the percent of respondents who agree that four trait descriptions describe Obama well: knowledgeable, moral, strong leader, and cares about people. As is immediately clear, Tea Party sympathizers, indicated in the first bar, are significantly less likely to agree with any of the positive traits descriptions. To illustrate, we find that 97 percent of Tea Party skeptics and 82 percent of those in the middle of the road say Obama is knowledgeable, compared to just 56 percent of Tea Party supporters. The separation between believers and skeptics is almost as large when it comes to perceptions about whether or not the president is moral, where 40 percentage points separate the two camps: 95 percent to 55 percent. Nor, relative to other groups, do Tea Party supporters think Obama is a good leader. Indeed, only 27 percent of them agree that Obama is a good leader versus 90 percent of skeptics and 69 percent of the people who are relatively indifferent to the Tea Party. Another gap between believers and everyone else is visible when we explore whether or not people perceive that Obama cares about them. Slightly more than half (53%) of believers think Obama cares about them versus 82 percent of those in the middle of the road and 96 percent of skeptics.

Across all dimensions measured in figure 5.3, Tea Party supporters demonstrate considerably lower opinions of the president than any other subgroup of Americans. We now investigate the extent to which the differences we observed are due to ideological differences. Again, one of the purposes for separating Tea Party conservatives from non–Tea Party conservatives is to examine the proposition that the former are more extreme than the latter. This is precisely what we find. In figure 5.4 we report results for self-described conservatives, with separate rows for those who support and do not support the Tea Party. Across all four traits, non–Tea Party conservatives show higher support for President Obama by 26 to 40 percentage points over Tea Party conservatives. For example, 72 percent of non–Tea Party conservatives say Obama is knowledgeable, but just 43 percent of Tea Party conservatives agree, and this trend holds for Obama's

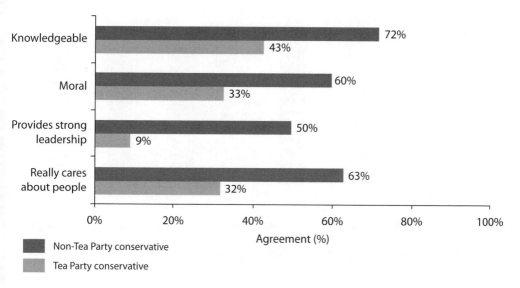

5.4. Attitudes toward Obama's traits among conservatives,
by Tea Party support
Note: Total conservative $N = 407$, with 204 true believers in the Tea Party;
relationships significant at χ^2 $p < 0.000$

morality, leadership, and connection with the American people. These findings suggest that ideology isn't driving the difference between Tea Party supporters and everyone else—at least as far as evaluations of President Obama are concerned.

Presidential Performance

Beyond these presidential traits, we are interested in how the public evaluates Obama's performance as president, but not in the traditional Gallup "job approval" fashion. Beginning in 2009, reputable mainstream polling outfits started to develop new questions of presidential performance, including whether or not the public wanted President Obama's policies to fail or succeed. In fact, just days before Obama's inauguration as the forty-fourth president of the United States, conservative talk radio host Rush Limbaugh said he hoped Obama's policies would fail. His comment created a bit of division among

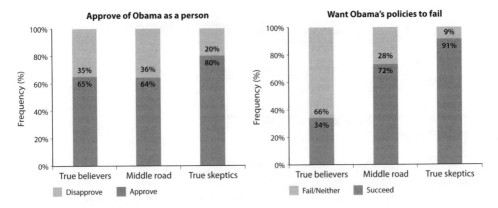

5.5. Attitudes toward Obama, by degree of Tea Party support
Note: Total $N = 1188$, with 308 true believers, 488 middle of the road,
and 392 true skeptics; relationships significant at $\chi^2\ p < 0.000$

Republicans, some of whom said they thought it wrong to wish
the president's policies would not succeed.[28] Others weren't so
reluctant to publicly wish failure on the new president, including Republican stalwarts Rick Santorum and Mike Pence.[29]
For more mainstream, "responsible" conservatives, it would
seem out of line to hope that any president's policies would
fail and likely result in instability in America; however, as we
have argued, Tea Party supporters may merely be reactionary
conservatives.

Moving on to figure 5.5, we find in other evaluations of
Obama that Tea Party sympathizers are clear outliers, holding
the most negative views toward the president. For instance, we
asked respondents, apart from his job performance as president,
what they thought of Obama as a person. Here, 80 percent of
Tea Party skeptics said they approved of Obama but just 65 percent of Tea Party supporters approved. A related question, we
asked whether respondents hoped the president's policies would
succeed or fail, and once again we found stark differences between Tea Party supporters and the general public. While just
9 percent of skeptics said they hoped Obama's policies would

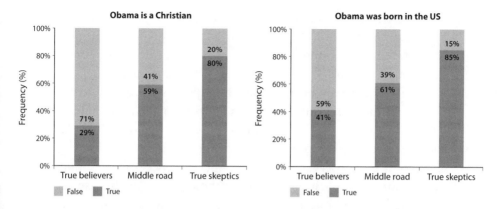

5.6. Facts about Obama's biography, by degree of Tea Party support
Note: Total $N = 1188$, with 308 true believers, 488 middle of the road, and 392 true skeptics; relationships significant at χ^2 $p < 0.000$

fail, a majority—66 percent—of Tea Party supporters said they wanted the president to fail. On both accounts this personal opposition to Obama, beyond just his policies, is distinct among Tea Partiers, and not found among mainstream conservatives.

Presidential Fact or Fiction?

Finally, in figure 5.6 we explore agreement with specific facts about Obama. In this case, we can determine if Tea Party supporters are opposed to Obama because they know nothing about him, or if they are familiar with his true biography but choose to support myths and conspiracy theory. As with our prior areas of analysis, we use this section to move beyond the traditional, more conventional assessment of presidential job approval. This section helps us understand how far believers may go in supporting conspiratorial beliefs about the president.

We asked true/false questions about different biographical statements of President Obama concerning his religion and nativity. Despite his repeated public statements that he is a devout Christian, including the considerable media attention and negative reaction to his Christian pastor Jeremiah Wright in 2008, a majority of Tea Party supporters do not believe Obama is a practicing Christian. When asked, just 29 percent of Tea Party supporters said Obama is Christian, compared to 80 percent of Tea Party opponents. Further, when probing the president's nativity, just 41 percent of Tea Party supporters believe Obama was actually born in the United States compared to 85 percent of those opposed to the Tea Party who believe the president was born in the United States. However, we don't believe these views come out of ignorance of the president.

Beyond the observed responses, the evidence suggests that people simply don't wish to answer these questions. In a separate analysis we conducted some time ago, we demonstrated that believers were more likely than any other groups to avoid answering this question, claiming either no knowledge of the president's background, or outright refusing to answer the question.[30] We find it hard to believe that supporters of the Tea Party, who tend to be more involved in politics and pay more attention to the news, would not be familiar with Barack Obama's biography and history. In fact, they are aware of these facts but choose to dispute them, as evidenced by Tea Party favorite Donald Trump and author Jerome Corsi,[31] both of whom question Obama's eligibility for the presidency.

In what by now should be a familiar pattern, we close this section with a comparison of self-identified conservatives. By comparing self-identified conservatives with different points of view concerning the Tea Party, we wish to test the proposition that what we have observed to this point is merely a matter of predispositional differences between skeptics and believers. Again, large differences emerge. As figure 5.7 clearly indicates, a 31-point difference separates the conservative camps on whether or not conservatives approve of Obama as a person. Another 17 points allows us to discriminate between conservative factions on whether or not people believe the president is a practicing Christian; a smaller, still significant difference (14 points) emerges between the groups when we asked whether or not people believed Obama was born in the United States. However, the most arresting finding by far is the number of Tea Party

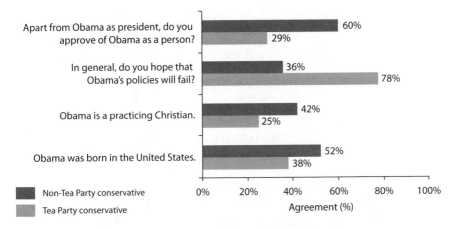

5.7. Attitudes and facts about Obama among conservatives, by Tea Party support
Note: Total conservative $N = 407$, with 204 true believers in the Tea Party;
relationships significant at $\chi^2\ p < 0.000$

conservatives who wish to see the president's policies *fail*: 78 percent of Tea Party conservatives versus 36 percent of non–Tea Party conservatives. This is a gap of 42 points, the largest among the four. If anything, we shouldn't expect any differences here because the question mentions policy explicitly, something on which conservatives tend to be in lockstep.

In this section, we attempted to gauge how people have evaluated President Obama along several dimensions. From presidential approval to what people believe to be true about President Obama, the way in which people view the Tea Party has much to say about how people perceive the president. We fully expected to find big differences between skeptics of the Tea Party and true believers. But even as we moved beyond crude comparisons between skeptics and believers to Tea Party and non–Tea Party, we were able to easily discriminate between conservative camps. Increasing the degree of difficulty for us, that is, confining the analysis to self-identified conservatives, has a side benefit, one coincidental with our enterprise. By illustrating that support for the Tea Party has an effect on the ways in which people view the president—beyond conventional conservatism—validates our theoretical claim that Tea Party conservatives aren't conservatives in the traditional sense: they're reactionary. The fact that so many of them wish to see the president fail should drive this point home.

OBAMAPHOBIA: IS IT REALLY ABOUT POLITICS OR SOMETHING ELSE?

So far, the results reviewed in this chapter are very clear. Compared to the general American public, it *seems* that Tea Party sympathizers hold significantly different, more negative opinions about President Obama. We have even held ideology constant, showing that even among self-identified conservatives, differences emerge between those who identify with the Tea Party and those who don't. Still, the above results are simple group-based comparisons between people who favor the Tea Party and those who aren't so favorably disposed to the message. If we are to have any confidence in our findings, we must account for competing influences on public opinion and attitudes toward the president.

There are several other factors that may attenuate the strength of relationship that we have so far observed. Partisanship, racism, socially dominant attitudes, authoritarianism, and ethnocentrism are the most important possible confounds. These competing explanations map well onto an assertion we made as we opened our book: politics and out-group antipathy have had much to say about American social and political life. It's only fitting that we take them into consideration in our assessment of a political figure in which both currents converge as never before.

We now turn to regression analysis, as we have before, as a means of testing our claim that support for the Tea Party helps to shape public opinion toward Obama, even as we account for the various alternative explanations outlined above. Our analysis above permits us to make definitive claims about the association between Tea Party support and perceptions of President Obama.[32] If we are correct, and believers are reacting to the president because they perceive him as an agent of subversion, support for the Tea Party will have an independent effect, over and above all the other explanations. If support for the Tea Party fails to emerge from the analysis with an independent effect, it suggests that what we observed in the preceding figures, in which believers were revealed to hold strong, negative opinions of Obama, was really about politics or out-group antipathy of some kind.

So far, we're sure that the reader probably presumes that direction of causality runs from support for the Tea Party to attitudes about Obama. While identification with the Tea Party may conceivably cause someone to believe Obama is not a practicing Christian, for instance, it may also be the case that the causal arrow is reversed. In other words, people may come to support the Tea Party because they don't like the president, or don't trust him. In the absence of experimental data, there's no way for us to know for sure what's causing what. Still, we think it's more likely that support for the Tea Party, net of other explanations, influences anti-Obama attitudes.

Our confidence rests on the role played by Fox News as a means of forging a collective identity among Tea Party elites, activists, and supporters.[33] As Kathleen Hall Jamieson and John Capella's research demonstrates, increasing exposure to conservative media tends to crystallize, even change opinion on important issues.[34] Moreover, they go on to show that the insularity of consumers of conservative media from more mainstream media outlets, in which they'd come across viewpoints counter to what they see on, say, Fox, tends to promote attitudes at variance with the rest of America. When one couples this with Fox News' demographic profile, one that's 85 percent white, middle-class, and middle-aged, it should come as no great shock that it plays an important role in sustaining the Tea Party movement, since they were likely part of Fox's audience before the Tea Party took off. Indeed, according to our data, 60 percent of Fox News' audience consists of true believers.[35] For this reason we also account for whether or not one turns to Fox News as their primary source of information.

For ease of presentation, we now turn to a series of regression results and predicted probabilities in which we modeled attitudes toward Obama. Figures 5.8 and 5.9 represent our findings. (For all models, the full regression results are reflected in table A5.1 in the appendix.) We begin the discussion of results with findings for attitudes on presidential trait characteristics. In order to capture a more complete assessment of President Obama, the four traits examined above are analyzed together as an index.[36] This allows for an examination of all the traits together, offering a more holistic evaluation. As we would expect, we find that individuals who are more conservative, Republican, hold socially dominant attitudes, and who are more racially resentful hold more negative attitudes toward Obama. Still, the association between support for the Tea Party and perceptions of Obama's traits remain intact. That is, beyond a respondent's political and social predispositions, support for the Tea Party has considerable influence on the way in which Americans view Obama. In fact, as figure 5.8 suggests, increasing support for the Tea Party indicates dampened perceptions of Obama's presidential traits more than anything else in the model, including social dominance and conservative ideology.[37] Substantively, the results indicate that support for the Tea Party dampens positive evaluations of Obama by 32 percent versus 20 percent and 10 percent for conservatism and social dominance orientation, respectively. Racial resentment reduces it by 6 percent.

On questions of personal approval, and hoping for the president's policies to fail, Tea Party supporters show a distinct and statistically significant relationship with anti-Obama opinions. With one exception, the association between Tea Party support and Obama-related attitudes is the most robust of all. For instance, as figure 5.9 shows, sympathizing with the Tea Party is associated with a 41 percent decrease in the probability of approving of Obama as a person, compared to decreases of 31 percent and 33 percent for racism and conservative ideology, respectively. Likewise, on issues of factual biographical information, we continue to find Tea Party sympathizers as statistical outliers. Our findings suggest that they are more likely than skeptics to believe conspiracy theories about President Obama's

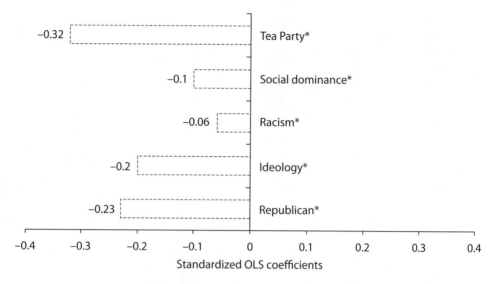

5.8. Agreement with positive Obama traits
*Significant at $p < 0.00$, one-tailed test

American citizenship and Christianity. For instance, supporting the Tea Party decreases the probability of believing Obama is Christian and an American citizen by 29 percent and 24 percent, respectively. Furthermore, along with a conservative ideology and racist attitudes, sympathizing with the Tea Party increases the probability of hoping Obama's policies fail by close to 20 percent. The remaining results are more of the same.

Throughout our analyses we have attempted to rule out any and all competing explanations that might possibly affect the observed relationship between Tea Party support and Obamaphobia. We have controlled for basic demographic characteristics of our respondents, such as age, education level, income level, gender, and race. We have also accounted for social and political predispositions, party affiliation, and ideology, as well as racial resentment, authoritarianism, ethnocentrism, and social dominance orientation. It didn't matter: support for the Tea Party remains wedded to Obama-related attitudes.

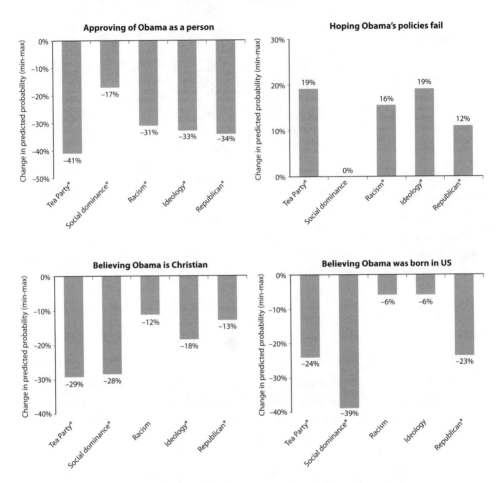

5.9. Association between Tea Party support and views toward Obama
*Significant at $p < 0.05$, one-tailed

These findings support our theoretical claim we made way back in chapter 1: support for the Tea Party is a proxy for reactionary conservatism. We arrive at this conclusion simply because even after we account for conservatism, support for the Tea Party continues to shape what people think about the president.[38] This suggests that there is a difference between Tea Party conservatives and non–Tea Party conservatives, or what we call reactionary conservatives. Of course, this lends support to our contention that Tea Party sympathizers are reactionary conservatives. Because support for the Tea Party continues to influence opinions on the president, we know it's not driven by ethnocentrism, racism, the feeling that Obama is out of compliance with social norms (authoritarianism), the belief that Obama symbolizes the rise of "Others" (social dominance), partisanship, or ideology. We're left with reactionary conservatism, a claim with which we feel comfortable, given the evidence supplied by our interviews, experimental results, and the content of Tea Party websites.

CONCLUDING THOUGHTS

In this chapter we have investigated the extent to which supporters of the Tea Party hold hostile views of President Obama. It is not a stretch to say that Tea Party sympathizers aren't keen on the president, but this is well known. By their own admission, and popular news stories, Tea Party supporters strongly oppose the president and campaigned vigorously in 2010 to regain control of the U.S. House of Representatives. What then is the contribution? We have demonstrated through both our review of Tea Party blog posts and our analysis of our survey evidence that Tea Party supporters go well beyond the simple Republican or conservative opposition to a Democratic president. Tea Party supporters have demonstrated a strong, negative reaction to the president, one that includes portraying him as un-American, immoral, and hoping that his policies fail.

Perhaps most important is the fact that support for the Tea Party continues to shape opinion after we account for alternative explanations, including ideology, partisan loyalty, and racism. This lends support for our claim that Tea Partiers are really reactionary conservatives, even as forces within the Tea Party maintain that the movement is mainstream. Therefore, if many of its supporters are in any way indicative of the larger movement, it's hard to make the case that it's mainstream.

6

Can You Hear Us Now?
Why Republicans Are
Listening to the Tea Party

I N THE PAST FEW CHAPTERS, we have focused on several issues of contemporary importance in America and to the Tea
Party. We've investigated freedom and patriotism. We also
explored the way people view policies geared to help marginalized groups get a fair shake in American society.[1] In chapter 5,
we explored public perceptions of the president. In each case,
the attitudes of Tea Party sympathizers represent a significant
departure, both substantively and statistically, from the rest of
the public. In this chapter we hope to illustrate why this matters. It's important, in our opinion, because it appears as though
the Tea Party and its supporters have the potential to convert
their sentiments into public policy. Of course, the principal vehicle for doing this is through political mobilization, pressuring
public officials to represent one's interests. If this doesn't happen, Americans who are dissatisfied with the performance of
their representatives will "throw the rascals out." Examples are

legion in which Tea Party–backed candidates supplanted establishment incumbents. So far, the Tea Party movement and its supporters appear to have followed through on this promise.

Throughout American history social movements have often been tied to political participation.[2] Social movements exist not just to bring attention to their issue, but also to capture the attention of public officials, often by promising to elect or eject from office key allies and opponents.[3] Based on their activism and political success in 2010, the Tea Party appears to be the most recent exemplar of the type of social movement capable of sparking political participation. Indeed, anecdotal accounts suggest the Tea Party was very active and engaged, holding hundreds of large and small rallies across all fifty states during the primaries and general election in 2010. News accounts declared that the Tea Party was motivated, enthusiastic, and ready to vote.[4]

It appears that Tea Party supporters participated at high levels. In 2010, Republicans won sixty-five seats in the House.[5] What's more, Tea Party–connected representatives made good on their promise to oppose the president's legislative agenda. To illustrate, 98 percent of the House Tea Party caucus voted against permitting sexual minorities from openly serving in the military, and 96 percent of them refused to support raising the debt limit.[6] Even so, since most of the evidence to date is anecdotal, it remains open to question whether or not the Tea Party is the mobilizing source people believe it to be.

From a distance, it appeared that Tea Party sympathizers were fully engaged in the political process. In fact, recent research on the Tea Party indicates that its members were deeply involved, to the point of knowing the legislative process in detail.[7] Still, it may well be the case that a pendulum merely swung back toward the Republican Party. Put differently, political independents and mainstream conservatives alike were more likely to vote, and to vote Republican. Such is often the case in American politics, with each political party gaining and losing momentum every four to six years, as voters, especially Independents, search for new ideas in government.

In 2006, Democrats made significant gains, claiming a majority in the U.S. House of Representatives after picking up additional House seats in 2008. Some analysts have argued that the Democrats overreached in those elections and the 2010 election was a mix of a natural correction, with some elevated enthusiasm for the Republican side, in which things simply "returned to equilibrium."[8] Thus, we have two competing stories about the 2010 election on which we can bring evidence to bear: Were Tea Party supporters more politically engaged than those unsympathetic to the aims of the Tea Party? Or did the 2010 election mark a normal return to equilibrium in which Republicans had a good year after two relatively poor showings in 2006 and 2008?

In this chapter, we explore the political consequences of the Tea Party as seen through its supporters. If Tea Party supporters were indeed more politically active, and politically cohesive, it brings even more relevance to their movement. Many social movements protest and call for change, but few ever get to the level of mobilizing millions of supporters, and like-minded individuals, to get involved in politics, to donate money to campaigns, to write letters lobbying Congress, and to vote en masse. When this transition does occur from protest to politics, it is often after years of organizing and mobilizing supporters. In the case of the Tea Party, it would appear that their movement went from inception to significant political influence in approximately eighteen months!

In fact, Tea Party supporters began to influence the political process early in the primary calendar, ousting Republican incumbents and party-anointed candidates in U.S. Senate contests in Utah and Kentucky. Recognizing this apparent advantage in political participation early on, Republican strategist Ed Goeas asked a key question in April 2010: "How long will this last [and] will that intensity be there in November?"[9] Indeed, this was the $64,000 question for a movement that burst onto the scene with no recognized leadership and no recognized structure: Would the Tea Party be able to generate mass mobilization and political participation and convert their loud voice into real political influence?

In what follows, we first discuss the relationship between social movements and political mobilization. We argue that the Tea Party is a hybrid of both, in which fear, anger, and anxiety at the perceived illegitimacy of Obama, and his policies, informs political behavior. We then canvass two modes of political activity: voting and nonvoting behavior. If our findings on Tea Party supporters are in any way indicative of the political engagement and mobilization of the Tea Party, we know why Republicans have listened to them: they are more likely than other segments of the mass public to pursue politics as a means of voicing their grievances. We then offer a few concluding thoughts.

From Mass Mobilization to Political Mobilization

A quick review of the political science literature on political participation reveals that most of the work conducted on mobilization separates social movements from other forms of political participation such as donating money to a campaign, writing your member of Congress, or voting. Social movement participation is clearly seen as a type of political participation, but ultimately scholars have sought to analyze it separately from other forms of political participation. As we scan notable social movements in past decades, it makes sense that social movement activism and protest seems to follow a different path than whether or not one votes in the midterm elections.

In describing various movements from pro-life, pro-choice, environmental, to civil rights, scholars tend to rely on what's come to be known as the "opportunity structure model." Here, movement leaders successfully rally their supporters at key intervals during which the political system is the most open to change.[10] Well-attended rallies and protests are often the principal objectives of movement organizers. The hope is that public officials will notice and work to assuage the movement's grievance(s). Of course, this is not always the case. Occasionally, social movements also encourage active political participation across the board, most notably voting.[11] We believe this is the case with the Tea Party.

Still, research on voter frustration, anger, and political alienation fails to conclude that such agitated voters will actually become more engaged in the political process. In fact, if their disgust and alienation is too strong, they may withdraw from formal participation in the political process altogether. People who are alienated may see formal participation, such as voting, as an act that makes no real difference. Some may turn to protest, instead, as a means of expressing their preferences without voting.[12] Some of the earliest work on political participation reveals that apathy and low levels of political efficacy, the perception that one's political participation will have some meaningful impact on the political system, may depress participation in engaging the political system.[13]

Moreover, a long line of research suggests that disapproval of government policy can create a sense of political alienation, or political disaffection, in which political engagement decreases.[14] It is certainly easy to describe Tea Party sympathizers as disapproving of nearly all government policy since the election of Barack Obama, and not just somewhat disapproving—they strongly disapprove of government policy under Obama. For instance, according to our 2011 poll, 79 percent of Tea Party supporters rejected health care reform versus 39 percent of everyone else. Likewise, for banking reform, our 2010 poll indicates that 58 percent of Tea Party sympathizers rejected banking reform compared to 22 percent for everyone else. The question, then, is whether or not Tea Party supporters feel politically alienated, or whether they maintain a sense of political efficacy and think they can influence change.

Fredric Templeton's study of political alienation in 1960 found that after adjusting for class, those with high levels of alienation were largely withdrawn from national politics, scored low on political knowledge, and told interviewers they were no longer interested in political affairs.[15] One problem Templeton notes is that alienated individuals tend to feel isolated and disconnected from networks in which people are active and engaged in the political process. Just as many pundits believe today, Templeton in 1966 blames the two major parties for having a stranglehold on national politics, which prevents viable alternative viewpoints from gaining salience, leaving frustrated Americans alienated.

This view is hard to square with the facts on the ground. As we have already indicated above, too many Tea Party–backed candidates won in 2010 for this to be true. Pushed by the perceived threat posed by Obama's presidency, and their frustration with the Republican Party under President Bush, it may be the case that once other factors are considered, Tea Partiers' political power may have been attenuated. In short, their political power may be an illusion, even if they don't necessarily abstain from political engagement. Since both Democrats and Republicans are seen as too institutionalized and mainstream, it may take the emergence of a right-wing (or left-wing) movement to capitalize on political disaffection, ultimately channeling this sentiment into political participation.

How can the politically disaffected reengage in the political process? The first step is to recognize the difference between alienation from the political *system*, and distrust of the current political *regime*. The political system is the long-standing political institutions that embody American government as a whole. Distrust of the political regime is directed at current (or recent) political authorities and political institutions that are characterized by individual political actors, making them less stable over time. In short, we doubt that Tea Party supporters have given up on the American political system, but we know they're upset with the current political regime insofar as the White House is now the target of their collective ire.

Second, we argue that Tea Party supporters are motivated to engage in politics for symbolic reasons: because it's a way to save "their" country. Let's be clear, we don't deny the possibility—even likelihood—that some believers participate in the political process because they derive some other benefit, including performing their duty as a citizen, among other things. But there's another benefit, a "purposive" benefit, one that accrues to one's participation in a worthy cause.[16] In this case, the cause is an opportunity for the Tea Party and its supporters to resist what they believe is the president's subversive policy agenda. To flesh this out a bit more, we turn to recent research in social psychology.

As we made clear in chapter 5, Tea Party supporters question the president's legitimacy. Here, we think it likely that, even though they may be politically disaffected, Tea Party supporters refused to sit on the sidelines in 2010 because they believed they needed to "take back their country" from a rogue president. Based on the evidence we have already presented, we don't think it's a stretch to say that Tea Party sympathizers question the legitimacy of the Obama administration. After all, we've already seen evidence of this in chapter 5, in which Tea Party supporters were more likely than the rest of the public to believe the president to be a Muslim and an alien (i.e., a noncitizen).

Toward this end, we turn to social psychology to suggest why politically disaffected individuals may dive into politics. One line of research suggests that illegitimacy, especially the perceived illegitimacy of political power, may serve as something of a mobilizing agent to prod the alienated to become involved in the political process.[17] The research suggests that if the group over whom power is wielded perceives that the power was either gained illegitimately or exercised illegitimately, the relatively powerless become angry, eventually challenging the perceived illegitimacy with all of the resources they have at their disposal. In this way, Tea Party supporters may turn political disaffection into symbolic political action, one representing their rejection of the policies of a president whom they believe illegitimate. In other words, despite their political disaffection, political engagement represents expressive political behavior, activism that goes beyond the material benefits that may accrue to taking the time to participate.[18]

The emergence of the Tea Party in 2009, and with it millions of sympathizers, presents something of a hybrid model of social movement and mass political mobilization. Rather than only staging large-scale protest events for media and policy-maker attention, Tea Party activists and supporters appeared to have a long-term agenda that expressly dealt with voter mobilization. Throughout their protest rallies, Tea Party supporters continued to call for new faces and new voices in our nation's capital, and specifically targeted Democratic and Republican incumbents to challenge and vote out of office. Thus, an integral part of what the Tea Party appeared to want was mass political participation in the 2010 primaries and general elections. Beyond just trying to influence the debate about health care or spending, Tea Party supporters claimed to be fed up with almost all politicians in Washington, D.C., and seemed to organize their social movement in tandem with mass political mobilization.

For a look at the hybrid model to which we refer, we need look no further than historical examples in which the Far Right proved effective at mixing social and political mobilization. Consider examples from the twentieth century. The Klan from the 1920s helped install state chief executives in Georgia, Oregon, and Maine. The Klan's political muscle wasn't restricted to state-level politics, either. Indeed, the Klan is credited with the election of a United States senator from Texas during this period.[19]

The John Birch Society (JBS) can't claim this type of success. Even so, it was effective in its own right. The JBS was considered a key player in successfully securing Senator Barry Goldwater's nomination to represent the GOP in the 1964 presidential election when he opposed President Lyndon B. Johnson. The JBS and its supporters are also credited with playing an important role in Ronald Reagan's successful candidacy in California's gubernatorial race in 1966, when he defeated two-term incumbent

Pat Brown. Most important, perhaps, is that the JBS is recognized for providing the foundation for the grassroots conservative movement that emerged in the 1960s, which eventually elevated the erstwhile Governor Reagan to the presidency in 1980.[20]

We expect to observe similar patterns with the Tea Party in its ability to mobilize the masses for sustained political action. If we are correct, and the Tea Party is really a vehicle for reactionary conservatism, we should expect their perceived illegitimacy of Obama's presidency to motivate their supporters' engagement in the political process. We realize some people may *legitimately* argue that Tea Party supporters are really motivated by their commitment to conservatism, or that they're committed Republican partisans, claims validated in chapter 2. Still, evidence presented in that chapter also squares with our claim: Tea Party sympathizers are motivated by something that transcends politics or conservatism.

In the present context, that is, political engagement, we argue that questioning the legitimacy of President Obama is an extension of reactionary conservatism. If we are correct, and the pattern we have observed throughout the book holds, we will ultimately find that the anxiety associated with the perception that an "illegitimate" president is prying the country away from them pushes believers to engage in politics beyond conventional explanations such as partisanship or even ideology. In sum, their anger, fueled by the perceived illegitimacy of the president, will help carry the day.

CONVENTIONAL EXPLANATIONS OF POLITICAL PARTICIPATION

While Tea Party supporters were new on the scene in 2009–10, a long-standing literature on political participation exists from which we can derive some expectations. Political science research points to a clear demographic pattern in political participation that could benefit Tea Party supporters. As the classic

The American Voter makes clear, and *The American Voter Revisited* further verified sixty years later,[21] age, class, and political interest are hallmarks of explaining participation. Older, more educated middle- and upper-income Americans are all more likely to participate in politics across a range of activities. The reasoning is simple: such Americans have more of a stake in the political system, and they have more to gain and lose. For these reasons, they are more likely to participate. Beyond a stake in the system, age, education, and income serve as resources on which citizens may draw, making them more effective at navigating the political system. Likewise, people who pay attention to current events, and who are politically interested, are much more likely to get involved. On both of these accounts, supporters of the Tea Party already fall into the "likely to participate" category. As we demonstrated in chapter 2, Tea Party sympathizers are, demographically, more likely to be older, somewhat more educated, and have a higher income.

However, this raises an important question of whether or not the political participation of the Tea Party is really about being a Tea Party supporter or just about being somewhat older and middle- to upper-class. We turn to this question later when we account for the influence of age, education, income, and political interest to determine if there is any isolated effect of being a Tea Party supporter on political participation in 2010. So, while we have good reason to suspect Tea Party supporters participated at high rates, we have little to go on beyond speculation. A quick glance at some empirical evidence suggests that some Tea Party supporters may have sat out the election.

In Washington State, Tea Party favorite and Palin endorsee, Clint Didier, lost his primary challenge to a mainstream and well-known Republican, Dino Rossi, in the 2010 U.S. Senate primary election. In the primary election, the two Tea Party stronghold counties in which Didier won voted at relatively high rates. Even so, in the November general election, these same two counties managed to generate relatively low turnout,[22] and the mainstream Republican Rossi narrowly lost to Democrat Patty

Murray. Stories like this abound with the Tea Party, in which they claim high levels of mobilization in some states but fail to live up to expectations in others.

Crucial to the story about Tea Party supporters is whether or not they carried their message beyond frustration and converted it into political engagement. This has implications not just for the 2010 election, but well beyond, as right-wing movements will likely accompany the duration of the Obama presidency in one form or another, and the political viability of such movements is quite important to the study of American politics. In this chapter we return to our Multi-State Survey of Race and Politics to assess the empirical evidence for whether or not Tea Party supporters actually took part across a range of political participation at higher rates than the general public.

TEA PARTY SUPPORTERS AND POLITICAL PARTICIPATION IN 2010

Our survey asked respondents a range of typical questions about how actively they participate in politics, which we group into two broad categories: nonelectoral and electoral participation. There are many ways through which citizens may attempt to influence the political system. We'd like to assess the extent to which believers were able to bridge the two different participation domains and transform the grassroots energy they so clearly possess into formal political participation. Turning to our 2011 public opinion survey, we asked all respondents, "In general, how interested are you in news about what's going on in government?" We followed this question with the following: "Now we'd like to know, in general, how politically and socially active you've been. Please indicate whether or not you've attended a political meeting." If a person said yes, we asked if they had done so in the last twelve months. Finally, we also asked if our survey participants voted in the 2010 general election, and whether they supported the Republican or Democratic candidate in the U.S. House of Representatives election.

Foreshadowing our findings, we discovered that Tea Party sympathizers did participate in both nonelectoral and electoral political activity at higher rates than the general public. Further, our results indicate that simple ideological opposition to a Congress controlled by Democrats failed to make a tangible difference. Even if we limit the analysis to self-identified conservatives, our results indicate that Tea Party conservatives outperformed non–Tea Party conservatives on almost every dimension of political participation. Of course, this result is consistent with our findings in every chapter of this book, in which we illustrate differences between Tea Party conservatives and non–Tea Party conservatives.

We begin our investigation with nonelectoral political engagement. Here, we explore modes of political participation that don't include voting. We then examine electoral participation. In the present case, we consider whether or not one voted in the midterm elections in 2010, and whether or not one voted for the Republican candidate to represent them in their respective congressional districts.

Nonelectoral Political Engagement

We start with nonelectoral forms of political participation, where we expect Tea Party *activists* were more involved in the political process but have less clarity about the extent to which *sympathizers* were engaged. We also examine whether or not we can make distinctions between them and the rest of the mass public, people who aren't too keen on the Tea Party. Interest in politics serves as an initial barometer of political engagement, something that's considered a gateway to other, more demanding political activities.[23] In this sense, it is the least demanding form of political engagement. If Tea Party supporters are participating at higher rates, then we should first expect them to be more interested in politics than anyone else. If they are truly reactionary, and driven by their perceived illegitimacy of the president, we should expect them to be more interested in politics than the rest of the public, even other conservatives. It may also be the case that the surge in Tea Party–backed candidates who won in 2010 were from districts that were so evenly balanced, they are susceptible to the above-mentioned pendulum effect, in which the electoral balance switches back and forth. In this case, the Republican surge we witnessed in 2010 may simply be the typical give-and-take that happens during alternating election cycles. If this is the case, we may find few national differences between Tea Party supporters and the rest of the mass public.

Along with assessing interest in politics, we also examine whether or not Tea Party sympathizers are more likely to attend a political meeting than those less supportive of the movement. Political meetings are conducive to the discussion of new ideas, and are a place in which individuals may voice their opinions and express their dissatisfaction with the status quo on a face-to-face basis. More important, attending a political meeting of some kind is indicative of increasing political engagement, certainly beyond political interest, because it requires more initiative. If Tea Party sympathizers are truly dissatisfied with President Obama, and perceive him as an illegitimate chief executive, then it shouldn't take much to coax them into attending a political meeting, relative to folks for whom the Tea Party movement is an annoyance. On the other hand, if Tea Party supporters are not reacting to the current political environment in a unique way, their attendance at meetings will mirror the rest of America.

Figure 6.1 represents the results for political interest and attending a political meeting in the past twelve months. We find that true believers in the Tea Party were statistically more likely to express an interest in politics, and take part in political meetings, than any other group. For example, 74 percent of Tea Party supporters reported high levels of political interest compared to 67 percent of movement skeptics and 61 percent of those in the middle of the road. Almost a third (32%) of Tea Party supporters attended a political meeting compared to 25 percent of Tea Party skeptics. Just 19 percent of respondents in the middle of the road attended a meeting, leaving Tea Party sympathizers close to 10 percentage points higher.

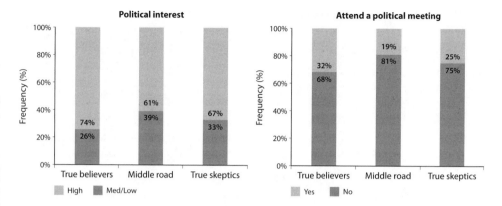

6.1. Nonelectoral engagement, by degree of Tea Party support
Note: Total N = 1188, with 308 true believers, 488 middle of the road,
and 392 true skeptics; relationships significant at χ^2 $p < 0.000$

Electoral Participation in 2010

In many ways, the nonelectoral participation may have laid the
groundwork for elevated voter turnout in 2010 by Tea Party
supporters. Scholars have long known that involvement or affiliation with political "groups" promotes electoral participation.[24]
Group-inspired political activity serves to keep the individual
focused on politics, provides information about candidates and
elections, and may even go so far as to organize get-out-the-vote
drives. When they weren't charging Obama with a socialist take-
over of America, or denouncing illegal immigrants and gays, Tea
Party activists often used their blogs, Listservs, and Facebook
networks to organize and promote electoral participation. Furthermore, participation in general is all the more important in
midterm elections, as research regularly reports a decrease in
turnout from the presidential election two years prior.[25]

   With this in mind, we expect that the Tea Party acted on their
anxiety and dissatisfaction, increasing the likelihood that, relative to Tea Party skeptics, they would vote. The need to recover
their country from, as we saw in chapter 1, their perception of
encroaching socialism, and to return America to its rightful heirs,

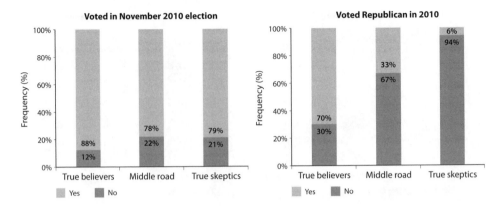

6.2. Electoral participation, by degree of Tea Party support
Note: Total N = 1188, with 308 true believers, 488 middle of the road, and 392 true skeptics; relationships significant at χ^2 $p < 0.000$

should have motivated and mobilized Tea Party sympathizers. Moreover, if we are correct, Tea Party supporters should have been actively working to oust supporters of President Obama and his political agenda at all costs, pushing their vote toward the Republican Party.

Turning to figure 6.2, the pattern of heightened Tea Party political participation is furthered in the electoral domain. A good 88 percent of Tea Party sympathizers reported voting. In contrast, 79 percent of Tea Party opponents and 78 percent of respondents in the middle of the road reported voting in 2010. The high turnout among Tea Party sympathizers is even more interesting considering the long tradition of reduced turnout in midterm elections in which public interest generally flags in the absence of a presidential campaign.

The final factor we consider is political choice. As we anticipated, Tea Party sympathizers voted overwhelmingly for Republican candidates to represent them in the House. Of course, skeptics went in the opposite direction, voting for Democrats. Overall, 70 percent of Tea Party sympathizers said they voted Republican, compared to just 6 percent of Tea Party opponents who voted Republican. Those in the middle failed to embrace the Republican Party, with only 33 percent voting for a Republican candidate.

While not surprising by the end of the 2010 election, this finding refutes some early accounts that the Tea Party had no real partisan leanings per se, and included large numbers of Democrats and Independents in its ranks.[26] This is simply not the case. Taking the above data into account, we find Tea Party supporters were quite active in the 2010 election. With high rates of political engagement, especially higher rates of voting, and voting Republican, it's hard to deny that Tea Party sympathizers' support was an important factor in Republicans retaking the House. If we consider the ways in which many House conservatives have often been steadfast in their refusal to compromise with President Obama, the influence of Tea Party sympathizers goes well beyond Election Day 2010.

Perhaps more important, the observed distinctions aren't simply about philosophical differences between true believers and nonbelievers. As figure 6.3 reveals, discrepancies also emerge between Tea Party conservatives and non–Tea Party conservatives. This is an important distinction, because a long line of research suggests that the party out of power, as far as the White House is concerned, generally mobilizes more than the party in the White House. This logic indicates that all conservatives may be politically motivated and active in 2010 across a variety of dimensions.

However, mainstream conservatives were not necessarily more active than anyone else. As the data reveals, Tea Party conservatives were the most active self-identified conservatives. For example, 40 percent of Tea Party conservatives attended a political meeting compared to just 18 percent of mainstream conservatives. Additionally, a full 85 percent of Tea Party conservatives reported high levels of political interest compared to 66 percent of other conservatives. The gap between Tea Party and non–Tea Party conservatives is maintained as the focus shifts to electoral participation. Continuing with results from figure 6.3, we

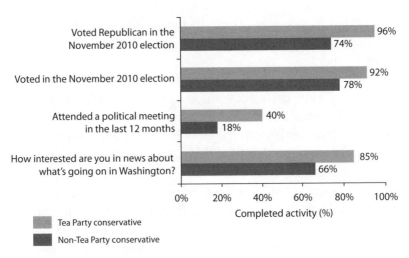

6.3. Political interest and participation in last twelve months among conservatives, by Tea Party support
Note: Total conservative N = 407, with 204 true believers in the Tea Party; relationships significant at χ^2 p < 0.000

note that among conservatives, Tea Party conservatives voted in the 2010 midterm elections at a higher rate (92 percent) than mainstream conservatives who voted at roughly the same rate as Tea Party opponents (78 percent). There is even more daylight separating conservative camps as we move beyond turnout and examine political choice. Our results indicate that 96 percent of Tea Party conservatives voted for their Republican House candidate while 74 percent of non–Tea Party conservatives did so. These results support our claim, first made in chapter 1, that Tea Party conservatives are different from non–Tea Party conservatives.

WERE TEA PARTY SUPPORTERS REALLY MORE COMMITTED THAN ANYONE ELSE?

Consistent with earlier chapters, we want to move beyond the comparative charts presented in figures 6.1 and 6.2 to determine whether or not being a Tea Party supporter has an independent effect on political participation beyond other factors that generally promote political engagement. Taking our cue from what's been written about political participation, we know well that a host of resource-based factors and political factors play a role in explaining who participates.[27] For example, it is well established that older, higher-income, and more educated individuals are more likely to participate in politics than those from other groups.[28] Furthermore, we know with almost certainty that taking an interest in politics and watching a great deal of political news coverage makes someone much more likely to participate in more time-consuming political activities than those who don't. In this section we adjust for the influence of these additional factors to isolate the Tea Party effect and determine if support for the Tea Party is associated with participation in 2010.

We first assess the influence of Tea Party support on political interest. From here, we take into account the influence of political interest when examining the predictive power of Tea Party support for our other, more intensive nonelectoral and electoral activities. Based on our earlier findings, our claim remains the same: fear, anger, and anxiety over the perceived illegitimacy of the Obama presidency should be associated with increased political engagement in 2010.

Across all four items, even after accounting for other factors that are also associated with political engagement, such as age, education, income, and political knowledge, we find Tea Party supporters are indeed more likely to participate. In other words, as attraction to the Tea Party increases, so too does the likelihood of having an interest in politics and attending a meeting. Specifically, figure 6.4 indicates that a believer in the Tea Party is 7 percent more likely than a skeptic to be interested in politics. Similarly, when it comes to attending a political meeting, attraction to the Tea Party appears to increase the probability by 4 percent that these people attended a political meeting in 2010 than skeptics. Yet, the difference between the two camps is essentially meaningless since the results aren't statistically significant. In other words, believers and skeptics are equally likely to attend meetings.

Moreover, as figure 6.4 shows, people who are more politically knowledgeable and conservative are more interested in politics than the politically ignorant and liberals, respectively. It's worth noting that once we switched from trying to understand what motivated political interest in 2010 to the motivation behind people attending meetings, we wished to gauge the relative importance of political interest when it comes to people attending political meetings. As it turns out, this has a more robust association with attending meetings than anything else. Interestingly, the importance of ideology is attenuated, suggesting that, for conservatives, attending meetings is really all about political interest.

If we found differences in political interest and attending meetings, both of which are relatively low-hanging fruit when it comes to political engagement, we should have no trouble finding differences as we move to voting behavior, for this entails a bit more initiative. As the results suggest, it will be a challenge for our proxy for reactionary conservatism, Tea Party support, to have a meaningful impact on electoral participation. Our model of voter turnout reveals a number of other important predictors.[29]

Still, beyond these well-established factors, we find evidence that Tea Party supporters were more likely to vote than Tea Party skeptics. Again, figure 6.4 shows that beyond the influence of other important factors generally associated with voting, such as political interest, knowledge, and ideology, supporting the Tea Party increases an individual's probability of voting by 5 percent. We're aware that this doesn't sound like much, but the fact that it's statistically significant is almost shocking, given all of the well-established explanations for voting for which we have accounted.

When it comes to gauging the party for whom one voted, we find the same trend. Even though there are several consistent predictors of voter choice, including controls for partisanship and ideology, sympathizing with the Tea Party increases the likelihood that respondents voted Republican in 2010. In fact,

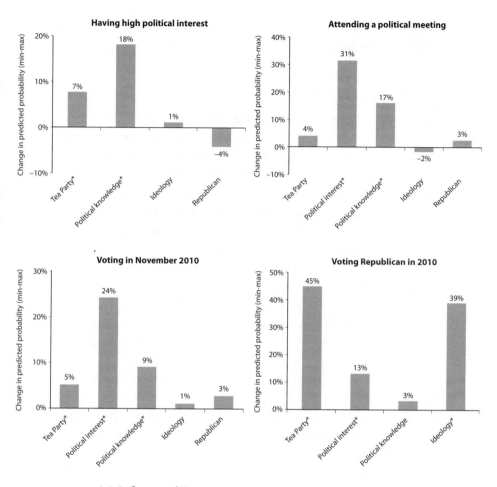

6.4. Influence of Tea Party support on political participation
*Significant at $p < 0.05$, one-tailed

when it comes to voting for a Republican candidate in 2010, the best predictor is whether or not someone is a Tea Party supporter. As figure 6.4 indicates, believers were 45 percent more likely than skeptics to vote for the GOP. The results also indicate the salience of other factors. For instance, the likelihood of voting for the Party of Lincoln increased by 13 percent, 3 percent, and 39 percent for those politically interested, knowledgeable, and conservative, respectively, over those who were politically apathetic, not very knowledgeable, and liberal.

■   ■   ■

Several chapters earlier, we mentioned a number of factors that may furnish the motivation for the Tea Party and its supporters. Specifically, in chapter 1, in which we conducted the long interviews, we detected both anger and fear in many of the responses surrendered by Tea Party sympathizers. Assessing political participation indirectly helps to adjudicate which emotion appears to have been the most prevalent among Tea Party supporters.

As social psychologists have discovered, anger, particularly intergroup anger, is most likely to flare when desired outcomes of the group to which one belongs is threatened by the actions of a different group. This is an extension of Richard Lazarus's work, in which he asserts that anger ensues when "a particular goal [is] frustrated . . . namely[,] the preservation or enhancement of ego-identity."[30] Since the individual generally derives her sense of self from membership in a particular social group,[31] it's logical to conclude that any perceived attempt to diminish the status of her group will be read as an assault on her status as well. Of course, we have argued all along that Obama, and what his presidency represents, is a threat to the social prestige of "real Americans." Given the fact that threat also induces anxiety, something that spurs political engagement,[32] we cannot afford to rule it out as a factor that motivates the political participation of believers. It seems, then, that we can rule out fear as something that motivates believers. We say so because it is associated with an immediate threat to one's physical safety that leads to the perception of insecurity and subsequent flight.[33] Extending this to political engagement, this suggests that fearful people will withdraw from politics.

At first glance, these don't seem like they're very important distinctions to make. Both are nothing more than negative emotions. Still, they're also associated with very different behavioral profiles. For instance, as psychologists have made clear, people who are full of fear tend to move away from the threat, avoiding behavior in any way associated with risk. In short, fearful people are inclined to adopt a defensive posture. People who are angry, on the other hand, tend to accept risk and confront threat, including threatening out-groups. In other words, they tend to favor offense over defense.[34]

To the extent that the Tea Party has demonstrated its courage, even aggression at times, it seems clear that most of the people associated with the movement are motivated more by anger than anything else. Extending this framework to political participation, we make no claims that voting or attending is at all risky in the present climate. Yet, it does represent going on the offensive versus staying home, and it's also consistent with reactionary tendencies discussed by Hofstadter and Rossiter.

Our results, moreover, add to a growing list in which solidarity and commitment push group members to overcome costs associated with participation in the political process. What's new and substantively significant about the Tea Party and its supporters, though, is that most of the time people are coaxed into political participation, it comes from the left, for the purpose of redistributing power and resources. One counterexample that's often offered is the New Right, where many attributed Ronald Reagan's victory in 1980 to a faction of the New Right: the Christian Right. But Clyde Wilcox, among many others, disproved that folk wisdom.[35]

After accounting for competing explanations, Wilcox found that the Christian Right failed to have a meaningful impact on political participation. The other examples we cited toward the beginning of this chapter, that is, the Klan and the JBS, have yet to have their political participation empirically scrutinized in the same fashion in which we've scrutinized the Tea Party's engagement. So, in addition to everything else, our findings indicate that identification with the Far Right is capable of sustaining political engagement beyond other factors, notably partisanship and ideology. This is key because, as Wilcox demonstrated, such political facts ultimately trumped what some believed to be the decisive impact of the Christian Right on Reagan's run for the White House in 1980.

Concluding Thoughts

The Tea Party and its supporters are admittedly upset, frustrated, and distrustful of government. Even so, they are clearly not politically alienated or withdrawn. On the contrary, in 2010, Tea Party supporters appeared eager to dive into politics, mobilizing in an effort to influence the political system. Recent events suggest their eagerness is paying off. Whether it was attending a political meeting or voting in the 2010 election, we found strong and consistent evidence that Tea Party sympathizers outperformed other Americans. Before the 2010 election, people speculated whether or not the Tea Party would have a real political impact. On the one hand, some social science theories suggest that political frustration and anger may lead to alienation and withdrawal. Elsewhere, some pundits suggested that the Tea Party effect was overstated and that 2010 was nothing more than a return to political equilibrium. Still, others suggested that *all* conservatives were fed up and ready to take political action, not just the Tea Party supporters.

Each of these ideas has some merit. Still, the data we have gathered suggests they all come up short, and that, in fact, Tea Party sympathizers were much more likely than others to wade into the political process. We maintain that their reaction to whom they perceive as an illegitimate president drove sympathizers' political engagement. How else can we explain it? Prior to our analysis a critic could credibly charge that Tea Party supporters were no more committed to opposing Obama's policies than other partisans and conservatives. Now, however, we know this isn't true: sympathizers are motivated by something else. Throughout, we have maintained that beneath the anger and anxiety demonstrated by Tea Party supporters is a sense that Obama and his confederates seek to destroy the country. This chapter demonstrates this sentiment isn't confined to perceptions of freedom and patriotism (chapter 3), intergroup relations (chapter 4), or how people view the president (chapter 5). Our results confirm the explanatory power of reactionary conservatism.

Conclusion

I T'S HARD TO OVERESTIMATE the Tea Party movement's impact on contemporary American politics since their emergence following Barack Obama's inauguration. With their assistance, Republicans have regained the majority in the U.S. House of Representatives, continue to make inroads in the U.S. Senate, and have won a majority in many statehouses across the country. What's more, in late 2011, CNN even hosted a "Tea Party Express" Republican Debate for the nine Republican presidential candidates, a nod to the growing influence of the movement. And throughout the lengthy Republican primary process in 2012, a key discussion point on almost every news show from Fox News to MSNBC was for whom Tea Party supporters voted.

We were motivated to write this book for two reasons. First, as we write this book, the Tea Party is an important player in American politics and, justifiably, the subject of great national interest. As social scientists, we sought to bring an objective, theory-driven, data-supported examination to the study of the Tea Party movement. Second, instead of focusing our study on Tea Party members and Tea Party organizations, we sought to explore the attitudes and behavior of Tea Party sympathizers. We did so primarily because relatively few people ever become an official member of a social movement. As our findings indicate, it's no different for the Tea Party. In our effort to focus on

Tea Party supporters instead of activists, we seek to shift the intellectual discussion from movement members and activists to movement sympathizers. We also sought to create a framework by which people can better understand right-wing movements in general, not just the Tea Party.

In fact, as we have mentioned, right-wing movements have been a topic of discussion for many years. With his book *The Paranoid Style in American Politics*, renowned historian Richard Hofstadter made a seminal contribution to the way we understand such movements. He explains that the paranoid "believes himself to be living in a world in which he is spied upon, plotted against, betrayed, and very likely destined for total ruin."[1] This sounds very similar to the sentiments of those who support the Tea Party. Many have said they believe President Barack Obama un-American in at least two ways: they see him as an alien and believe him to be a socialist. As a consequence, they perceive Obama is in the process of dismantling the "real" America they know and love. Again, we believe this perception of threat to America is something that ultimately results in Tea Party supporters' subscription to reactionary conservatism.

As we mentioned in the book's introduction, approximately 450,000 people are official members of the national Tea Party movement, but approximately 45 million Americans identify with the Tea Party. A better understanding of the political success of the Tea Party, therefore, requires us to move beyond its core members and focus instead on a much larger segment of the population: people who are attracted to the movement and its ideology, but who for various reasons cannot or will not officially join it. Ultimately, this permits us to gain a better understanding of the broader impact of the movement, in addition to appreciating why some are motivated to support the Tea Party.

We opened this book by asking two basic questions, both of which play off opposing sides in a clash between people who support the Tea Party and those critical of the movement. The first question has to do with the motivation(s) of the Tea Party and its supporters. The Tea Party and their sympathizers claim to be motivated by conservative principles and nothing more. Critics are skeptical of that claim, charging that the movement is motivated more by out-group hostility than anything else. Our claim was simply that neither out-group hostility nor adherence to conservative principles are the *only* ways of understanding why people are sympathetic to the aims of the Tea Party. We argued that Tea Party support is also associated with social change perceived as subversion. Our position is that the election and subsequent presidency of Barack Obama represents change that the movement and its supporters *just simply can't believe in*. In fact, they seek to resist it. For the second question, we sought to confront the consequences of supporting the Tea Party. We argued that support for the Tea Party is really a proxy for reactionary conservatism. As such, we anticipated that it would provide a different motivation for various attitudes and behavior associated with current political and policy issues. Both claims were confirmed.

We are not the first to claim that the Tea Party is, at least in part, a response to Obama's presidency. Nor are we the first to link the Tea Party to various outcomes. Others, most notably, Skocpol and Williamson, make similar claims.[2] Still, our study differs from the others in manifold ways. First, for reasons discussed above, our focus resides with Tea Party supporters, not members or activists. Second, we elaborate and test a theory of Tea Party support. In doing so, we account for several competing explanations in our analysis beyond the usual suspects: partisanship, ideology, demographics, and even racism. Indeed, we also rule out other forces that may lead some to support the Tea Party, including the desire for social conformity (authoritarianism), preference for one's in-group, and the belief that some groups aren't fit to be equal (social dominance orientation). Third, we subject our claims about the meaning of Tea Party support to rigorous tests across several domains using multiple evidentiary sources, including historical analysis, content analysis of Tea Party websites, in-depth interviews, and a comprehensive public opinion survey. Fourth, we link the Tea Party to national right-wing movements in the twentieth century.

At this point in the book, we realize that we've given the reader much to digest. In the interest of crystallizing the main takeaway points for the reader, in the balance of the conclusion, we shall revisit our main points and place our findings into a broader context. However, prior to elaborating on these points below, we'd like to first distill them. All of our evidence, including the survey data, interviews, and content analysis of official Tea Party websites, converge on the following:

- Among other things, support for the Tea Party is ultimately driven by threat associated with a perception on the part of supporters that their country is slipping away, something linked to Obama's presidency.

- Support for the Tea Party is a proxy for reactionary conservatism, something quite different from more mainstream conservatism. As we detail below, this is a crucial distinction.

- This finding, therefore, undermines the claim that Tea Party supporters are committed conservatives.

- The evidence undermines the claim that Tea Party supporters are no more than average—if somewhat angry—Americans.

- Contrary to their stated position, Tea Party supporters don't always support freedom.

- If patriotism is defined as sacrifice, that is, placing the needs of the nation above one's self-interest, Tea Party supporters aren't necessarily patriotic.

- Politics, a preference for social conformity, and various sources of group-based intolerance cannot account for Tea Party supporters' hostility toward minorities.

- Politics, group-based intolerance, and racism cannot completely account for the contempt with which Tea Party supporters hold their president.

- Tea Party supporters are politically engaged, far more so than those who have a less-than-flattering impression of the movement, and more than non–Tea Party conservatives.

- The Tea Party is the latest representation of right-wing social movements that periodically crop up when dominant groups perceive their way of life is threatened.

Taken together, these ten points represent the larger message we hope the reader takes from the book. Below, we elaborate on these points. In what follows, we first recap our principal findings. Along the way, we respond to possible objections critics may raise. We then make the case for why this book transcends the Tea Party and its sympathizers, and why the framework we have worked out will help us better understand right-wing movements. We cap the conclusion, and the book, with a discussion of the implications attached to our findings.

PRINCIPAL FINDINGS

In the book's introduction, we observed that Americans have debated about the proper role of government in American social and economic life for quite some time, and that this would likely affect people's attachment to the Tea Party. While not stating it in these terms, the Tea Party and its supporters, from the beginning of the movement, have declared their fidelity to conservative principles. It's true that Tea Party supporters are conservative; still, our findings indicate that they aren't the kind of conservatives with which conservative intellectuals feel comfortable. In fact, we show throughout the book that Tea Party supporters, as conservatives, are quite distinct from non–Tea Party conservatives.

As we demonstrated in chapter 1, we must be careful to distinguish Tea Party conservatives from more moderate conservatives because there are marked differences between the two. At both the elite and mass levels, Tea Party conservatives tend to buy into conspiratorial beliefs about President Obama, far more so than non–Tea Party conservatives. As the late conservative political theorist Clinton Rossiter suggests in his work on conservatism, this tendency toward hyperbole and exaggeration is commensurate with a belief system removed from the conservative mainstream, in which a premium is placed on order and stability, and cautions against buying into demagoguery. Furthermore, as historian Geoffrey Kabaservice details in a recent book on the demise of moderate Republicans since the 1950s, more mainstream conservatives are inclined to pragmatic solutions to the nation's problems; more extreme conservatives, not so much.[3]

The distinction between mainstream and reactionary conservatives should not be taken lightly.[4] Consider some of the policy preferences and positions most recently taken by the Tea Party. Their willingness to risk potential economic disaster during the first debt-ceiling standoff, and threats to repeal parts of the Fourteenth Amendment, suggests that Tea Party conservatives appear committed to something other than conservative principles. Indeed, these policy preferences and aims appear at variance with some of the most prominent conservative thinkers of the twentieth century, including Robert A. Taft, Russell Kirk, and William Buckley, insofar as each believed in the preservation of social unity and social order. Of course, the difference between Tea Party conservatives and the conservative mainstream reminds us of a similar split among conservatives fifty years ago when Governor Nelson Rockefeller led the more mainstream conservatives, and Senator Barry Goldwater was associated with something akin to the reactionary conservatives of their day: the John Birch Society.[5]

Hostility directed toward out-groups broadly defined, of course, represents the other long-standing influence on American social and political life. The Tea Party and its sympathizers are steadfast in their denial that out-group hostility of any kind has anything to do with the movement. Ultimately, however, we found that racism and a preference for maintaining a social order in which egalitarianism isn't a priority (social dominance orientation) does motivate people to support the Tea Party. The critics are correct. Based on the composition of the Tea Party, and many incidents in which the Tea Party has been accused of bigoted behavior, these findings shouldn't come as a complete surprise. Even so, we wish to make it clear that the results fail to suggest that *all* Tea Party supporters are against egalitarianism, or that *all* of them are racist. In like fashion, our findings don't completely exonerate those who hate the Tea Party: some opponents of the Tea Party are, themselves, racist. Instead, a fair interpretation of the evidence indicates that, on average, true believers in the Tea Party tend to harbor *much, much* more group-based hostility than true skeptics of the movement.

This brings us to the significance of the confirmation of our first claim. The fact that both critics and supporters' claims about the Tea Party are correct, and that we still find support for the association between affinity for the movement and fear and anxiety associated with Barack Obama's presidency, suggests that our findings are genuine. Validating our hunch, after accounting for all of the other explanations related to other long-standing predispositions, like partisanship and limited government, tells us that at least some of the sentiment associated with the Tea Party is reactionary, driven by the perception that the president is a threat to the country, leader of a conspiracy to ruin America, or not even a real American himself. If this is true, and our evidence suggests that it is, believers sound a whole lot like the Far Right that Hofstadter references when he describes them as full of "heated exaggeration, suspiciousness, and conspiratorial fantasy."[6]

The second question for which we sought an answer revolves around the consequences associated with supporting the Tea Party. We argued that identification with the Tea Party serves as a rough proxy for reactionary conservatism. As such, we claimed that it has something to say across a range of contemporary beliefs, issues, and behavior in American politics. Even after accounting for predispositions central to American social and political life, approval of the Tea Party can tell us how

Americans view patriotism and freedom, how they see marginalized groups, and whether or not they're actively engaged in politics. Of course, support for the Tea Party is connected to the way people perceive President Obama. Beyond the fact that Tea Party supporters are energized, having the courage of their convictions to make necessary noise and to press politicians to listen, what else are we to glean from our results?

For one thing, by virtue of their commitment to their cause, as their engagement in politics suggest, their patriotism is evident. This is squarely in accord with the more classic definition of patriotism outlined in chapter 3, as one's willingness to sacrifice one's self-interest for the good of the community. Still, as our results from the same chapter make clear, the patriotism of Tea Party believers has limits.

Patriotism, for sympathizers, doesn't extend to minorities in search of equality, nor does it attach to providing the less fortunate access to better education, even if it means strengthening the country. It really all comes down to how one defines patriotism. If patriotism is about individualism and self-interested behavior, the Tea Party may rightly celebrate its patriotism. If, however, patriotism is about self-sacrifice, placing the common good (as it applies to all, minorities included) and therefore the good of the country before self-interest, the Tea Party cannot be considered patriotic. We think their rejection of self-sacrificial patriotism may have something to do with the groups who stand to benefit: racial and sexual minorities. After all, as sociologist John Skrentny points out, it's generally people from marginalized groups with whom fights over rights are identified,[7] and these are the people from whom the Tea Party wishes to retrieve their country.

Ultimately, it's the same story for freedom, for which we used civil liberties as a proxy. The Tea Party often claims it wishes to limit the reach of government, yet its supporters are okay with racial profiling? Again, this seems more about "taking back their country" than limiting big government, since whites are far less likely to be subjected to racial profiling than any other group. In contrast, true believers wished to limit the intrusion of government when it came to the protection of free speech. But since we considered possible alternative explanations that included conservative principles and the desire for social conformity, we're left with the likelihood that the selection of civil liberties in this case is more about resisting big government under the control of someone they perceive is destroying the country than resisting big government out of principle. At the end of the day, it's hard to say that the Tea Party and its supporters stand by their claims of patriotism and liberty. Rather, it seems that they stand for the selective application of patriotism and liberty, reserving it for like-minded Tea Party supporters.

The results are similar when it comes to the extension of equal treatment to "Others." Since we accounted for every conceivable alternative explanation, we are left to consider only that believers are motivated to oppose more egalitarian policies out of threat they believe to be masked as change: that they're losing their country to groups they fail to recognize as "real" Americans. Similarly, attitudes directed toward President Obama aren't totally about ideology or partisanship. Nor are they even completely driven by racism. Instead, it seems likely that the connection between support for the Tea Party and beliefs about Obama is motivated by a fear on the part of believers that the president is an alien, out to destroy the United States as they know it.

If we take a step back, it's possible to see a theme emerging. Groups beyond the boundaries of what's recognized as the American norm, that is, white, native-born, and heterosexual, are shunned. These are the groups from whom the Tea Party hopes to wrest the country. Using Frank Rich's article in the *New York Times* as the datum for our narrative, a reference first identified in the introduction, we've now come full circle. Indeed, our analysis parallels his observations that Obama and minority groups signal a change in which the Tea Party cannot believe. Only our analysis is far more rigorous. In fact, our data confirms an observation made many years ago by Lipset and Raab. Surveying a swath of time spanning almost two hundred years, they observed a pattern among right-wing movements in which there is "a tendency to treat cleavage . . . as illegitimate."[8] Difference of any kind, in other words, is not tolerated.

At this point, we'd like to identify at least three such objections to our findings. The first one is that our survey, on which we lean so heavily, is limited to just thirteen states. A critic may credibly charge that our conclusions are valid only for those states. Even though our survey didn't cover the entire country, it compares very favorably to several contemporaneous national surveys in which support for the Tea Party was a principal focus.[9]

A second objection is related insofar as it touches on methodology. Some may well wonder how we can use Tea Party support as something we attempt to determine in chapter 2, only to turn around and use it to determine various attitudes and behaviors in subsequent chapters. For those who have difficulty with us using Tea Party support like this, we turn to theory as a means of explaining our reasoning. Theoretically, as we have already made clear, reactionary conservatism, for which Tea Party support is a proxy, is a predisposition: a product of social learning. Thus, we thought it wise to assay it's determinants first. Since it is ontologically prior to the attitudes and behaviors investigated in chapters 3–6 (it's a predisposition), we used Tea Party support as a means to explore just how much reactionary conservatism is capable of explaining. This process is similar to the ways in which scholars in the social sciences introduce (or revise) major theoretical interventions.[10]

The third, perhaps more serious charge is that we overlooked something fairly obvious in our search for sources and consequences of Tea Party support: moral outrage. Sociologist James Jasper's work makes a strong case for placing more emphasis on the moral dimension of social protest in which activists are moved to act out of a perceived violation of values.[11] According to Tea Party activists and supporters, fiscal responsibility and small government are among their most important value-based objectives. Hence, applying the moral outrage framework may explain their opposition to President Obama and what they believe are his big government policies, not perceived subversion masquerading as change, which we claim. In other words, it could be the perceived violation of values associated with fiscal responsibility and economic individualism on the part of the president (or Democrats) that raises the hackles of Tea Party supporters.

This is a point we readily concede. We don't make a case for moral outrage, but we have reasons for not doing so. We won't list them all here, but we'd like to emphasize at least one. If the Tea Party and its followers were genuinely driven by moral outrage, we should have seen it during George W. Bush's presidency. During President Bush's first term, the federal deficit expanded more than it ever had in our nation's history. While the Bush tax cuts benefited a segment of the population, they limited revenues available to the federal government, and accounted for almost a third of the cumulative deficit during the Bush administration.[12] Certainly, the wars in Afghanistan and Iraq were expensive; however, Bush also increased discretionary spending by 49 percent during his presidency, spending twice as much as his predecessor, Democrat Bill Clinton. On Bush's watch, adjusting for inflation, the federal budget increased by 104 percent compared to the Clinton-era increase of 11 percent. Finally, when Bush took over as president, he inherited a $700 billion surplus from his predecessor. Upon departing office, he left his successor, Barack Obama, a $1.3-trillion deficit—a $2 trillion swing. Mulling over the facts, conservative economist Chris Edwards has gone so far as to call President Bush "The Biggest Spender since LBJ."[13] While we think moral outrage may well help explain the emergence of the Tea Party, and frame its objectives, we find no evidence to support that position.

WHY IT MATTERS, TAKE 1: CONTINUITIES WITH THE FAR RIGHT

From the beginning, we have been careful to reference right-wing movements only as a means of situating the Tea Party historically, and to provide a rough model for our theoretical framework. Now, after exhaustive analysis, we have arrived at a point at which we feel the data are very clear. In this case, the facts suggest that the Tea Party and its supporters look a lot like the Ku Klux Klan of the 1920s and the John Birch Society (JBS) of the 1960s. Consider the demographic composition of all three groups: white, middle-class, middle-aged, heterosexual (at least on the surface) men. We have already documented this in chapter 1 for the Klan and the JBS, and for our survey, this is recorded in chapter 2. Our findings are confirmed by several contemporaneous studies.[14]

The Far Right has been the subject of intellectual inquiry for a long time. The work of Hofstadter and his colleagues in the 1950s and 1960s is probably the best of the lot. Hofstadter's work is both widely praised and criticized.[15] For our money, he probably received too much of both. Nonetheless, among the many allegations leveled by Hofstadter, Lipset, and others against the Far Right is its aversion to change, something that is perceived as a threat to its constituents' way of life. For the Klan of the 1920s, as we have discussed, blacks, Jews, Catholics, the increasing independence of women, and labor radicalism were all perceived as threats to the America that Klansmen and their followers had come to know and love. The JBS blamed the "eastern elites" for the swarm of communism that threatened the country. Communism was attached to almost anything that failed to conform to the "American" way of life, including racial equality, gay rights, women's rights, and programs designed to alleviate (if not eliminate) poverty. With the Tea Party and its supporters, change and the attendant threat are associated with the president and the malign intent the movement assigns his policies.

It's also hard to dismiss the tendency of all three to buy into conspiracy theories of some kind. For the Klan, blacks, Jews, Catholics, and labor radicals were going to destroy the country if they weren't stopped. The JBS believed eastern elites and their communist allies had put the United States on the road to totalitarianism. It was left up to the JBS and its supporters to prevent this from happening. The Tea Party and its allies, as we have seen, believe President Obama is out to destroy the country, or that he is a secret Muslim, or that he was not born in America. Of course, this would undermine his status as a "real" American. Thus, they are firm in their commitment to stop him. Agree or disagree with their methods or objectives, they are well on their way to accomplishing their task. We must commend them for their commitment.

All three are also hard to defend as conservative movements. We first consider the Klan of the 1920s. The Klan sought to enforce white supremacy and strict adherence to a moral code they thought appropriate through the implied and manifest use of violence. For instance, intimidation and violence were employed as a means of keeping "uppity" African Americans in their place. Similarly, coercion and violence was used as a tool to police wayward, irresponsible husbands from public drunkenness, squandering their earnings on vice, and mistreating their families. The Klan's violation of conservatism is pretty clear. Vigilantism does everything but encourage social order and stability.

The JBS insisted that the evil of communism would destroy the country—from the inside out. As we touched on in the introduction, the founder of the JBS, Robert Welch, never hesitated to identify levels of communist infiltration, which reached as far as the White House and the Supreme Court, among other institutions. And, as we mentioned, there is some evidence to suggest that rank-and-file members failed to embrace what boiled down to charging former supreme Allied commander and current president Dwight D. Eisenhower, and a sitting Supreme Court chief justice and former governor of California, Earl Warren, with treason. Even so, local chapters engaged in a massive letter-writing campaign in a bid to impeach the chief justice. They did, however, believe the struggle against the communist way of life to be a good-versus-evil, life-and-death battle. So, there was what bordered on a maniacal preoccupation with big government "collectivism," a situation that was perceived as threatening a pillar of "true Americanism": the autonomy for one to make one's own choices and bear responsibility for the results. For the most part, these were scared, suspicious people, folks afraid they'd lost control of their lives.[16]

Thus, the JBS ran afoul of conservatism in a number of ways. First, the policy preferences flowing from the JBS would lead to instability. Refusing to recognize the legitimacy of the Supreme Court flies in the face of more traditional conservatism in which the rule of law is of critical importance for the maintenance of a free society, in which the court serves as a bulwark against the passions of the masses.[17] Moreover, the discord sewn by the JBS toward core institutions such as churches and schools—not to mention the central government—affected the social unity for which conservatism calls. Finally, casting as treasonous those whose beliefs failed to align with JBS doctrine represents a flagrant violation of freedom, a chief goal of conservatism.

It appears, then, that a case can be made that the Klan and the JBS, and the reactionary conservatism to which they appeared wedded, were beyond traditional conservatism, something on which a parade of conservative intellectuals have agreed. There are differences between the two in the extent to which each departed from conservative principles. Both were reactionary in that they failed to embrace the change that took place and stressed a desire to recapture principles associated with an America of bygone times.

The Klan departed in both thought and deed from conservatism. Its intolerant creed, masquerading as "Americanism," clashed with conservative principles. While the Klan drew on conventional means to achieve its ends, its violent and coercive methods carried it beyond the bounds of conservatism. The tactics of the JBS and its supporters, including the letter-writing campaigns and store boycotts, were squarely within accepted political practices. Indeed, this organization hardly accepted the violence or overt racial and religious intolerance associated with the Klan. Yet the tactical goals of the JBS, especially its founder, Robert Welch, were anything but conservative.

Doubting the legitimacy of a sitting president? This is patently unpatriotic, an offense for which arguably the most dominant conservative intellectual at the time, William Buckley Jr., ejected the JBS from the conservative movement in 1965.[18] Sowing distrust between citizens and key institutions—by seeing anything that so much as suggested social progress as a communist plot—accomplished very little beyond posing a threat to order and stability. In short, these are all serious violations of the tenets of conservatism.

For now, the Tea Party is still in its infancy, but as our data suggests, it seems a lot like its twentieth-century forbears. We'd be more skeptical if all of our data didn't point in the same direction, but it does. If our interpretation is correct, the Tea Party seems very much like a reactionary movement. How else does one explain doubting the legitimacy of a sitting president? What about the desire to fiddle with the Constitution, the document they claim to revere, over birthright citizenship? What about Tea Party elites, like Sarah Palin, placing crosshairs on congressional districts in which the representatives cooperated with the president on health care reform? How does one account for a group that pressures its representatives in the House to refuse to meet the president and the Democrats halfway on raising the debt ceiling? We'll allow the reader to draw his or her own conclusions. But the parallels between the Tea Party and national right-wing movements of the past seem striking to us. They all appear to be reactionary.

WHY IT MATTERS, TAKE 2: CONTEMPORARY POLITICS

Understanding the roots of Tea Party support and its reactionary lineage may encourage better understanding of contemporary politics. Studying Tea Party sympathizers may help us better understand the ways in which public opinion affects public policy, as well as how right-wing movements come and go in the twenty-first century. Drawing on democratic theory and the assumption that politicians wish to retain their seats, scholars have forcefully argued that public opinion is an important part of the policy process, insofar as politicians use it to gauge constituent sentiment.[19] Recent work in social movement theory includes public opinion as a means of explaining the extent to which it is a factor in movements' achieving their goals. Research suggests that the interplay between public opinion and the disruption associated with movement activity ultimately contributes to movements' achieving some of their policy-related goals. We believe the Tea Party movement increases the salience of issues for the public, who in turn become more interested and more likely to make demands of their representatives. In short, exploring Tea Party sympathizers, not members or activists, may help us get a handle on, and anticipate, policy change and the congressional agenda.[20]

Another implication has to do with the extent to which support for the Tea Party will affect partisan polarization.[21] Over the past decade, scholars of the legislative branch have noted an increase in the degree of party polarization in Congress. Not restricted to Washington, D.C., public opinion scholars have likewise found that the American public itself is becoming increasingly polarized along partisan lines. As we have demonstrated, the Tea Party and its supporters make a clear case of further polarization through their extreme viewpoints, which go beyond mainstream conservatives. Now, with dozens of members of the House and Senate sympathetic to the Tea Party, scholars of congressional polarization will certainly turn their attention to not just Tea Party supporters but how the newly elected Tea Party members of Congress shape the next wave of partisan polarization.

And as we found in chapter 6 Tea Party supporters were quite likely to be involved in politics in 2010. Already, research on voter attitudes and the psychological processes of trust in government, efficacy, and ultimately civic participation are turning to questions of Tea Party support. At the 2011 annual research conference of the American Political Science Association, dozens of papers were delivered on how the Tea Party is influencing voting behavior, and entire panels were devoted to trying to forecast Tea Party influence in the 2012 elections.

Our book also has the ability to inform ongoing discussions about the Far Right, which remains vital in Europe. Most of the Far Right political parties in Europe, as well as other industrialized democracies, are a response to immigration. As political scientist Terri Givens illustrates in her work, "radical Right" parties in Austria, Denmark, France, and Germany share at least two common themes. First, as we have already suggested, they demand immigration reform: more strict immigration controls, the expulsion of unemployed immigrants, and the restriction of social welfare and employment to citizens. Second, the radical Right prefers to work within the existing political system, although they consider themselves "antiestablishment."

A third factor that contributes to the rise of the radical Right is an unbending commitment to nationalism.[22] Givens, and many other scholars on the radical Right in Europe, tend to stress institutional mechanisms, such as party competition, to explain the rise of the radical Right.[23] Our approach is more social psychological than anything else. Based on a brief canvass of the vast literature on the Far Right in Europe, we ran across a few that adopted a similar theoretical approach, but none that brings to bear the array of evidence that we marshal in this book. We also focus on movement sympathizers, where much of the existing work on Europe focuses on movement activists.[24]

As we close, we'd like to highlight the importance of the contemporary relevance of the Tea Party and where they're headed. First, whether or not one is a true believer or true skeptic of the Tea Party, we must acknowledge the impact they've had on contemporary American politics. For this reason, this book is an important contribution, because it permits a better understanding of what motivates people to support such movements, especially the idea that their country is slipping away from them. It also hints at the consequences of right-wing movements. In the current climate, the Tea Party is moving the Republican Party even further to the right. But this isn't much different than the effect the John Birch Society had on the Republican Party in the early 1960s when it contributed to the decline of liberal and moderate conservatives. In both cases, fear and anxiety tend to fuel policy preferences that militate against social and economic progress. This is difficult to reconcile with the love for America that the Far Right often professes.

POSTSCRIPT: THE 2012 ELECTION

In the early months of the Republican primary debates and elections, the Tea Party maintained considerable influence. Many of the leading candidates who emerged enjoyed robust ties to the Tea Party, most notably Michele Bachmann, the head of the Tea Party congressional caucus. Joining Bachmann as Tea Party loyalists were Rick Santorum, Herman Cain, and Rick Perry. For months, business mogul Donald Trump fueled speculation that he would run for president. In the end, he failed to enter the race, but not before questioning the legitimacy of Obama's presidency on the grounds that the president wasn't born in the United States. Indeed, Tea Party voters made a strong showing in the Republican primaries and caucuses, ultimately influencing the direction of the party, pushing it further to the right.

Throughout the primaries, candidates campaigned feverishly to win over local and statewide Tea Party leaders and elected officials, all in an effort to position themselves as the most conservative candidate in the field. In fact, the influence of the Tea Party was so notable that questions about it became a permanent fixture of the Republican primary exit polls, with every network reporting how Tea Party Republicans and non–Tea Party Republicans had voted. Pundits of all stripes often wondered whether it was possible for a Republican candidate to win the nomination in the absence of strong support from the Tea Party. The eventual Republican nominee, Mitt Romney, was generally perceived as the establishment (or more traditional) Republican candidate, and not identified as a Tea Party favorite.[25] However, Romney felt the pressure of the Tea Party faithful and made many significant overtures to the Tea Party.[26] He embraced the Tea Party's anti-immigrant policies, he repeatedly called Obama's policies European-style big government, and, probably most critical, he selected as his running mate Paul Ryan, called by many the biggest star of the Tea Party movement.[27] Romney's move to the right worked: he won 87 percent of the Tea Party vote.[28] But it turned out to be a Pyrrhic victory: the Romney-Ryan ticket ultimately lost the election.

In addition to their influence in national presidential politics, the Tea Party once again backed several candidates for House and Senate across the country. In the U.S. Senate, Tea Party–backed candidates upended mainstream Republicans in the Missouri, Indiana, and Texas primaries. As was the case in 2010, some of these right-wing challengers, such as Ted Cruz in Texas, were successful in gaining a seat in the U.S. Senate, while others, such as Todd Akin in Missouri and Robert Murdoch in Indiana, were judged too reactionary to win in the general election. In the U.S. House of Representatives, Tea Party candidates fared much better in districts geared toward a more conservative voting base. According to the Institute for Research & Education on Human Rights, Tea Party–backed candidates won at a 92 percent clip in the House.[29] The forty-eight Republican members of the House, then, constitute more than one-fifth of the Republican caucus. This likely explains Speaker Boehner's hesitation to accommodate more moderate positions. Until very recently, the speaker has had a tough time corralling his caucus.[30]

As the Republican Party moves forward from its national defeat in 2012, the Tea Party and its sympathizers may become more relevant than ever, not less. The Tea Party delegation seems to have drawn a clear line in the sand and doubled down on their opposition to President Obama.[31] As we write, they continue to oppose any tax or spending compromise, and continue to oppose immigration reform. In fact, in the immediate days after the 2012 election, a local Tea Party leader and Republican county chairman in Texas suggested that they should start a movement to secede from the Union because they no longer wanted to be part of Obama's America. He went further in expressing his opposition to the coalition of blacks, Latinos, and Asian Americans that was widely credited with delivering victory for President Obama: he asserted that "maggots re-elected Obama," and that his party should oppose the president at every chance.[32]

Why would they continue on this course, given the shifting demography of America? It's really quite simple: the constituencies of these representatives continue to pull them to the Far Right. Even if Tea Party rallies aren't drawing the crowds they once did, people continue to support the Tea Party and its agenda.[33] This brings us full circle, back to our central point: we need to better understand Tea Party sympathizers. The following quote from a Tea Party supporter, sent in an email to one of us just days after the election, crystallizes why we believe Tea Party sympathizers remain important:

> How dare you state that Republicans are criticizing Barrack Obama because he is black? What evidence do you have of that? We judge him by the content of his character, not the color of his skin. We criticize him because his ignorance, incompetence, and arrogance is destroying this country, the greatest one on earth.

As Obama serves his second term in office, we expect reactionary conservatives to dig in their heels, continuing to resist his agenda along with his legitimacy. Without question, the election of Barack Obama is truly *change they can't believe in.*

APPENDIX

THE FOLLOWING APPENDIX CONTAINS the detailed methodological procedures for the evidence presented in the book. We presented two types of evidence. We drew on content analysis and long, open-ended interviews for the qualitative component. More quantitative evidence was drawn from original surveys we conducted through the Survey Research Lab at the University of Washington. Our pilot survey, conducted in the winter of 2010, provided the initial datum for this book. Based on the preliminary findings in our pilot study, we used long interviews to reinterview a sample of our original respondents, hoping to better understand our initial results. It was clear to us that we needed to field another survey so that we might better understand the relationship between support for the Tea Party and various social and political predispositions, including social dominance orientation, authoritarianism, and ethnocentrism. We also deepened our battery of questions on President Obama, among other things. Finally, our content analysis of Tea Party websites and the *National Review Online* permits us to move beyond the masses to examine elite and citizen activist discourse.

Description of Multi-State Survey of Race and Politics (MSSRP) and Telephone Survey Methodology

Public opinion data for this book are drawn from two primary sources: the 2010 and 2011 Multi-State Survey of Race and Politics. Both studies were implemented by the Center for Survey Research at the University of Washington using undergraduate college students as live telephone interviewers, and under the direction of Professor Christopher Parker, director of the center. Research for these two surveys was supported through a grant from the University of Washington Research Royalty Fund, the Department of Political Science, and the Washington Institute for the Study of Ethnicity and Race. No private or programmatic grants were used to fund this study. Parker is the principal investigator.

In February–March 2010, we fielded an original public opinion survey called the Multi-State Survey of Race and Politics (MSSRP) as a pilot study to examine what Americans thought about issues of race, public policy, national politics, and President Obama, exactly one year after the inauguration of the first African American president. The survey was drawn from a probability sample of 60,000 household records, stratified by state, and resulted in 1,006 completed interviews. The completed sample included 505 white non-Hispanics, 312 African Americans, 99 Latinos, and 90 "other" (those who refused to answer race). The results were weighted to the 2009 U.S. Census American Community Survey estimates for the adult population in the seven states with respect to gender, age, educational attainment, income, and race.

Our 2010 study included seven states, six of which were politically competitive states in 2008, including Georgia, Michigan, Missouri, Nevada, North Carolina, and Ohio. For its diversity and its status as an uncontested state, California was also included for comparative purposes. To conduct the study, we used live telephone callers to a mix of landline and cell phone–

only households. The study was in the field from February 8 to March 15, 2010. We received a cooperation rate of 47 percent, with a margin of error of plus or minus 3.1 percent for the full sample.

In 2011 we decided to replicate and extend the MSSRP study to include a larger sample size of thirteen states and a greater number of completed interviews. Given the growth and influence of the Tea Party movement from 2010 to 2011, we decided to add new states to the study in 2011 in addition to surveying all seven of the original states in the 2010 survey. In 2011 we added Arizona, Colorado, Florida, Pennsylvania, South Carolina, and Wisconsin. These six states represent an additional layer of politically competitive states, especially in state-level politics, and also had notable Tea Party–backed candidates for office. Since we are ultimately interested in studying Tea Party supporters, we specifically sought to include states that did have at least some Tea Party presence.

Like the study in 2010, the 2011 study was conducted using live telephone callers to a mix of landline and cell phone–only households. The 2011 version averaged about 40 minutes in length, and was in the field from January 24 to March 4, 2011. The survey was drawn from a probability sample of 90,000 household records, stratified by state, and resulted in 1,504 completed interviews. The completed sample included 903 white non-Hispanics, 379 African Americans, 115 Latinos, and 107 of "other" (those who refused to answer race). In this survey, we achieved a cooperation rate of 56 percent with a margin of error of plus or minus 2.5 percent for the full sample. The results are weighted to the 2010 U.S. Census estimates for the adult population in the thirteen states we surveyed with respect to gender, age, educational attainment, income, and race.

Because the data are drawn from a stratified state-based sample, we opt to cluster our standard errors by state, since we expect errors are correlated for the respondents within each state.[1] This approach is common with geographically stratified data and follows established research practices.[2] Without clustering errors at the state level, the intraclass correlation would generate misleading results. In further analysis, we estimate a two-way fixed effects model and examine varying slopes and intercepts by state and region. All models are estimated using clustered standard errors.[3]

Question Wording and Coding: Dependent Variables
SUPPORT FOR THE TEA PARTY

This question measured a respondent's approval of the Tea Party movement: "Based on what you have heard, do you approve or disapprove of the Tea Party movement?" The question was coded on a three-point scale (0–1), such that "true believers" in the Tea Party = 1, "true skeptics" of the movement = 0, and those in the "middle of the road" = 0.5.

DETAIN SUSPECTS

This question measured whether or not a respondent agreed with the detainment of terrorist suspects: "Some people say law enforcement should be able to arrest and detain anyone indefinitely if that person is suspected of belonging to a terrorist organization or in the process of committing a terrorist act. Others say that no one should be held for a long period of time without being formally charged with a crime." The question was recoded (0–1) such that 1 = agreement with detention.

RACIAL PROFILING

This question measured whether or not a respondent agreed with racial profiling: "Some people say that law enforcement should be able to stop or detain people of certain racial backgrounds if these groups are thought to be more likely to commit crimes. This is called racial profiling. Others think racial profiling should not be done because it harasses many innocent people on account of their race." The question was recoded (0–1) such that 1 = agreement with racial profiling.

MEDIA FREE SPEECH

This question measured whether or not a respondent agreed with free speech for media professionals: "Some people say that media professionals should be able to say whatever they wish even if what they say intentionally misleads people or may even ultimately result in violence of some kind. Others say that media professionals should be prevented from saying things that are intentionally misleading or may ultimately result in violence." The question was recoded (0–1) such that 1 = agreement with free speech.

BLIND PATRIOTISM

This question measured whether or not a respondent agreed with supporting their country no matter the circumstances: "Some people say that patriotism is about supporting your country, right or wrong. In other words, Americans shouldn't criticize the country even if they disagree with its policies. Others say that criticism is necessary and that true patriots must challenge America to live up to its values." The question was recoded (0–1) such that 1 = high levels of blind patriotism.

PATRIOTIC REDISTRIBUTION

This question measured whether or not a respondent agreed that redistribution is patriotic: "Some people say that it's our patriotic duty to help subsidize an education for those without access to good schools, something that will ultimately strengthen the United States. Others say that redistributing the money of hardworking Americans is wrong because it takes money away from the people who earned it and gives it to people who didn't work for it." The question was recoded (0–1) such that 1 = agreement with redistribution as patriotic.

CRITICAL PATRIOTISM

This question measured whether or not a respondent agreed that pushing for equality is patriotic: "Some people say that true patriotism is about pushing America to realize its promise of equality, even if it means enacting new laws to ensure everyone is treated equally. Others think it is unnecessary to enact new laws to prevent discrimination, especially if these laws are already in place." The question was recoded (0–1) such that 1 = agreement with critical patriotism.

DREAM Act

This question asked whether or not respondents supported or opposed the DREAM Act: "The DREAM Act would allow illegal immigrants who came to the U.S. as very young children to eventually gain legal status if they attend college or serve in the U.S. military. Do you support or oppose the DREAM Act?" The question was recoded (0–1) such that 1 = support for the DREAM act.

Repeal Citizenship

This question measured respondents' attitudes about repealing the constitutional right of birthright citizenship: "Do you think we should continue to grant citizenship to all children born in the U.S., or do you think the Constitution should be changed so children of illegal immigrants are not automatically granted citizenship?" The question was recoded (0–1) such that 1 = support for repealing birthright citizenship.

Immigrant Political Power

This question measured respondents' perceived political power in relation to the political influence of immigrants: "The more influence that immigrants have in politics the less influence people like me will have in politics." The question was on a five-point scale from strongly disagree to strongly agree (0–1) such that 1 = agreement with the statement.

Immigrants Increase Crime in America

This question measured respondents' views toward immigrants contributing to increasing levels of crime in America: "New immigrants have increased the level of crime in the United States." The question was on a five-point scale from strongly disagree to strongly agree (0–1) such that 1 = attitudes in agreement with the statement.

GAYS AND LESBIANS IN THE MILITARY

This question measured respondents' feelings about gays and lesbians openly serving in the U.S. military: "How about the decision to repeal Don't Ask, Don't Tell and allow gays and lesbians to serve openly in the U.S. military? Do you support or oppose it?" The question was on a five-point scale from strongly oppose to strongly support (0–1) such that 1 = opposition toward gays and lesbians openly serving in the U.S. military.

GAYS AND LESBIANS TOO POLITICALLY POWERFUL

This question asked whether or not gays and lesbians are too politically powerful: "As a group, do lesbians and gay men have too much political power, not enough political power, or just about the right amount of political power?" The question was on a three-point scale from too much to not enough (0–1) such that 1 = the belief that gays and lesbians are too politically powerful.

SAME-SEX MARRIAGE

This question measured whether or not respondents support same-sex marriage: "Some people say that gay and lesbian couples should be given the right to get married, while others say that the government should not provide legal recognition of same-sex marriage. Which comes closer to your view?" The question was recoded (0–1) such that 1 = opposition to same-sex marriage.

GAYS AND LESBIANS KEEPING PRIVATE IN SOCIETY

This question measured whether or not respondents' agreed with gays and lesbians talking about their sexual orientation openly in society: "Is society better when it encourages gay men and lesbians to be open and talk about their sexual orientation publicly or when it encourages them to keep their sexual orientation to themselves?" The question was recoded (0–1) such that 1 = opposition to gays and lesbians openly discussing their sexual orientation.

BARACK OBAMA TRAITS

This question indexed the following traits about President Barack Obama:

In your opinion, how well do the following describe Barack Obama:

(1) Knowledgeable

(2) Strong leader

(3) Moral

(4) Really cares about people

The items were scaled (0–1) such that 1 = positive traits accurately describe President Barack Obama. Reliability: $\alpha = 0.87$.

FAVORABILITY OF BARACK OBAMA AS A PERSON

This question measured how respondents' felt about Barack Obama aside from his job as president: "Apart from whether you approve or disapprove of the way Barack Obama is handling his job as president, what do you think of Obama as a person?" The question was recoded on a five-point scale from strongly disapprove to strongly approve (0–1) such that 1 = approval for Obama as a person.

PRESIDENT OBAMA POLICY SUCCESS

This question measured whether or not respondents wanted President Obama's policies to succeed or fail: "In general, do you hope that Barack Obama's policies will succeed, or do you hope his policies will fail?" The question was on a three-point scale from hoping Obama's policies succeed to hoping they fail (0–1) such that 1 = hope Obama's policies fail.

President Obama Is a Christian

This question measured whether or not respondents thought President Obama is a Christian by asking if the following statement is true: "Obama is a practicing Christian." The question was recoded (0–1) such that 1 = true.

President Obama Was Born in the United States

This question measured whether or not respondents thought President Obama was born in the United States by asking if the following statement is true: "Obama was born in the United States." The question was recoded (0–1) such that 1 = true.

Political Interest

This question measured a respondents' political interest: "In general, how interested are you in news about what's going on in government and politics?" The question was on a five-point scale from not at all interested to extremely interested (0–1) such that 1 = high levels of political interest.

Attend Political Meeting

This question asked respondents whether or not they had attended a political meeting in the last twelve months. The question was recoded (0–1) such that 1 = yes.

Vote in 2010

This question asked respondents whether or not they voted in the 2010 general election in November. The question was recoded (0–1) such that 1 = voted.

Vote Republican in 2010

This question asked respondents whether or not they had voted for a Republican candidate for the U.S. House of Representatives in the 2010 general election: "Did you vote for the Republican candidate or the Democratic candidate for the U.S. House of Representatives?" The question was recoded (0–1) such that 1 = voted Republican.

Question Wording and Coding: Independent Variables
FEAR OF BARACK OBAMA

This question measured a respondent's attitude toward President Obama and socialism: "When it comes to Barack Obama's policies, please tell me which statement you agree with most: (a) I support Obama's current policies; (b) Obama's policies are pushing the country toward socialism; (c) Obama's policies are misguided and wrong, but they are not socialism." The question was on a three-point scale (0–1) such that 0 = support for Obama's current policies and 1 = agree that Obama is pushing country toward socialism.

SOCIAL DOMINANCE

Social dominance is indexed by the following items:

(1) If certain groups of people stayed in their place, we would have fewer problems.

(2) Inferior groups should stay in their place.

(3) Sometimes other groups must be kept in their place.

(4) We should do what we can to equalize conditions for different groups.

(5) Group equality should be our ideal.

(6) We should increase social equality.

The items were scaled (0–1) such that 1 = higher levels of social dominance. Reliability: $\alpha = 0.69$.

RACISM

Racism is indexed by the following items:

(1) Irish, Italians, Jews, and many other minorities overcame prejudice and worked their way up. Blacks should do the same without any special favors.

(2) Generations of slavery and discrimination have created conditions that make it difficult for blacks to work their way out of the lower class.

(3)   Over the past few years, blacks have gotten less than they deserve.

(4)   It's really a matter of some people not trying hard enough; if blacks would only try harder they could be just as well off as whites.

The items were scaled (0–1) such that 1 = low levels of racism. Due to survey question order, this scale is coded in reverse order from the other attitude measures. Reliability: α = 0.72.

Authoritarianism

Authoritarianism is indexed by the following items:

Which one do you think is more important for a child to have:

(1)   Independence or respect for elders?

(2)   Curiosity or good manners?

(3)   Obedience or self-reliance?

(4)   Considerate or well behaved?

The items were scaled (0–1) such that 1 = high levels of authoritarianism. Reliability: α = 0.67.

Ethnocentrism

Ethnocentrism is indexed using a scale measuring how a respondent felt about African Americans, Hispanic Americans, Asian Americans, and white Americans when it comes to being hard-working versus lazy, intelligent versus unintelligent, and trustworthy versus untrustworthy. Respondent's answers for each racial group were indexed, and then the difference between the scores for African Americans, Hispanic Americans, and Asian Americans from respondent's scores for white Americans was calculated. These differences were added together and rescaled (0–1) such that 1 = high levels of ethnocentrism.

Limited Government

This question measured a respondent's support for limited government by indexing the following items:

Next, I am going to ask you to choose which of two state-ments I read comes closer to your own opinion. You might agree to some extent with both, but we want to know which one is closer to your own views.

(1) ONE, the main reason government has become bigger over the years is because it has gotten involved in things that people should do for themselves; or TWO, government has become bigger because the problems we face have become bigger.

(2) ONE, we need a strong government to handle today's complex economic problems; or TWO, the free market can handle these problems without the government being involved.

(3) ONE, the less government, the better; or TWO, there are more things that government should be doing.

The items were scaled (0–1) such that 1 = support for limited government. Reliability: $\alpha = 0.70$.

ECONOMIC ANXIETY

This question measured a respondent's anxiety toward his or her own economic situation: "Now, thinking about your OWN economic situation. Some people are very anxious about their OWN economic situation, while other people are not anxious at all. How anxious are you about your OWN economic situation?" The question was on a four-point scale from not at all anxious to very anxious (0–1) such that 1 = high economic anxiety.

RELIGIOUS ATTENDANCE

This question measured a respondent's religious attendance by the following: "Aside from weddings and funerals, how often do you attend religious services? Would you say never, less often than a few times a year, a few times a year, once or twice a month, once a week, or more than once a week?" The question was on a six-point scale from never to more than once a week (0–1) such that 1 = high levels of religious attendance.

Evangelical

This measured whether or not a respondent considered themselves an evangelical or born-again Christian. The question was recoded (0–1) such that 1 = yes, the respondent considers himself or herself an evangelical Christian.

Traditionalism

This measured respondents' attitudes about how people should conduct their lives in America by indexing the following items:

(1) The newer lifestyles are contributing to the breakdown of our society.

(2) This country would have many fewer problems if there were more emphasis on traditional family ties.

The items were scaled (0–1) such that 1 = agreement with the moral attitude statements. Reliability: $\alpha = 0.65$.

Ideology

This question measured a respondent's ideology by asking how liberal, moderate, or conservative one felt they were. The question was on a three-point scale from liberal to conservative (0–1) such that 0 = Liberal, 0.5 = Moderate, and 1 = Conservative.

Party ID

This question measured a respondent's political party identification. The question was separated into three dummy variables for Democrat, Independent, and Republican, each recoded (0–1) such that 1 = either Democrat, Independent, or Republican.

Education

This question determined the respondent's highest level of education: "What is the highest level of education you completed?" The question was recoded on a six-point scale from grades 1 through 6 to postgraduate (0–1) such that 1 = postbaccalaureate degree.

GENDER

This question determined the respondent's gender. It was recoded (0–1) such that 1= male.

AGE

This question asked for actual age in years and was compressed into a four-point scale (0–1), such that 1 = the oldest age cohort.

INCOME

This question measured the household income of the respondent: "What was your total combined household income in 2010 before taxes?" This question was recoded on a seven-point scale from less than $20K to more than $150K (0–1) such that 1 = the highest income levels.

POLITICAL KNOWLEDGE

Political knowledge is indexed by the following questions:

(1) Do you happen to know who has the final responsibility to decide whether or not a law is constitutional?

(2) Do you happen to know what job or political office is now held by Joseph Biden?

(3) Which political party currently has the most seats in the House of Representatives in Washington, D.C.?

The items were scaled (0–1) such that 1 = high levels of political knowledge. Reliability: $\alpha = 0.57$.

FOX NEWS

This question asked respondents "From which station do you get most of your information?" The question was recoded (0–1) such that 1 = Fox News and 0 = other options, including MSNBC, PBS, ABC, CBS, NBC, and so on.

RACIAL GROUP MEMBERSHIP

This question measured a respondent's racial identity. The question was recoded (0–1) such that 1 = black and 0 = all other races.

White Interviewer

This question asked respondents what they perceived the racial background of their survey interviewer to be. For ease, this question was coded as a dummy variable comparing respondents who perceived their interviewer's race as white to those who did not. The question was recoded (0–1) such that 1 = white and 0 = every other racial group.

Experiment Methodology and Results

Chapter 1 Results

Due to social desirability issues, it's likely that very few people who truly believe the president will destroy the country will answer a question asking this honestly. To compensate for social desirability, we use what is called "The List Experiment," a methodological technique developed by James Kuklinski and Matthew T. McClure, professors of political science at the University of Illinois, to illicit answers to sensitive questions. The experiment works as follows. In the baseline condition, half of the respondents are read four relatively innocuous statements; in the treatment condition, the other half are read the same four basic statements, plus the sensitive statement. In our experiment the baseline statements were: *I have money invested in an individual retirement account, I have sometimes been unable to pay my bills, I usually choose to buy organic foods,* and *I usually shop at Walmart.* The sensitive statement was: *I think Barack Obama will destroy the country.* To reduce the likelihood of social desirability, respondents are simply asked how many statements are true for them, not which ones. If the treatment is effective, the mean number of items in this condition should always exceed the mean number of items in the baseline condition, where only four statements were read. The difference between the baseline and treatment conditions, multiplied by 100, indicates percentage of a given group affected by the treatment.

TABLE A1.1

Mean level of those who believe Obama will destroy the country, by type of conservatism

Condition	All Conservatives	Non-TP Conservatives	TP Conservatives
Baseline	2.01	2.11	1.89
	(.058)	(.084)	(.079)
N	230	123	107
Treatment	2.36	2.17	2.60
	(.058)	(.098)	(.106)
N	223	123	100
% Believe Obama will Destroy Country	35%	6%	71%
Total N	453	246	207

Source: Multi-State Survey of Race and Politics (2011).

In the present case (table A1.1), moving from left to right, all conservatives ($N = 453$) are in the first column, non–Tea Party conservatives ($N = 246$) are in the middle column, and Tea Party conservatives ($N = 207$) occupy the third column. So, doing the math, we see that 35 percent of all conservatives believe Barack Obama is destroying the country (2.36 – 2.01 × 100). As we become more discriminating when it comes to self-identified conservatives, big differences emerge. For instance, as we move to the middle column, we see that 6 percent of non–Tea Party conservatives believe the president is destroying the country versus 71 percent of Tea Party conservatives who believe this to be true.

Content Analysis and Interviews

Our analysis first examines content from the *National Review Online* (NRO) compared to content from major Tea Party websites. A comparison of the two sources provides insight into how the current political environment is interpreted by mainstream conservative elites and citizen activists within the Tea Party. If the Tea Party is truly about mainstream conservatism, the content frames on their websites should reflect those in the *NRO*.

NATIONAL REVIEW ONLINE

The content for the *NRO* consists of 3,891 articles from the online website from 2008 to 2010. The *NRO* content was sampled by examining every Monday, Wednesday, and Friday in 2008 and 2010, and every Tuesday, Thursday, and Saturday in 2009 to achieve a random, yet representative sample of each year. Content from Tea Party websites was collected from major websites in five states identified by a Rasmussen report as top Tea Party venues, as well as from nine additional states from the 2011 Multi-State Survey of Race and Politics. The five states identified as top Tea Party venues from the 2010 Rasmussen report are: Alabama, Arizona, Colorado, Georgia, and Kentucky. In addition, California, Florida, Missouri, Nevada, North Carolina, Ohio, Pennsylvania, South Carolina, and Wisconsin are included in the analysis as states from the 2011 MSSRP. The entire Rasmussen report can be found at Rasmussen Reports, http://www.rasmussenreports.com/public _content/most_recent_videos/2010_06/where_is_the_tea _party_strongest. A total of 3,948 articles and postings from forty-two major Tea Party websites (websites that represent the state in its entirety, such as the Arizona Tea Party, or websites from a major city or region of the state) were examined dating back no further than 2009. By limiting our examination to these websites, we are focusing on online dialogue by the communication leaders, or citizen activists, within the Tea Party.

When possible, the content from these websites was examined in its entirety. When the website content was overwhelming, a random sample was examined in order to accurately represent all of the content within the website over time. When a random sample was used, every tenth post on the website was sampled. Each post or article was coded for one main topic based on the initial paragraph as well as the overall theme. The analysis was limited to websites and blogs that represent the state, a major city or region within the state, and only blogs with official domain names. Additionally, the comments on blog posts and articles were excluded from our analysis. The content analysis finished with an intercoder reliability of 0.82.

Frame Description

Eight frames are compared to assess the extent to which the Tea Party websites reflect mainstream conservatives: four frames that focus on conservative issues (foreign policy/national security, big government/states' rights, patriotism/take country back, and values/morals), and four frames that represent topics beyond traditional conservatism (conspiracy, personal attacks on Obama, immigration, and race/racism).

BIG GOVERNMENT AND STATES' RIGHTS

This frame describes content making a case against or criticizing government expansion or a large national government in general. This also contains content arguing for the expansion of states' rights. Content generally focuses on limiting government expansion, especially in relation to nationalization of health care and government bailouts of large corporations.

CONSPIRACY AND GOVERNMENT DESTROYING COUNTRY

This frame describes conspiratorial content claiming that the government or the president is a socialist or communist, or is leading the country to destruction. This frame also describes content that claims an Obama-led government, or the national government in general, is bad for the country and ruining America. Content generally describes the president as a socialist or communist and as ruining America. This content often accompanies derogatory language toward the president and his supporters.

FOREIGN POLICY AND NATIONAL SECURITY

This frame describes content about international affairs and countries other than the United States. Content generally describes global warming and environmental issues, as well as international conflict. This frame also describes content that focuses on protecting the country from outside and internal threats. Content generally describes new security measures to protect the United States, as well as terrorism updates.

Patriotism and Take Back Country

This frame describes content that focuses on the importance of loving America and remaining loyal, as well as rhetoric on taking one's country back. Content generally describes how much an author of the post or article loves their country. Content also relays the importance of taking their country back and making it their own once again. This content is often in reference to an American holiday, such as the Fourth of July or Veterans Day.

Personal Attacks on President Obama

This frame describes content personally attacking President Obama beyond his politics and policies. The content generally describes the president in derogatory language, often insulting his intelligence and the intelligence of his wife and family. Content personally attacking the president also describes how un-American he is and contains racist sentiments.

Immigration

This frame describes content on immigration policy, immigrants, and illegal immigrants. It also contains content on immigration workers or the immigration policy stances of politicians, including the president. Content generally describes the drawbacks of illegal immigration and also expresses sentiments condemning illegal immigrants.

Race and Racism

This frame describes content in which the author used racially derogatory names to describe nonwhite groups, mainly blacks and Latinos. This frame also contains references to stereotypes generally associated with the groups.

Values and Morals

This describes content about religion, moral predispositions, and general attitudes on what is right and wrong. Content generally focuses on the importance of religion within American culture, as well as the immorality of homosexuality. Evangelical sentiments were also a focus of this content frame.

Major Tea Party Websites

A total of forty-two websites were examined from March 2009 through the midterm elections of November 2010. As major Tea Party websites were selected based on official domain names and state or regional representation, the number of websites examined in each state varies; at least two and as many as four major Tea Party websites may have existed in any given state.

TABLE A1.2
Major Tea Party websites by state

State	Major Tea Party Website
Pennsylvania	Pennsylvania TP Patriots
	Pennsylvania Tea Party
	Pittsburgh Tea Party
Wisconsin	Wisconsin TP Patriots
	Fight Back Wisconsin
	La Crosse Tea Party
Nevada	Nevada Tea Party Patriots
	Carson City Tea Party
North Carolina	North Carolina Tea Party
	North Carolina TP Patriots
	Asheville Tea Party
Michigan	Michigan TP Patriots
	Tea Party of W. Michigan
	Lansing Michigan TP
Missouri	Missouri Tea Party Patriots
	St. Louis Tea Party

TABLE **A1.2** (*continued*)

State	Major Tea Party Website
Ohio	Ohio Tea Party Patriots Cincinnati Tea Party Portage County Tea Party Dayton Tea Party
California	California Tea Party California Tea Party Patriots Central Valley Tea Party Southern California Tax Revolt Coalition
Georgia	Georgia Tea Party Atlanta Tea Party The Columbus Georgia Tea Party Georgia Tea Party Patriots
Colorado	Colorado Tea Party Colorado Tea Party Patriots Northern Colorado Tea Party
Kentucky	Northern Kentucky Tea Party Kentucky Tea Party Patriots
Alabama	Alabama Tea Party Alabama Tea Party Patriots
Arizona	Arizona Tea Party Arizona Tea Party Patriots
Florida	Florida Tea Party South Florida Tea Party Florida Tea Party Patriots
South Carolina	South Carolina Tea Party South Carolina Tea Party Patriots

Long Interviews

In the summer of 2010, we conducted interviews to complement the pilot survey we conducted in the winter of 2010. We conducted these interviews to further flesh out our findings from the survey. We wished to gain better insight on the attitudes that were reported in our pilot study. We wanted to investigate the extent to which negative or positive emotions are associated with their impressions of President Obama and various out-groups. To do so, we reinterviewed a subset of our original respondents. Our goal was to reinterview at least thirty people, ten for each category of Tea Party support: believers, middle-of-the road(ers), and skeptics. We also stratified by gender, hoping to reinterview at least fifteen women, half of the sample. We were successful on both counts. The interviews were also stratified by state: California, Georgia, Missouri, Michigan, Nevada, North Carolina, and Ohio were states in the original 2010 survey. The reinterviews were conducted from August 15 to August 30, 2010. The interviews averaged twenty-five minutes in length.

Interview Questionnaire

Hi. I'm calling on behalf of the University of Washington Survey Research Center.

We are conducting a short survey about issues related to the 2010 election.

We would like to ask you a few questions about current political issues and groups in America today.

I'm going to first ask whether or not you have positive or negative feelings, after which I'll ask you to be more specific.

If your feelings are positive, we're going to ask you if you feel enthusiastic, interested, inspired, proud, or excited. If your feelings are negative, we're going to ask whether or not you feel scared, angry, nervous, guilty, or pity.

Finally, I will ask you why you feel the way you feel.

This gives you a chance to say anything you want at all.

Okay, to get started:

I. Feelings about the Country
   a. How do you feel about the United States today? Do you have positive or negative feelings about the country?
   b. Do you feel enthusiastic/scared, interested/angry, inspired/nervous, proud/guilty, or excited/pity when it comes to the United States? Or, Yeah, a lot of people

we talk to have mixed feelings. Do you feel enthusiastic, angry, inspired, scared, proud, or nervous
when it comes to the United States?

   c. Why do you feel that way?

II. Feelings about the Political System

   a. In a few words, how would you define the American
political system?

   b. Do you have positive or negative feelings about the
American political system?

   c. Do you feel enthusiastic/scared, interested/angry,
inspired/nervous, proud/guilty, or excited/pity when
it comes to the American political system? Or, Yeah,
a lot of people we talk to have mixed feelings. Do
you feel enthusiastic, angry, inspired, scared, proud,
or nervous when it comes to the American political
system?

   d. Why do you feel that way?

III. Feelings about Equal Rights

   a. How does it make you feel living in a country
where, regardless of political or religious beliefs,
everyone has the same rights?

   b. Do you have positive or negative feelings about
everyone having equal rights?

   c. Do you feel enthusiastic/scared, interested/angry,
inspired/nervous, proud/guilty, or excited/pity about
everyone having equal rights? Or, Yeah, a lot of
people we talk to have mixed feelings. Do you feel
enthusiastic, angry, inspired, scared, proud, or nervous about everyone having equal rights?

   d. Why do you feel that way?

IV. Feelings about Government Surveillance

   a. How do you feel about governmental surveillance
when the country may be in danger?

   b. Do you have positive or negative feelings when it
comes to surveillance?

    c. Do you feel enthusiastic/scared, interested/angry, in-spired/nervous, proud/guilty, or excited/pity when it comes to surveillance? Or, Yeah, a lot of people we talk to have mixed feelings. Do you feel enthusiastic, angry, inspired, scared, proud, or nervous when it comes to surveillance?

    d. Why do you feel that way?

  V. Feelings about President Obama

    a. How do you feel about President Obama?

    b. Do you have positive or negative feelings about President Obama?

    c. Do you feel enthusiastic/scared, interested/angry, inspired/nervous, proud/guilty, or excited/pity when it comes to Barack Obama? Or, Yeah, a lot of people we talk to have mixed feelings. Do you feel enthusiastic, angry, inspired, scared, proud, or nervous when it comes to Barack Obama?

    d. Why do you feel that way?

 VI. Feelings about Health Care

    a. How do you feel about the recent health care bill passed by Congress in March 2010?

    b. Do you have positive or negative feelings?

    c. Do you feel enthusiastic/scared, interested/angry, inspired/nervous, proud/guilty, or excited/pity when it comes to health care? Or, Yeah, a lot of people we talk to have mixed feelings. Do you feel enthusiastic, angry, inspired, scared, proud, or nervous when it comes to health care?

    d. Why do you feel that way?

VII. Feelings about the Tea Party

    a. How do you feel about the Tea Party?

    b. Do you have positive or negative feelings about the Tea Party?

    c. Do you feel enthusiastic/scared, interested/angry, in-spired/nervous, proud/guilty, or excited/pity when it comes to the Tea Party? Or, Yeah, a lot of people we talk to have mixed feelings. Do you feel enthusiastic, angry, inspired, scared, proud, or nervous when it comes to the Tea Party?

    d. Why do you feel that way?

VIII. Feelings about Approval

    a. What does it mean to you when somebody says they approve/disapprove of the Tea Party?

IX. Feelings about Immigrants

    a. How do you feel about illegal immigrants?

    b. Do you have positive or negative feelings about illegal immigrants?

    c. Do you feel enthusiastic/scared, interested/angry, inspired/nervous, proud/guilty, or excited/pity when it comes to illegal immigrants? Or, Yeah, a lot of people we talk to have mixed feelings. Do you feel enthusiastic, angry, inspired, scared, proud, or nervous when it comes to illegal immigrants?

    d. Why do you feel that way?

X. Feelings about Blacks

    a. How do you feel about blacks?

    b. Do you have positive or negative feelings about black Americans?

    c. Do you feel enthusiastic/scared, interested/angry, inspired/nervous, proud/guilty, or excited/pity when it comes to blacks? Or, Yeah, a lot of people we talk to have mixed feelings. Do you feel enthusiastic, angry, inspired, scared, proud, or nervous when it comes to blacks?

    d. Why do you feel that way?

XI. Feelings about Women

    a. How do you feel about the push for women's equality?

    b. Do you have positive or negative feelings when it comes to women having equal rights?

    c. Do you feel enthusiastic/scared, interested/angry, inspired/nervous, proud/guilty, or excited/pity when it comes to women having equal rights? Or, Yeah, a lot of people we talk to have mixed feelings. Do you feel enthusiastic, angry, inspired, scared, proud, or nervous when it comes to women having equal rights?

    d. Why do you feel that way?

XII. Feelings about gays and lesbians

    a. How do you feel about gays and lesbians?

    b. Do you have positive or negative feelings about gays and lesbians?

    c. Do you feel enthusiastic/scared, interested/angry, inspired/nervous, proud/guilty, or excited/pity when it comes to gays and lesbians? Or, Yeah, a lot of people we talk to have mixed feelings. Do you feel enthusiastic, angry, inspired, scared, proud, or nervous when it comes to gays and lesbians?

    d. Why do you feel that way?

Thank you; that is all the questions we have for you.

TABLE A1.3
Selected demographic characteristics of interviewees

Respondent	Tea Party Opinion	Gender	State	Year of Birth	Education
1	Approve	Male	Nevada	1935	16
2	Approve	Female	Missouri	1965	18
3	Approve	Male	North Carolina	1940	14
4	Approve	Female	Nevada	1947	18
5	Approve	Female	California	Refused	14
6	Approve	Female	Michigan	1943	16
7	Approve	Male	Nevada	1952	14
8	Approve	Female	Georgia	1959	16
9	Approve	Male	Ohio	1976	16
10	Approve	Female	Georgia	1952	16
11	Approve	Male	Georgia	1952	16
12	Middle of the Road	Female	North Carolina	1941	14
13	Middle of the Road	Female	Nevada	1940	18
14	Middle of the Road	Female	Ohio	1963	14
15	Middle of the Road	Male	Missouri	1942	16
16	Middle of the Road	Female	North Carolina	1960	14
17	Middle of the Road	Male	Ohio	1971	14
18	Middle of the Road	Male	Missouri	1977	14
19	Middle of the Road	Male	California	1934	16
20	Middle of the Road	Female	California	1935	12
21	Disapprove	Female	California	1981	16
22	Disapprove	Female	Missouri	1931	14
23	Disapprove	Female	Missouri	1934	18
24	Disapprove	Male	Georgia	1961	14
25	Disapprove	Female	Nevada	1972	16
26	Disapprove	Female	Ohio	1940	12
27	Disapprove	Female	North Carolina	1948	14
28	Disapprove	Male	Michigan	1972	14
29	Disapprove	Male	Missouri	1948	18
30	Disapprove	Male	North Carolina	1955	16
31	Disapprove	Female	Georgia	1937	16

Note: Data collected by authors 2010.

Table A2.1
Comparison of MSSRP 2011 with contemporaneous national polls by Tea Party support and selected demographics

	2011 MSSRP (All respondents)	MSSRP "True Believers"	PEW "True Believers"*	NYT/CBS "True Believers"***	USA Today/Gallup "True Believers"****	Blair-Rockefeller "True Believers"*****
Age						
18–29	19%	11%	19%	7%	16% (18–29)	—
30–44	23%	23%	20%	16%	34% (30–49)	37% (<45)
45–64	38%	43%	43%	46%	29% (50–64)	63% (>45)
65+	20%	23%	18%	29%	21% (65+)	—
Education						
Less HS	13%	8%	2%	4%	—	7%
HS Grad	30%	40%	27%	26%	34% (No College)	28%
Some College	26%	26%	40%	33%	34%	39%
College Grad	31%	26%	31%	37%	31%	28%
Income						
<$20K	17%	11%	23%	18% (<$30K)	19% (<$30K)	—
$20–40K	23%	26%	16%	17% ($30–50K)	26% ($30–50K)	—
$40–60K	17%	15%	18% ($40–75K)	25% ($50–75K)	55% (>$50K)	36% (<$40K)
$60–100K	23%	24%	21% ($75–100K)	11% ($75–100K)	—	50% ($40–100K)
>$100K	20%	24%	22%	20% (>$100K)	—	14% (>$100K)
Ideology						
Liberal	29%	9%	4%	4%	7%	—
Moderate	37%	25%	8%	20%	22%	—
Conservative	34%	66%	88%	73%	70%	—

	*	**	***	****	
Party ID					
Democrat	41%	10%	5%	8%	—
Independent	27%	36%	36%	43%	—
Republican	32%	54%	54%	49%	55%
Race					
Black	20%	3%	—	6%	—
Latino	9%	1%	—	—	—
White	71%	96%	89%	79%	91%
Gender					
Male	52%	54%	59%	55%	58%
Female	48%	46%	41%	45%	42%
Tea Party support†					
"True Believers"	26%	24%	18%	28%	10.6%
"Middle of the Road"	41%	53%	—	46%	—
"True Skeptics"	33%	23%	—	26%	—

*Nationwide telephone interviews of 1,503 adults conducted in January 2011. *Source:* Princeton Survey Research Associates International for the Pew Research Center.

**Nationwide telephone poll with 1,580 adults conducted April 5–12, 2010. *Source:* http://www.nytimes.com/interactive/2010/04/14/us/politics/2010414-tea-party-poll-graphic.html?ref=politics#tab=9.

***National landline telephone interviews with 1,033 adults conducted March 26–28, 2010. *Source:* http://www.gallup.com/poll/127181/tea-partiers-fairly-mainstream-demographics.aspx.

****Nationwide Internet-based knowledge networks survey of 3,406 adults conducted in November 2010. *Source:* http://blairrockefellerpoll.uark.edu/5146.php.

†Those who answered "Don't Know" are excluded from the MSSRP analysis; however, even when including these respondents, the 19 percent of Tea Party "True Believers" is comparable to other polls at the time that find support for the Tea Party in the "teens" when including respondents who answer "Don't Know" (such as a July 2010 Gallup poll found here: http://www.gallup.com/poll/148940/tea-party-sparks-antipathy-passion.aspx; and a July *Washington Post*/ABC News poll found here: http://www.washingtonpost.com/wp-srv/politics/polls/postabcpoll_071711.html).

TABLE A2.2
Determinants of support for the Tea Party (ordered logistic regression)

Predictor	b
Fear of Obama	1.12*
	(.241)
Age	−0.01
	(.101)
Education	−0.06
	(.142)
Income	−0.13*
	(.054)
Male	0.34*
	(.128)
Black	−0.05
	(.204)
Republican	1.04*
	(.288)
Independent	0.72*
	(.160)
Limited Govt.	0.84*
	(.315)
Economic Anxiety	0.06
	(.098)
Ideology	0.21*
	(.045)
Political Knowledge	−0.29
	(.372)
Authoritarianism	0.03
	(.126)
Evangelical	0.29*
	(.148)
Ethnocentrism	0.67
	(1.08)
Racism	−0.25*
	(.095)
Social Dominance	0.19*
	(.062)
FOX News	1.13*
	(.338)
/cut1	0.94
	(1.21)
/cut2	2.12
	(1.20)
/cut3	4.00
	(1.27)
Pseudo R-squared	0.2885
N	719

Note: Clustered standard errors are in parentheses.
*Sig. at $p < 0.05$, one-tailed test; DV is coded 1–4; DV coded such that 4 = high Tea Party support.

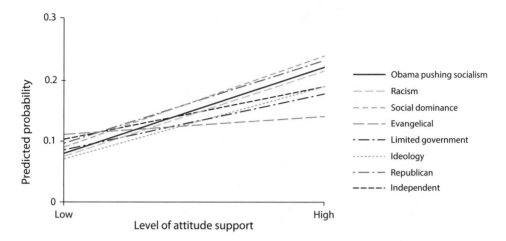

A2.1. Change in the probability of supporting the Tea Party
Note: All predictors shown significant at $p < 0.05$, one-tailed

CHAPTER 3 RESULTS

TABLE A3.1
Predicting support for civil liberties (logistic regression)

Predictor	Support Free Speech	Support Detainment	Support Racial Profiling
Tea Party support	0.50*	−0.01	0.34*
	(.149)	(.076)	(.053)
Social dominance	0.08	0.28*	0.39*
	(.069)	(.060)	(.107)
Republican	−0.05	0.10	0.45
	(.462)	(.251)	(.368)
Independent	−0.03	−0.04	0.43
	(.230)	(.211)	(.289)
Ideology	−0.08	0.17*	0.11
	(.065)	(.052)	(.071)
Authoritarianism	−0.47*	0.60*	0.24
	(.180)	(.158)	(.231)
Ethnocentrism	1.60	−0.77	1.54
	(1.16)	(1.69)	(1.62)
Male	0.49*	−0.29*	0.20
	(.191)	(.141)	(.164)
Age	−0.10	0.14*	0.23*
	(.082)	(.072)	(.105)
Income	0.04	0.05	0.14
	(.053)	(.056)	(.083)
Education	0.05	−0.02	−0.01
	(.133)	(.076)	(.122)
Black	−0.40*	0.09	−1.38*
	(.143)	(.186)	(.393)
Political knowledge	0.40	−0.27	0.87*
	(.250)	(.335)	(.409)
Constant	−2.54	−2.89	−6.87
	(.794)	(1.03)	(.916)
Pseudo R-squared	0.0913	0.0974	0.2391
N	796	857	857

Note: *Clustered* standard errors are in parentheses.
*Sig. at $p < 0.05$, one-tailed test; all variables coded 0–1; DVs coded such that 1 = high support for freedom.

TABLE A3.2
Determinants of various forms of patriotism (logistic regression)

Predictor	(Un)Critical Patriotism	Egalitarian Patriotism	Economic Patriotism
Tea Party support	0.21*	−0.32*	−0.27*
	(.065)	(.082)	(.079)
Social dominance	0.30*	−0.38*	−0.24*
	(.060)	(.064)	(.044)
Republican	−0.35	−0.95*	−0.79*
	(.442)	(.190)	(.365)
Independent	−0.22	−0.54*	−0.38†
	(.309)	(.286)	(.217)
Ideology	−0.06	−0.25*	−0.24*
	(.061)	(.057)	(.055)
Authoritarianism	0.69*	−0.35*	−0.22
	(.224)	(.175)	(.165)
Ethnocentrism	−1.39	−0.23	0.24
	(1.93)	(1.37)	(1.13)
Male	−0.18	0.11	−0.16
	(.193)	(.236)	(.171)
Age	0.04	−0.05	−0.12*
	(.179)	(.101)	(.074)
Income	0.12	−0.08*	−0.01
	(.116)	(.036)	(.050)
Education	−0.40*	0.04	−0.20
	(.145)	(.114)	(.125)
Black	0.21	0.07	0.92*
	(.345)	(.245)	(.285)
Political knowledge	−0.62	0.37	−0.12
	(.353)	(.293)	(.285)
Constant	−2.74	4.64	3.62
	(1.49)	(1.08)	(.662)
Pseudo R-squared	0.1070	0.2538	0.2148
N	857	857	857

Note: *Clustered* standard errors are in parentheses.
*Sig. at $p < 0.05$, one-tailed test; all variables coded 0–1; DVs coded such that 1 = agreement.

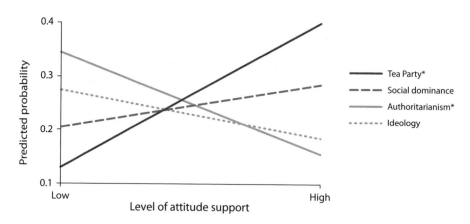

A3.1. Change in the probability of supporting free speech
*Significant at $p < 0.05$, one-tailed

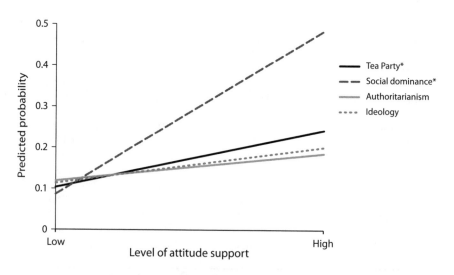

A3.2. Change in the probability of supporting racial profiling
*Significant at $p < 0.05$, one-tailed

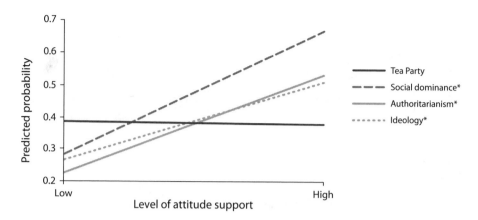

A3.3. Change in the probability of supporting indefinite detainment
*Significant at $p < 0.05$, one-tailed

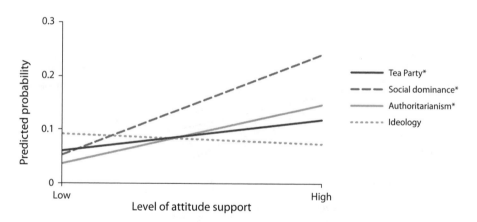

A3.4. Change in the probability of supporting (un)critical patriotism
*Significant at $p < 0.05$, one-tailed

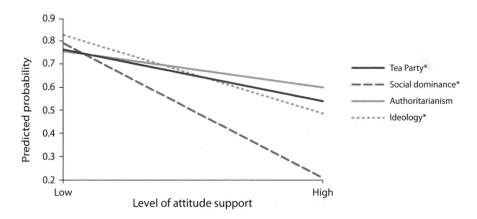

A3.5. Change in the probability of supporting economic patriotism
*Significant at $p < 0.05$, one-tailed

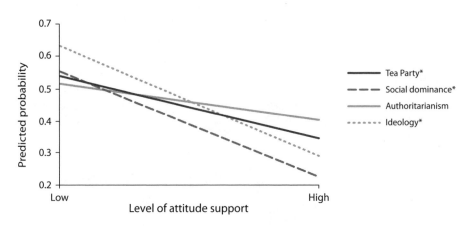

A3.6. Change in the probability of supporting egalitarian patriotism
*Significant at $p < 0.05$, one-tailed

Table A4.1
Determinants of attitudes toward immigrants and immigration policy
(ordered logistic regression)

Predictor	Support DREAM Act	Repeal Citizenship**	New Immigrants Criminal	Too Powerful
Tea Party approval	−0.66*	0.43*	0.16*	0.44*
	(.147)	(.211)	(.070)	(.178)
Social dominance	−2.05*	0.71*	0.28*	−1.93*
	(.385)	(.281)	(.081)	(.375)
Ethnocentrism	0.05	0.14	2.37*	0.10
	(1.28)	(1.52)	(1.12)	(1.59)
Authoritarianism	0.01	0.93*	0.15	0.83*
	(.291)	(.496)	(.128)	(.317)
Age	−0.07	0.04	−0.00	0.16*
	(.078)	(.069)	(.089)	(.072)
Income	0.02	0.03	−0.13	−0.12*
	(.045)	(.033)	(.048)	(.051)
Education	−0.04	−0.11*	0.16	−0.10
	(.074)	(.086)	(.136)	(.109)
Male	0.13	0.14	0.15	0.06
	(.174)	(.135)	(.135)	(.111)
Black	−0.12	−0.11	0.10	−0.12
	(.154)	(.234)	(.154)	(.110)
Republican	−0.75*	0.23	0.07	−0.11
	(.266)	(.257)	(.265)	(.206)
Independent	−0.35*	0.19	0.04	−0.10
	(.131)	(.204)	(.154)	(.172)
Ideology	−0.22*	0.09*	−0.01	0.02
	(.047)	(.058)	(.056)	(.051)
/cut1	−3.44		1.04	−1.28
	(.718)		(.901)	(1.20)
/cut2	−2.95		2.37	−0.32
	(.706)		(.895)	(1.16)
/cut3	−2.75		3.16	−0.02
	(.738)		(.922)	(1.15)
/cut4	−1.52		3.40	0.99
	(.738)		(.914)	(1.12)
Constant		−1.81		
		(.932)		
Pseudo R-squared	0.1025	0.0565	0.0357	0.0473
N	878	908	857	908

Note: *Clustered* standard errors are in parentheses.
*Sig. at $p < 0.05$, one-tailed test; all variables coded 0–1; DVs coded such that high values = support for issue or policy.
**Logistic regression.

TABLE A4.2
Determinants of attitudes toward gays and lesbians and gay rights (logistic regression)

Predictor	Anti-Gays in Military**	Gays Too Powerful	Anti-Gay Marriage	Gays Keep Private
Tea Party approval	0.19*	0.04	0.19*	0.50*
	(.062)	(.144)	(.084)	(.024)
Social dominance	0.15*	0.23*	0.19*	1.05
	(.073)	(.103)	(.079)	(.665)
Ethnocentrism	0.53	−0.39	0.80	3.38†
	(1.40)	(1.56)	(1.16)	(1.73)
Authoritarianism	−0.03	0.11	0.37	0.59
	(.095)	(.231)	(.235)	(.527)
Age	0.03	0.30*	0.26	0.05
	(.099)	(.168)	(.175)	(.138)
Income	−0.01	0.00	0.07	−0.15*
	(.053)	(.067)	(.079)	(.054)
Education	−0.05	0.02	−0.00	−0.10
	(.064)	(.166)	(.180)	(.114)
Male	0.38*	0.60*	0.38*	0.15
	(.128)	(.186)	(.194)	(.196)
Black	0.28	−0.11	0.80*	0.57*
	(.171)	(.286)	(.355)	(.254)
Ideology	0.23*	0.30*	0.26*	0.22*
	(.031)	(.093)	(.061)	(.040)
Morals	0.36*	0.56*	0.83*	2.74*
	(.073)	(.112)	(.083)	(.594)
Evangelical	0.55*	0.30	1.11*	0.57*
	(.158)	(.194)	(.215)	(.241)
/cut1	1.30			
	(.706)			
/cut2	2.04			
	(.722)			
/cut3	2.50			
	(.702)			
/cut4	3.06			
	(.711)			
Constant			−3.19	−1.67
			(.977)	(.981)
Pseudo R-squared	0.1087	0.2573	0.3766	0.2722
N	782	719	753	759

Note: Clustered standard errors are in parentheses.
*Sig. at $p < 0.05$, one-tailed test; all variables coded 0–1; DVs coded such that high values = anti-gay attitudes.
**Ordered logistic regression.

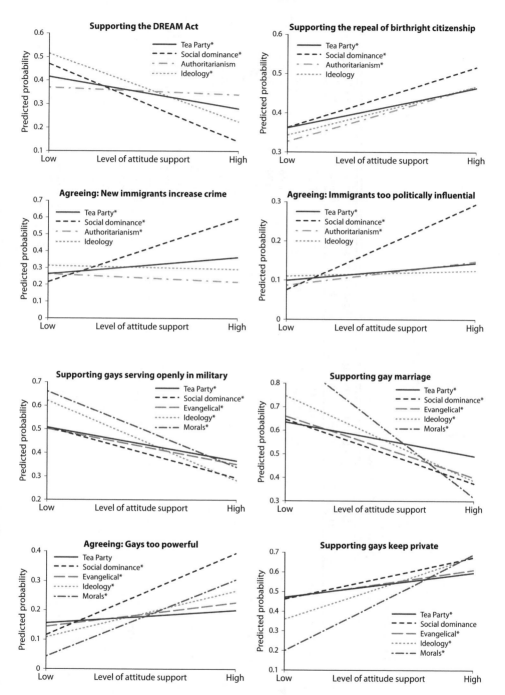

A4.1. Change in the probability of attitudes toward immigrants and sexual minorities
*Significant at $p < 0.05$, one-tailed

TABLE A5.1
Determinants of attitudes toward President Obama

Predictor	Positive Traits**	Obama Personal Approval***	Want Obama to Fail***	Obama Christian**	Obama Born U.S.**
Tea Party approval	-0.18*	-1.74*	2.20*	-1.33*	-1.57*
	(.017)	(.323)	(.405)	(.298)	(.283)
Social dominance	-0.12*	0.88†	0.07	-1.48*	-2.20*
	(.030)	(.508)	(.599)	(.584)	(.449)
Ethnocentrism	0.08	-0.69	-1.60	-1.80	2.05
	(.068)	(1.80)	(1.86)	(1.63)	(1.29)
Racism	0.05*	1.26*	-1.88*	0.53	0.48
	(.027)	(.428)	(.524)	(.431)	(.441)
Authoritarianism	-0.02	-0.61	0.44	-0.63	-1.14*
	(.031)	(.380)	(.508)	(.477)	(.402)
Age	-0.01	-0.07	0.11	-0.01	-0.30*
	(.006)	(.076)	(.098)	(.103)	(.108)
Income	-0.00	-0.12*	0.05	0.05	-0.03
	(.004)	(.042)	(.062)	(.051)	(.055)
Education	-0.01	0.12	0.18	0.16	0.11
	(.008)	(.101)	(.171)	(.099)	(.132)
Male	-0.01	-0.19	-0.10	0.17	0.09
	(.014)	(.169)	(.184)	(.134)	(.270)

	(1)	(2)	(3)	(4)	(5)
Black	0.08*	1.06*	−1.35*	0.67*	−0.35
	(.016)	(.285)	(.339)	(.218)	(.296)
Republican	−0.13*	−1.46*	1.21*	−0.58*	1.12*
	(.019)	(.215)	(.232)	(.237)	(.312)
Ideology	−0.03*	−0.24*	0.43*	−0.16*	−0.04
	(.005)	(.051)	(.061)	(.030)	(.064)
Fox News	−0.08*	−0.65*	0.63*	−0.39*	−0.24
	(.014)	(.243)	(.192)	(.177)	(.236)
Evangelical	0.01	−0.05	0.27*	0.41*	−0.37*
	(.011)	(.191)	(.121)	(.165)	(.221)
/cut1		−5.40	4.17		
		(.839)	(.690)		
/cut2		−5.04	4.95		
		(.840)	(.724)		
/cut3		−4.47			
		(.863)			
/cut4		−2.67			
		(.828)			
Constant	1.02			2.65	3.27
	(.056)			(.861)	1.04
Pseudo R-squared	.1521	0.2652	0.3846	0.2457	0.2499
N	891	863	859	892	892

Note: Clustered standard errors are in parentheses.

*Sig. at $p < 0.05$, one-tailed test; all variables coded 0–1; DVs coded such that high values = agreement.

**Logistic regression.

***Ordered logistic regression.

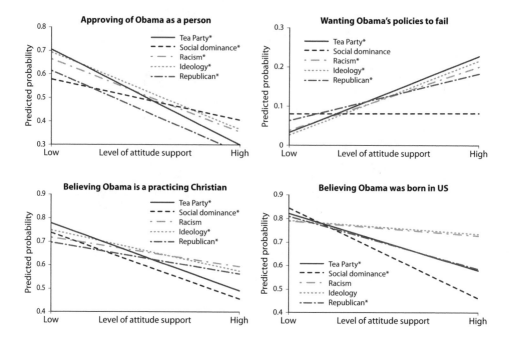

A5.1. Association between Tea Party support and attitudes and facts toward Obama
*Significant at $p < 0.05$, one-tailed

CHAPTER 6 RESULTS

TABLE **A6.1**
Determinants of political participation (logistic regression)

Predictor	High Interest**	Attend Meeting	Vote 2010	Vote Republican
Tea Party approval	0.41*	0.23	0.79*	2.91*
	(.213)	(.191)	(.358)	(.249)
Age	0.34*	−0.06	0.46*	0.15
	(.060)	(.071)	(.163)	(.167)
Income	0.08*	0.12*	0.21*	0.11*
	(.043)	(.056)	(.095)	(.053)
Education	0.13*	0.15	0.21*	0.20
	(.070)	(.135)	(.128)	(.138)
Male	−0.01	−0.20	−0.39*	0.06
	(.120)	(.157)	(.233)	(.182)
Black	0.33*	0.41*	0.70*	−1.52*
	(.170)	(.171)	(.199)	(.277)
Republican	−0.21	0.15	0.41	1.96*
	(.170)	(.213)	(.382)	(.327)
Ideology	0.01	−0.02	0.02	0.47*
	(.027)	(.044)	(.099)	(.087)
Political knowledge	1.25*	0.91*	1.10*	0.49
	(.206)	(.289)	(.452)	(.448)
Political interest		0.51*	0.57*	0.15
		(.099)	(.140)	(.103)
/cut1	−1.19			
	(.315)			
/cut2	0.01			
	(.279)			
/cut3	1.64			
	(.288)			
/cut4	4.04			
	(.326)			
Constant		−3.99	−3.08	−6.84
		(.534)	(.578)	(.448)
Pseudo R-squared	0.0345	0.0637	0.1681	0.5443
N	1032	1032	1032	1032

Note: *Clustered* standard errors are in parentheses.
  *Sig. at $p < 0.05$, one-tailed test; all variables coded 0–1; DVs coded such that high values = high participation.
  **Ordered logistic regression.

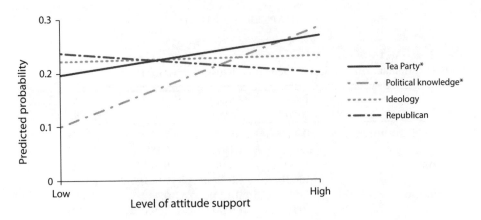

A6.1. Change in the probability of expressing high political interest
*Significant at $p < 0.05$, one-tailed

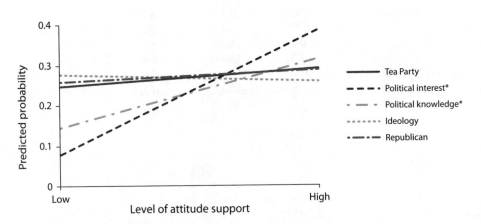

A6.2. Change in the probability of attending a political meeting
*Significant at $p < 0.05$, one-tailed

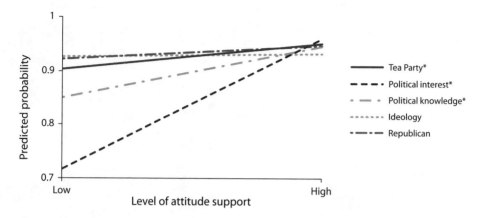

A6.3. Change in the probability of voting in the November 2010 elections
*Significant at $p < 0.05$, one-tailed

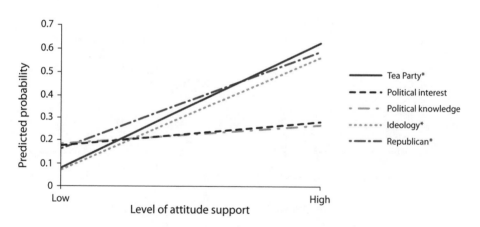

A6.4. Change in the probability of voting Republican in the
November 2010 elections
*Significant at $p < 0.05$, one-tailed

NOTES

INTRODUCTION

1. These quotes and observations are based on a first-person account undertaken by Mike Edra, "The Second Annual Oregon Tea Party Celebration: A Movement in Which Ideas Seem to Have Growing Importance," Institute for Research & Education on Human Rights (IREHR), May 31, 2011, http://irehr.org/issue-areas/tea-parties/19-news/83-the-2nd-annual-oregon-tea-party-celebration-a-movement-in-which-ideas-seem-to-have-growing-importance.

2. These quotes and observations are based on a first-person account undertaken by Devin Burghart, "Tea Time with the Posse Inside an Idaho Tea Party Patriots Conference," IREHR, April 18, 2011, http://irehr.org/issue-areas/tea-parties/19-news/79-tea-time-with-the-posse-inside-an-idaho-tea-party-patriots-conference.

3. Theda Skocpol and Vanessa Williamson, *The Tea Party and the Remaking of Republican Conservatism* (New York: Oxford University Press, 2012), 6.

4. For Peggy Noonan's observations, see "Why It's Time for the Tea Party," *Wall Street Journal* online, http://online.wsj.com/article/SB10001424052748703440604575496221482123504.html; for Juan Williams's observations, see "Tea Party Anger Reflects Mainstream Concerns," http://online.wsj.com/article/SB10001424052702304252704575155942054483252.html.

5. See, among others, Mark A. Smith, *The Right Talk: How Conservatives Transformed the Great Society into the Economic Society* (Princeton: Princeton University Press, 2007); Clinton Rossiter, *Conservatism in America* (Cambridge, MA: Harvard University Press, 1982).

6. Dick Armey, *Give Us Liberty: A Tea Party Manifesto* (New York: William Morrow, 2010).

7. Thierry Devos and Mahzarin R. Banaji, "American = White?," *Journal of Personality and Social Psychology* 88, no. 3 (2005): 447–66; and Margot Canaday, *The Straight State: Sexuality and Citizenship in Twentieth Century America* (Princeton: Princeton University Press, 2009).

8. Daniel Bell, ed., *The New American Right* (New York: Criterion, 1955); and Seymour Martin Lipset and Earl Raab, *The Politics of Unreason: Right-Wing Extremism in American Politics, 1790–1970* (New York: Harper and Row, 1970).

9. Richard Hofstadter, *The Paranoid Style in American Politics* (New York: Vintage Books, 1952), 29.

10. Ibid., 32.

11. Seymour Martin Lipset and Earl Raab, *The Politics of Unreason: Right Wing Extremism in America, 1790–1977* (Chicago: University of Chicago Press, 1978).

12. For more, see, among others, Tyler Anbinder, *Nativism and Slavery: The Northern Know Nothings and the Politics of the 1850s* (New York: Oxford University Press, 1992); see also, Bruce Levine, "Conservatism, Nativism, and Slavery: Thomas R. Whitney and the Origins of the Know-Nothing Party," *Journal of American History* 88, no. 2 (2001): 455–88.

13. Nancy MacLean, *Behind the Mask of Chivalry: The Making of the Second Ku Klux Klan* (New York: Oxford University Press, 1994); Rory McVeigh, *The Rise of the Ku Klux Klan: Right-Wing Movements and National Politics* (Minneapolis: University of Minnesota Press, 2009); and Lipset and Raab, *The Politics of Unreason.*

14. See J. Allen Broyles, *The John Birch Society: Anatomy of a Protest* (Boston: Beacon Press, 1966); Benjamin R. Epstein and Arnold Forster, *The Radical Right: Report on the John Birch Society and Its Allies* (New York: Vintage Books, 1967); and Robert Welch, *The Blue Book of the John Birch Society* (self-published, 1961).

15. Stanley B. Greenberg, James Carville, Jim Gerstein, Peyton M. Craighill, and Kate Monninger, "Special Report on the Tea Party Movement: The Tea Party—An Ideological Republican Grass-roots Movement; but Don't Mistake It for a Populist Rebellion," Democracy Corps, 4. Available at http://www.democracycorps.com/attachments/article/821/Tea-Party-Report-FINAL.pdf.

16. Andrew Perrin, Steven J. Tepper, Neal Caren, and Sally Morris, "Cultures of the Tea Party," *Contexts* 10, no. 2 (2011): 74–75.

17. Frank Rich, "The Rage Is Not About Health Care," *New York Times* online, http://www.nytimes.com/2010/03/28/opinion/28rich.html?_r=0.

18. For an excellent rendering of the relationship between homosexuality and American identity, see Margot Canaday, *The Straight State.*

19. For more on social learning theory, see, among others, Albert Bandura and Richard H. Walters, *Social Learning and Personality Development* (New York: Holt, Rinehart and Winston, 1963). For its application to reactionary movements, see Ira S. Rohter, "Social and Psychological Determinants of Radical Rightism," in *The American Right Wing: Readings in American Political Behavior,* ed. Robert A. Schoenberger (New York: Holt, Rinehart, and Winston, 1969), 193–238.

20. For more on reactionary conservatism, something we explore in greater detail in chapter 1, see Clinton Rossiter, *Conservatism in America.* For an alternative view of conservatism, one that sees no daylight separating reactionary from moderate, traditional conservatives, see Corey Robin, *The Reac-*

tionary Mind: Conservatism from Edmund Burke to Sarah Palin (New York: Oxford University Press, 2011). Rest assured, we put these competing views on conservatism to an empirical test in chapter 1.

21. Dean Reynolds, "Palin: 'It's Time to Take Our Country Back,'" CBS News.com, http://www.cbsnews.com/8301-503544_162-20016903-503544.html.

22. Bernard Bailyn, *The Ideological Origins of the American Revolution* (Cambridge, MA: Harvard University Press, 1992); and Gordon S. Wood, *The Creation of the American Republic, 1776–1787* (Chapel Hill: University of North Carolina Press, 1969).

23. For political elites, see James T. Patterson, *Mr. Republican: A Biography of Robert A. Taft* (Boston: Houghton Mifflin) and *Congressional Conservatism and the New Deal: The Growth of the Conservative Coalition in Congress, 1933–1939* (Lexington: University of Kentucky Press, 1967). For the reaction of business elites, see Kim Phillips-Fein, *Invisible Hands: The Making of the Conservative Movement from the New Deal to Reagan* (New York: W. W. Norton, 2009).

24. Mark Williams's original blog post has been removed. However, the following link contains a reproduction: http://gawker.com/5588556/the-embarrassing-racist-satire-of-tea-party-leader-mark-williams.

25. See "Mary Davenport, Tea Party Activist and Republican, Should Resign Over Racist 'Ape' Photo of Obama," Tuscon Citizen.com, http://tucsoncitizen.com/arizona-hispanic-republicans/2011/04/18/marilyn-davenport-tea-party-activist-and-republican-should-resign-over-racist-ape-photo-of-obama/.

26. Michele Bachmann, "Obama Needs to Stand for His Own Statements Regarding His Faith and Citizenship," YouTube video, http://www.youtube.com/watch?v=8uZEmee_c4o.

27. See, among others, Rogers M. Smith, *Civic Ideals: Conflicting Visions of Citizenship in U.S. History* (New Haven: Yale University Press, 1997), chapter 2.

28. David G. Gutierrez, *Walls and Mirrors: Mexican Americans, Mexican Immigrants, and the Politics of Ethnicity* (Berkeley: University of California Press, 1995), chapter 1.

29. Mae M. Ngai, *Impossible Subjects: Illegal Aliens and the Making of Modern America* (Princeton: Princeton University Press, 2004).

30. The literature here is wide-ranging and deep. We simply cite a few here. For a comprehensive review of racial issues across a range of racial categories, see the entire volume by Neil J. Smelser, William Julius Wilson, and Faith Mitchell, *America Becoming: Racial Trends and Their Consequences*, vol. 1 (Washington, DC: National Research Council, 2001). For the relationship

between race, incarceration, and employment, see Bruce Western, *Punishment and Inequality in America* (New York: Russell Sage, 2006); and Devah Pager, *Marked: Race, Crime, and Finding Work in an Era of Mass Incarceration* (Chicago: University of Chicago Press, 2007). For race and wealth, see Melvin L. Oliver and Thomas M. Shapiro, *Black Wealth/White Wealth: A New Perspective on Racial Inequality* (New York: Routledge, 1995). For race and residential segregation, see Douglas S. Massey and Nancy M. Denton, *American Apartheid: Segregation and the Making of the Underclass* (Cambridge, MA: Harvard University Press, 1993). For the relationship between race and poverty, see William J. Wilson, *The Truly Disadvantaged: The Inner City, the Underclass, and Public Policy* (Chicago: University of Chicago Press, 1987). Finally, for an excellent overview of the life chances of Latinos, see Edward E. Telles and Vilma Ortiz, *Generations of Exclusion: Mexican Americans, Assimilation, and Race* (New York: Russell Sage, 2008).

31. See, among others, Thomas C. Holt, *Children of Fire: A History of African Americans* (New York: Hill and Wang, 2010); and Desmond S. King and Rogers M. Smith, *Still a House Divided: Race and Politics in Obama's America* (Princeton: Princeton University Press, 2011).

32. For the record, we define racism as the way(s) in which skin color identifies "natural" differences between the racial "norm" and racial "Others." These differences—based, among other things, on intelligence and carriage—"justifies" the establishment of "practices, institutions, and structures" that secure permanent dominion of the in-group over the out-group. See George M. Fredrickson, *Racism: A Short History* (Princeton: Princeton University Press, 2002), 6.

33. Barbara J. Fields, "Ideology and Race in American History," in *Region, Race and Reconstruction: Essays in Honor of C. Vann Woodward*, ed. J. Morgan Kousser and James M. McPherson (New York: Oxford University Press, 1982), 143–77.

34. Joseph Lowndes, Julie Novkov, and Dorian Warren, eds., *Race and American Political Development* (London: Routledge, 2008); and Timothy Messer-Kruse, *Race Relations in the United States, 1980–2000* (Westport, CT: Greenwood, 2008); Matthew Lassiter and Joseph Crespino, eds., *The Myth of Southern Exceptionalism* (Oxford: Oxford University Press, 2009).

35. For other studies of right-wing movements that draw on symbolic politics, see Pamela Conover and Virginia Gray, *Feminism and the New Right: Conflict over the American Family* (New York: Praeger, 1983); and Clyde Wilcox, *God's Warriors: The Christian Right in Twentieth-Century America* (Baltimore: Johns Hopkins University Press, 1992).

36. Murray Edelman, *The Symbolic Uses of Politics* (Urbana: University of Illinois Press, 1965); Charles D. Elder and Roger W. Cobb, *The Political Uses of Symbols* (New York: Longman, 1983); David O. Sears, "Symbolic Politics:

A Socio-Psychological Theory," in *Explorations in Political Psychology*, ed. Shanto Iyengar and William J. McGuire (Durham, NC: Duke University Press, 1993), 113–49; see also Raymond Firth, *Symbols: Public and Private* (Ithaca: Cornell University Press, 1973).

37. For an account that's balanced, see Kate Zernike, *Boiling Mad: Inside Tea Party America* (New York: Times Books, 2010). For more partisan accounts, see Will Bunch, *The Backlash: Right-Wing Radicals, High-Def Hucksters, and Paranoid Politics in the Age of Obama* (New York: HarperCollins, 2010); and Scott Rasmussen and Douglas Schoen, *Mad as Hell: How the Tea Party Movement Is Fundamentally Remaking Our Two-Party System* (New York: HarperCollins, 2010).

38. For more, see Jill Lepore, *The Whites of Their Eyes: The Tea Party's Revolution and the Battle over American History* (Princeton: Princeton University Press, 2010); and Elizabeth Price Foley, *The Tea Party: Three Principles* (Cambridge: Cambridge University Press, 2012).

39. Skocpol and Williamson, *The Tea Party and the Remaking of Republican Conservatism.*

40. Devin Burghart, "Mapping the Tea Party caucus in the 112th Congress," IREHR, http://irehr.org/issue-areas/tea-party-nationalism/tea-party-news-and-analysis/item/355-mapping-the-tea-party-caucus-in-the-112th-congress.

41. "How the Tea Party Helped GOP Find a Path to Election Day Success," *Christian Science Monitor* online, http://www.csmonitor.com/USA/Elections/Tea-Party-Tally/2010/1102/How-the-tea-party-helped-GOP-find-a-path-to-Election-Day-successes/%28page%29/2; and Michael Cooper, "Victories Suggest Wider Appeal of Tea Party," *New York Times* online, http://www.nytimes.com/2010/11/03/us/politics/03tea.html?partner=rss&emc=rss.

42. Devin Burghart, "What Didn't Happen in Vegas: Tea Party Nation Ordered to Pay Up," IREHR, http://irehr.org/issue-areas/tea-party-nationalism/tea-party-news-and-analysis.

43. These figures are available here: http://www.irehr.org/the-data/tea-party-growth-chart.

44. For the numbers of Tea Party "agreement," see Pew's Political and Media Survey, Pew Research Center for the People and the Press, July 20–24, 2011.

45. We arrived at roughly 45 million by multiplying the voting-age population as of 2008 (225.5 million) by the 20 percent of the population that "agrees" with the Tea Party.

46. For the Tea Party's involvement in the voter ID efforts, see http://www.huffingtonpost.com/2012/10/05/true-the-vote-target-for-_n_1943329.html; for the number of citizens likely affected by the voter ID laws, see Wendy R. Weiser and Lawrence Norden, "Voting Law Changes in 2012," Brennan Center

for Justice, October 2011. For the Tea Party's involvement in the War on Women, see http://truth-out.org/news/item/8603-how-the-war-on-women-became -mainstream?tmpl=component&print=1.

47. Rory McVeigh, *The Rise of the Ku Klux Klan*, 32–33.

48. Sara Diamond, *Roads to Dominion: Right-Wing Movements and Political Power in the United States* (New York: Guilford Press, 1995).

49. We referenced the following sources for the demographic and attitudinal data on which we reported in the text: Kevin Arceneaux and Stephen P. Nicholson, "Reading Tea Party Leaves: Who Supports the Tea Party Movement, What Do They Want, and Why?" (unpublished manuscript, 2011); see also Gary C. Jacobsen, "The President, the Tea Party, and Voting Behavior in 2010: Insights from the Cooperative Congressional Election Study," paper presented at the Annual Meeting of the American Political Science Association, Seattle, WA, September 1–4, 2011. Finally, see Angela Maxwell, "Tea Party Distinguished by Radical Views and Fear of the Future," Blair-Rockefeller Poll, http://www.uark.edu/rd_arsc/blairrockefellerpoll/5295.php, retrieved July 6, 2011.

50. For the Klan, see MacLean, *Behind the Mask of Chivalry*. For interpretations of the John Birch Society, see J. Allen Broyles, *The John Birch Society*; Epstein and Forster, *The Radical Right*; and Robert Welch, *The Blue Book of the John Birch Society* (self-published, 1961). For interpretations of the Tea Party, see Devin Burghart and Leonard Zeskind, "Tea Party Nationalism: A Critical Examination of the Tea Party Movement, and the Size, Scope, and Focus of Its National Factions," IREHR, Fall 2010. See also, Skocpol and Williamson, *The Tea Party and the Remaking of Republican Conservatism*.

51. Bert Klandermans and Dirk Oegema, "Potentials, Networks, Motivations, and Barriers: Steps towards Participation in Social Movements," *American Sociological Review* 52 (1987): 519–31.

52. Ibid., 529.

53. For a more cost-benefit approach to social movement participation, see Dirk Oegema and Bert Klandermans, "Why Social Movement Sympathizers Don't Participate: Erosion and Nonconversion of Support," *American Sociological Review* 59 (1994): 703–22.

54. For accounts of the ways in which life circumstances promote or dampen prospects for activism, see Doug McAdam, *Freedom Summer* (New York: Oxford University Press, 1988). For an updated version, see Doug McAdam and Ronnelle Paulsen, "Specifying the Relationship between Social Ties and Activism," *American Journal of Sociology* 99, no. 3 (1993): 640–67. For a slightly different take, one in which commitment to movement-related issues happen *after* mobilization, see Ziad Munson, *The Making of Pro-Life*

Activists: How Social Movement Mobilization Works (Chicago: University of Chicago Press, 2008).

55. Munson, *The Making of Pro-Life Activists*.

CHAPTER ONE

1. For a more contemporary version of this view, see Elizabeth Theiss-Morse, *Who Counts as an American? The Boundaries of National Identity* (New York: Cambridge University Press, 2009), chapter 3. For a more historical version of the same argument based on different evidence, see Smith, *Civic Ideals*.

2. Richard Hofstadter, *The Paranoid Style in American Politics*, chapter 1.

3. We are aware that at least some in the Tea Party see Parker as a turncoat. Still, see criticism of the Tea Party here: Kathleen Parker, "The Tea Fragger Party," *Washington Post* online, http://www.washingtonpost.com/opinions/the-tea-fragger-party/2011/07/29/gIQA23pAiI_story.html.

4. Work conducted by Edwin Amenta and his colleagues suggests that movement influence may be gleaned from the extent to which it receives news coverage. The Klan and the John Birch Society, as representatives of larger right-wing movement "families," received the most coverage in the *New York Times*. Because we're interested in the largest, mass-based right-wing movements, identified using the aforementioned criteria, several well-known movements are excluded, including the Christian Anticommunism Crusade, Young Americans for Freedom, and so on. On the grounds that it was a regional movement confined to the South, we also exclude the White Citizens' Councils. For more measuring of the influence of social movements, see Amenta et al., "All the Movements Fit to Print." Furthermore, to the extent that some argue that the Tea Party is an "Astro Turf" movement, one run by billionaire and advocacy groups from the top down, recent scholarship casts doubt on that claim. According to Skocpol and Williamson, the Tea Party movement combines three forces: grassroots troops, deep-pocketed billionaires and free-market advocacy groups, and conservative media. See, *The Tea Party and the Remaking of Republican Conservatism*.

5. We recognize that the New Right is a sensible candidate for comparison, but it's too diverse to classify as a unified movement. The New Right included the Religious Right and the Secular Right. The Religious Right mobilized against abortion and the Equal Rights Amendment, among other issues. The Secular Right's principal focus centered on economic issues but included family issues, to the extent that they overlapped with economic productivity. But each wing of the New Right splintered into dozens of social movement organizations. Moreover, because of its sheer diversity, the New Right isn't listed

as one of the most influential right-wing movements of the twentieth century. See Amenta et al., "All the Movements Fit to Print: Who, What, When, Where, and Why SMO Families Appeared in the New York Times in the Twentieth Century." For the diversity of the New Right, see Pamela Conover and Virginia Gray, *Feminism and the New Right: Conflict over the American Family* (New York: Praeger, 1983).

6. We rely on Clinton Rossiter's interpretation of reactionaries; see *Conservatism in America*.

7. Richard Hofstadter, *The Paranoid Style in American Politics*, 23.

8. Seymour Martin Lipset and Earl Raab, *The Politics of Unreason*, 19.

9. Ibid.; Richard Hofstadter, *Paranoid Style in American Politics*; see Daniel Bell, "Interpretations of American Politics," in *The Radical Right*, ed. Daniel Bell (New Brunswick, NJ: Transaction Publishers, 2008), 47–74.

10. McVeigh, *The Rise of the Ku Klux Klan*.

11. Roland G. Fryer Jr. and Steven D. Levitt, "Hatred and Profits: Getting Under the Hood of the Ku Klux Klan," *NBER Working Paper Series*, Working Paper #13417, National Bureau of Economic Research, 2007.

12. Quoted in MacLean, *Behind the Mask of Chivalry*, xii.

13. Ibid., 5.

14. See, among others, David M. Chalmers, *Hooded Americanism: The History of the Ku Klux Klan* (Durham, NC: Duke University Press, 1987); Kenneth T. Jackson, *The Ku Klux Klan in the City, 1915–1930* (New York: Oxford University Press, 1967); and MacLean, *Behind the Mask of Chivalry*.

15. Seymour Martin Lipset notes a similar trend in Europe, in which the petit bourgeois are attracted to right-wing movements. See his *Political Man: The Social Bases of Politics* (Garden City, NY: Doubleday, 1960).

16. For economic competition, see McVeigh, *The Rise of the Ku Klux Klan*, chapter 4. For the Klan's interpretation of what constitutes American values, see MacLean, *Behind the Mask of Chivalry*, chapter 7.

17. Paul Kleppner, *The Cross of Culture: A Social Analysis of Midwestern Politics, 1850–1900* (New York: Free Press, 1970).

18. Fred W. Grupp Jr., "The Political Perspectives of Birch Society Members," in *The American Right Wing: Readings in Political Behavior*, ed. Robert A. Schoenberger, 83–118.

19. Epstein and Forster, *The Radical Right*, chapter 14.

20. Ibid.; see also Lipset and Raab, *The Politics of Unreason*, chapter 8.

21. Epstein and Forster, *The Radical Right.*

22. J. Allen Broyles, *The John Birch Society.*

23. Ibid.

24. Richard Hofstadter, *The Paranoid Style in American Politics.*

25. Darren Dochuk, *From Bible Belt to Sunbelt: Plain-Folk Religion, Grassroots Politics, and the Rise of Evangelical Conservatism* (New York: W. W. Norton, 2011); Hofstadter, *Paranoid Style*, chapter 3; see also John Higham, *Strangers in the Land: Patterns of American Nativism, 1860–1925* (New Brunswick, NJ: Rutgers University Press, 1955).

26. See, among others, Norman H. Nie, Jane Junn, and Kenneth Stehlik-Barry, *Education and Democratic Citizenship in America* (Chicago: University of Chicago Press, 1996).

27. While acknowledging the less attractive beliefs and practices of the Klan, there are some who argue that the Invisible Empire was a middle-class, neopopulist movement. Scholars like historian Leonard J. Moore recognize the ugliness for which the Klan is known, but he suggests that these beliefs and practices must be seen in context. That is, during this time, bigotry-driven white supremacy of all types, especially in Klan country (i.e., the Midwest and the South), was common, even de rigueur. The Klan's belief in the piety of Protestantism was no less dominant than its subscription to white supremacy. Klan members, according to the revisionist scholarship on the Invisible Empire, were therefore no different than most of white Protestant society. In other words, the Klan "represented mainstream social and political concerns, not those of a disaffected fringe group." For more on this revisionist account of the 1920s Klan, see, among others, Leonard J. Moore, *Citizen Klansmen: The Ku Klux Klan in Indiana, 1921–1928* (Chapel Hill: University of North Carolina Press, 1991); Shawn Lay, *Hooded Nights on the Niagara: The Ku Klux Klan in Buffalo, New York* (New York: New York University Press, 1995); and Glenn Feldman, *Politics, Society and the Klan in Alabama, 1915–1949* (Tuscaloosa: University of Alabama Press, 1999). For the quote, Leonard J. Moore, "Historical Interpretations of the 1920s Klan: A Traditional View and the Populist Revision," *Journal of Social History* 24 (1990): 342.

28. Critchtlow, *Conservative Ascendancy.*

29. Joseph R. Gusfield, *Symbolic Crusade: Status Politics and the American Temperance Movement* (Urbana: University of Illinois Press, 1963), 10–12, 16. For a closer look at status politics as protection of a group's way of life, see Ann L. Page and Donald A. Clelland, "The Kanawha County Textbook Controversy: A Study of the Politics of Lifestyle," *Social Forces* 57 (1978): 265–81. In his analysis of survey data collected in the 1960s, James McEvoy III arrives at a similar conclusion: the Goldwater and Wallace movements were driven by

the perception of declining social prestige. These movements, in other words, sought to "defend challenges to the normative patterns of established groups [in which] these reactionary groups are responding to perceived threats to prestige . . . and . . . [the] need for further acceptance into the moral, economic, and political orders of society." See McEvoy, *Radicals or Conservatives? The Contemporary American Right* (Chicago: Rand, McNally, 1971), 153.

30. Gusfield, *Symbolic Crusade*; for an account of the fallout associated with the perception of declining social prestige during the 1960s, see Ira S. Rohter, "Social and Psychological Determinants of Radical Rightism," in *The American Right Wing: Readings in American Political Behavior, ed.* Robert A. Schenberger, 193–238.

31. Roderick M. Kramer, "Paranoid Social Cognition in Social Systems: Thinking and Acting in the Shadow of Doubt," *Personality and Social Psychology Review* 2, no. 4 (1998): 251–75; the quote may be found on 254.

32. Susan T. Fiske, Beth Morling, and Laura E. Stevens, "Controlling Self and Others: A Theory of Anxiety, Mental Control, and Social Control," *Personality and Social Psychology Bulletin* 22, no. 2 (1996): 115–23; the quote can be located on 122.

33. For social-scientific approaches to paranoia, see, among others, M. Fornells-Ambrojo and P. A. Garety, "Understanding Attributional Biases, Emotions, and Self-esteem in 'Poor Me' Paranoia: Findings from an Early Psychosis Sample," *British Journal of Clinical Psychology* 48, no. 2 (2009): 141–62; Richard P. Bentall, Peter Kinderman, and Sue Kaney, "The Self, Attributional Process and Abnormal Beliefs: Towards a Model of Persecutory Delusions," *Behavioral Research and Therapy* 32 (1994): 331–41; and Peter Kinderman and Richard P. Bentall, "Causal Attributions in Paranoia and Depression: Internal, Personal, and Situational Attributions for Negative Events," *Journal of Abnormal Psychology* 106, no. 2 (1997): 41–45. For more on the relationship between power and intergroup relations, see Fiske, Morling, and Stevens, "Controlling Self and Others: A Theory of Anxiety, Mental Control, and Social Control"; and Eric Depret and Susan T. Fiske, "Perceiving the Powerful: Intriguing Individuals versus Threatening Groups," *Journal of Experimental Social Psychology* 35 (1999): 461–81.

34. Lawrence D. Bobo and Mia Tuan, *Prejudice in Politics: Group Position, Public Opinion, and the Wisconsin Treaty Rights Dispute* (Cambridge, MA: Harvard University Press, 2006).

35. Jennifer A. Whitson and Adam D. Galinsky, "Lacking Control Increases Illusory Pattern Perception," *Science* 322 (2008): 115–17.

36. We note this because it's a wash between the Klan and the JBS on other issues. For instance, the JBS suffered from an absence of representation in the White House, where President Dwight D. Eisenhower's eight-year stint was the

sole interruption of what would have otherwise been three and a half decades of Democrats in the White House. The Klan could claim no such frustration, for with the exception of Woodrow Wilson's time in office, Republicans occupied the Oval Office more than twenty years. The Klan's embrace of bigger government in the form of progressive policies differs from the JBS's fatigue of big government, a backlash with roots in resistance to the New Deal.

37. Maxwell, "Tea Party Distinguished by Racial Views and Fear of the Future."

38. Conover and Gray, *Feminism and the New Right*.

39. For a historical take on the phenotypical American, see Smith, *Civic Ideals*; for a more contemporary illustration, see Devos and Banaji, "American = White?"

40. For the president as the government personified, see Theodore J. Lowi, *The Personal President: Power Invested, Promise Unfulfilled* (Ithaca: Cornell University Press, 1985).

41. David Easton and Jack Dennis, *Children in the Political System: Origins of Political Legitimacy* (Chicago: University of Chicago Press, 1969).

42. Edelman, *The Symbolic Uses of Politics*.

43. Charles D. Elder and Roger W. Cobb, *The Political Uses of Symbols*; see also Firth, *Symbols: Public and Private*.

44. See Devos and Banaji, "American = White?"; Thiess-Morse, *Who Counts as an American?*; and Deborah J. Schildkraut, *Americanism in the Twenty-First Century: Public Opinion in the Age of Immigration* (New York: Cambridge University Press, 2011).

45. Hofstadter's impression is supported by Depret and Fiske, "Perceiving the Powerful." For pessimism associated with Tea Party supporters, see Maxwell, "Tea Party Distinguished by Racial Views and Fear of the Future."

46. Psychologist Agnieszka Golec de Zavala and her colleagues have demonstrated that aggression is linked to perceptions that one's group has been disrespected. See Agnieszka Golec de Zavala, Aleksandra Cichocka, Roy Eidelson, and Nuwan Jayawickreme, "Collective Narcissism and Its Social Consequences," *Journal of Personality and Social Psychology* 97, no. 6 (2009): 1074–96.

47. For estimates of the effect of the stimulus, see "Estimated Impact of the American Recovery and Reinvestment Act on Employment and Economic Output from January 2011 through March 2011," Congressional Budget Office, May 2011. For the estimated financial impact of health care reform, see Congressional Budget Office, letter to the Honorable John Boehner concerning the Patient Protection and Affordable Care Act (February 18, 2011).

48. For estimates of the effect of the stimulus, see "Estimated Impact of the American Recovery and Reinvestment Act on Employment and Economic Output from October 2011 through December 2011," Congressional Budget Office, February 2012.

49. Michael Tesler, "The Spillover of Racialization into Health Care: How President Obama Polarizes Public Opinion by Racial Attitudes and Race," 2010, paper prepared for the Annual Meeting of the International Society of Political Psychologists, July 2010.

50. Daniel Bell, "The Dispossessed," in *The Radical Right*, 3rd edition, ed. Daniel Bell (New York: Transaction Press, 2008), 2–3.

51. See Christopher S. Parker, Mark Q. Sawyer, and Christopher Towler, "A Black Man in the White House? The Role of Racism and Patriotism in the 2008 Presidential Election," *Du Bois Review* 6, no. 1 (2009): 193–17; and Matthew O. Hunt and David C. Wilson, "Race/Ethnicity, Perceived Discrimination, and Beliefs about the Meaning of an Obama Presidency," *Du Bois Review* 6, no. 1 (2009): 173–92.

52. People who support the Tea Party tend to be more conservative than Republicans overall in that 54 percent identify with the Republican Party while 73 percent consider themselves conservative. For this reason we emphasize ideology. For details, see Kate Zernike and Megan Thee-Brenan, "Poll Finds Tea Party Backers Wealthier and More Educated," *New York Times* online, April 14, 2010; available at http://www.nytimes.com/2010/04/15/us/politics/15poll.html. For more on attitudes toward policy domains, see Maxwell, "Tea Party Distinguished by Racial Views and Fear of the Future."

53. Patrick Allitt, *The Conservatives: Ideas and Personalities throughout American History* (New Haven: Yale University Press, 2009), chapter 1.

54. See Crawford, *Thunder on the Right*; Rossiter, *Conservatism in America*; Viereck, "The Philosophical 'New' Conservatism," and Kevin P. Phillips, *Post-Conservative America: People, Politics, and Ideology* (New York: Random House, 1982).

55. There were also internal divisions among conservatives, mainly between traditionalists and the new conservatives that revolved around industrialism. The type of conservatism pushed by industrial capitalists departed in several ways from traditional conservative doctrine. Laissez-faire conservatism, as late political theorist Clinton Rossiter called it, departed from more traditional conservatism in the following ways. Going back to Edmund Burke and John Adams, traditional conservatives valued community; laissez-faire conservatives valued rugged individualism; the former preferred harmony where the latter preferred competition; laissez-faire conservatives were the first conservatives in modern history to say that government could only hurt, not help people; traditional conservatives didn't associate capital accumulation with

helping the general welfare, or invention with progress, as did laissez-faire conservatives; traditional conservatives believed in charity, cooperation, and sensitivity to the plight of their compatriots, while for laissez-faire conservatives it was "every man for himself." For more details, see Rossiter, *Conservatism in America*; see also, Russell Kirk, *The Conservative Mind: From Burke to Eliot* (Washington, DC: Regnery, 2001); and Allitt, *The Conservatives*.

56. Ibid.

57. Rossiter, *Conservatism in America*, 177.

58. Patrick Allitt, *The Conservatives*; and Kirk, *The Conservative Mind*.

59. More on changing the Fourteenth Amendment for reasons related to immigration can be found here: http://teapartyamerica.blogspot.com/2010/08/change-14th-amendment-no-more-anchor.html.

60. Sam Tanenhaus, *The Death of Conservatism* (New York: Random House, 2009).

61. Corey Robin, *The Reactionary Mind: Conservatism from Edmund Burke to Sarah Palin* (New York: Oxford University Press, 2011).

62. Smith, *The Right Talk*, chapter 5.

63. George H. Nash, *The Conservative Intellectual Movement in America since 1945* (New York: Basic Books, 1976); see also Jerome Himmelstein, *To the Right: The Transformation of American Conservatism* (Berkeley: University of California Press, 1990).

64. According to CheckSiteTraffic.com, the *National Review Online* has the most unique visitors per month at 755K, versus 643K for the *American Spectator*, and 406K for the *Weekly Standard*.

65. David A. Snow and Robert D. Benford, "Master Frames and Cycles of Protest," in *Frontiers in Social Movement Theory*, ed. Aldon D. Morris and Carol McClurg Mueller (New Haven: Yale University Press, 1992); Mayer N. Zald, "Culture, Ideology, and Strategic Framing," in *Comparative Perspectives on Social Movements: Political Opportunities, Mobilizing Structures, and Cultural Framings*, ed. Doug McAdam, John D. McCarthy, and Mayer Zald (New York: Cambridge University Press, 1996); see also David A. Snow, E. Burke Rockford Jr., Steven K. Worden, and Robert D. Benford, "Frame Alignment Processes, Micromobilization, and Movement Participation," *American Sociological Review* 51, no. 4 (1986): 464–81.

66. John R. Zaller, *The Nature and Origins of Mass Opinion* (Cambridge: Cambridge University Press, 1992); see also Shanto Iyengar, Mark Peters, and Donald Kinder, *News that Matters* (Chicago: University of Chicago Press, 1987).

67. Taeku Lee, *Mobilizing Black Opinion: Black Insurgency and Racial Attitudes in the Civil Rights Era* (Chicago: University of Chicago Press, 2002), chapter 5.

68. Other frames are used to capture the online content in its entirety, but are excluded from the analysis because they are not relevant to our assessment of mainstream conservatism. All of the frames used to examine the online content are explained in the chapter 1 results given in the appendix under the heading "Frame Description." Additionally, posts or articles that are administrative in nature—informing readers of events, soliciting membership, and so on—are also framed; however, because a large number of posts and articles fell into this frame and there is very little substantive value in examining them, administrative posts are removed from the analysis altogether.

69. Michael Barone, "Big Government Forgets How to Build Big Projects," *National Review* online, http://www.nationalreview.com/articles/244117/big-government-forgets-how-build-big-projects-michael-barone, August 19, 2010.

70. We are aware that most of the public doesn't really know what it means to be a socialist or communist. It's a better bet that most don't know the distinction between the two. However, this isn't important for our purpose. Since most Tea Party activists tend to be middle-aged and older, they're baby boomers, born and socialized during the Cold War when socialism and communism were dirty words, often used by the Far Right to discredit progressive causes. More important, during the Cold War, black leaders and community activists had to work hard to avoid being labeled communist or socialist, lest they risk compromising their work on civil rights. In short, the Tea Party activists need not know the real meaning of communism or socialism in order to apply it to Obama. It's intended to discredit him and his policies. For more on the ways in which black civil rights organizations had to avoid being labeled communist or socialist, see Carol Anderson, *Eyes off the Prize: The United Nations and the African American Struggle for Human Rights, 1944–1955* (New York: Cambridge University Press, 2003); and Epstein and Forster, *The Radical Right*.

71. Rossiter, *Conservatism in America*; Allitt, *The Conservatives*; and Kirk, *The Conservative Mind*.

72. For a summary of the conditions under which change is feared, see John T. Jost, Jack Glaser, Arie W. Kruglanski, and Frank Sulloway, "Political Conservatism as Motivated Social Cognition," *Psychological Bulletin* 129, no. 3 (2003): 339–75. One will notice that fear of subversion is conspicuously absent from their list of conditions.

73. Content from Tea Party websites was collected from major websites in five states identified by a Rasmussen report as top Tea Party venues, as well as from ten additional states from the 2011 Multi-State Survey of Race and Politics. The five states identified as top Tea Party venues from the 2010 Ras-

mussen report are Alabama, Arizona, Colorado, Georgia, and Kentucky. In addition, California, Florida, Missouri, Nevada, North Carolina, Ohio, Pennsylvania, South Carolina, and Wisconsin are included in the analysis as states from the 2011 MSSRP. (The entire Rasmussen report can be found at http://www.rasmussenreports.com/public_content/most_recent_videos/2010_06/where_is_the_tea_party_strongest.) A total of 3,948 articles and postings from forty-two official Tea Party websites (websites that represent the state in its entirety, such as the Arizona Tea Party, or websites from a major city or region of the state) were examined dating back no further than 2009. By limiting our examination to these websites, we are focusing on online dialogue by the communication leaders, or citizen activists, within the Tea Party.

74. Website content and quotes are from the Atlanta Tea Party (June 30, 2009, www.atlantateaparty.net); the Northern Kentucky Tea Party (May 31, 2010, www.nkyteaparty.org); and the Alabama Tea Party Patriots, Concerned Americans of Lee County Alabama (May 2, 2010 and March 22, 2010, www.teapartypatriots.org/state/Alabama).

75. Mark Fenster, *Conspiracy Theories: Secrecy and Power in American Culture* (Minneapolis: University of Minnesota Press, 1999), 8.

76. David Brion Davis, *The Slave Power Conspiracy and the Paranoid Style* (Baton Rouge: Louisiana State University Press, 1969), 11.

77. Michael Rogin, *Ronald Reagan: The Movie, and Other Episodes in Political Demonology* (Berkeley: University of California Press, 1988), chapter 9.

78. We realize that it's possible that *National Review* journalists may well agree with Tea Party positions and tactics, but, for the sake of providing a more learned perspective, one that the moderates must take seriously, they may try to avoid some of the hyperbolic claims made on Tea Party websites.

79. Before dismissing the importance of "new media" on politics and society, we recommend reading David D. Perlmutter's *Blogwars* (New York: Oxford University Press, 2008).

80. Lepore, *The Whites of Their Eyes*; see also Skocpol and Williamson, *The Tea Party and the Remaking of Republican Conservatism*.

81. Please see the appendix for a description of the Multi-State Survey of Race and Politics (MSSRP).

82. For more on "The List Experiment," see James H. Kuklinski and Michael D. Cobb, "Racial Attitudes and the 'New South,'" *Journal of Politics* 59, no. 2 (1997): 323–49; and Matthew J. Streb, Barbara Burrell, Brian Fredrick, and Michael A. Genovese, "Social Desirability Effects and Support for a Female American President," *Public Opinion Quarterly* 72, no. 1 (2008): 76–89.

83. Skocpol and Williamson, *The Tea Party and the Remaking of Republican Conservatism*.

84. Please see the appendix for information about our 2010 Multi-State Survey of Race and Politics.

85. Drawing from the Positive and Negative Affect Schedule (PANAS), respondents were first asked whether their initial emotions toward a specific person or object were positive or negative. Following their initial response, respondents were then asked to expand on their feelings and prompted with positive or negative emotions to describe their attitudes, depending on the initial emotion. If a respondent's emotions were positive, they were then asked to further expand on what negative emotions describe their feeling best— enthusiastic, interested, inspired, proud, or excited. If they first provide a negative response, they are prompted with scared, angry, nervous, guilty, or pity. Respondents with neither a positive nor negative initial response were prompted with a combination of positive and negative emotions. See chapter 1 results in the appendix for the complete interview questionnaire. Also, for more of the PANAS scale, see D. Watson, L. A. Clark, and A. Tallegen, "Development and Validation of Brief Measures of Positive and Negative Affect: The PANAS Scale," *Journal of Personal and Social Psychology* 54, no. 6 (1988): 1063–70.

86. Respondents who did not express an opinion for or against the Tea Party, as well as those who were misinformed or not informed about the Tea Party at all, were considered to have "no strong opinion" of the movement.

87. Timothy D. Wilson and Jonathan W. Schooler, "Thinking Too Much: Introspection Can Reduce the Quality of Preferences and Decisions," *Journal of Personality and Social Psychology* 60, no. 2 (1991): 181–92.

88. Jon A. Krosnick, "The Role of Attitude Importance in Social Evaluation: A Study of Policy Preferences, Presidential Candidate Evaluations, and Voting Behavior," *Journal of Personality and Social Psychology* 55, no. 2 (1988): 196–210.

CHAPTER TWO

1. For a reference to Obama as anti-American, see Norman Podhoretz's editorial, "What Happened to Obama: Absolutely Nothing," *Wall Street Journal*, August 13–14, 2011, A13. For an exceptional account of placing homosexuality beyond American norms, see, among many others, Margot Canady, *The Straight State: Sexuality and Citizenship in Twentieth-Century America* (Princeton: Princeton University Press, 2009). And for an excellent study of discourse around illegal immigrants, see Otto Santa Ana, *Brown Tide Rising: Metaphors of Latinos in Contemporary American Public Discourse* (Austin: University of Texas Press, 2002).

2. See Howard Schuman, *Method and Meaning in Polls and Surveys* (Cambridge, MA: Harvard University Press, 2008), chapter 3.

3. The remaining 20 percent of the responses were difficult to place into any single category.

4. Similarly, the remaining 14 percent of the response were too fractious to constitute a coherent category.

5. These figures stack up well with contemporaneous studies, including an Associated Press/GfK poll conducted in April 2010. If we included only those with opinions of the Tea Party, 29 percent of those polled had a "very favorable" opinion of the Tea Party, and 28 percent of those with an opinion had a "very unfavorable" impression of them. Similar to our poll, in which 33 percent had no opinion of the Tea Party, in the AP poll, 33 percent had no opinion.

6. Typically, 5 percent of sympathizers join formal organizations. Bert Klandermans and Dirk Oegema, "Potentials, Networks, Motivations, and Barriers: Steps towards Participation in Social Movements," *American Sociological Review* 52, no. 4 (1987): 519–31.

7. Doug McAdam, *Freedom Summer* (New York: Oxford University Press, 1988). For an updated version, see Doug McAdam and Ronnelle Paulsen, "Specifying the Relationship between Social Ties and Activism, *American Journal of Sociology* 99, no. 3 (1993): 640–67. For a slightly different take, one in which commitment to movement-related issues happen *after* mobilization, see Ziad Munson, *The Making of Pro-Life Activists: How Social Movement Mobilization Works* (Chicago: University of Chicago Press, 2008).

8. For more, see Robert D. Putnam and David E. Campbell, *American Grace: How Religion Divides Us and Unites Us* (New York: Simon and Schuster, 2010), chapter 1.

9. See Dochuk, *From Bible Belt to Sunbelt.*

10. Hofstadter, *The Paranoid Style in American Politics*, chapter 3.

11. McClean, *Behind the Mask of Chivalry*, chapter 4. See also, Hofstadter, *The Paranoid Style in American Politics.*

12. See table A2.1 in the appendix, "Comparison of MSSRP 2011 with contemporaneous national polls by Tea Party support and selected demographics."

13. Donald P. Green, Bradley Palmquist, and Eric Schicler, *Partisan Hearts & Minds: Political Parties and the Social Identity of Voters* (New Haven: Yale University Press, 2002).

14. The literature on partisanship is voluminous. Instead of citing it in its entirety, we will simply cite a few classics. For the most recent work, see Zoltan L. Hajnal and Taeku Lee, *Why Americans Don't Join the Party: Race, Immigration, and the Failure (of Political Parties) to Engage the Electorate* (Princeton: Princeton University Press, 2011); for partisanship as a cue, see an

updated version of the classic *The American Voter*, by Michael Lewis-Beck, William G. Jacoby, Helmut Norpoth, and Herbert F. Weisberg, *The American Voter Revisited* (Ann Arbor: University of Michigan Press, 2008). For the classical work on partisanship as psychological attachment, see Angus Campbell, Philip E. Converse, Warren E. Miller, and Donald E. Stokes, *The American Voter* (New York: Wiley, 1960). For the classical work relating partisanship to information and rational choice, see Anthony Downs, *An Economic Theory of Democracy* (New York: HarperCollins, 1957). For an approach that draws on social identity theory, see Green, Palmquist, and Schicler, *Partisan Hearts & Minds*.

15. Diamond, *Roads to Dominion*; and Sheilah R. Koeppen, "The Republican Radical Right," *Annals of the American Academy of Political and Social Science* 382 (1969): 73–82. See also, Michael Rogin, *The Intellectuals and McCarthy: The Radical Specter* (Cambridge, MA: MIT Press, 1967).

16. Lewis-Beck, Jacoby, Norpoth, and Weisberg, *The American Voter Revisited*.

17. Michael Freeden, *Ideology: A Short Introduction* (New York: Oxford University Press, 2003), 123.

18. A debate has raged for years in political science over the extent to which people have the ability to think in ideological terms, where public attitudes across a range of issues are consistently liberal, conservative, or moderate. For the classic credited with starting the debate, see Philip E. Converse, "The Nature of Belief Systems in Mass Publics," *Ideology and Discontent*, ed. David Apter (New York: Free Press, 1964), 206–61; see also, Eric R.A.N. Smith, *The Unchanging American Voter* (Berkeley: University of California Press, 1989). On the other side of the debate, see Robert E. Lane, *Political Ideology: Why the American Common Man Believes What He Does* (New York: Free Press, 1962); Norman H. Nie, Sidney Verba, and John R. Petrocik, *The Changing American Voter* (Cambridge, MA: Harvard University Press, 1976); William G. Jacoby, "The Structure of Ideological Thinking in the American Electorate," *American Journal of Political Science* 39, no. 2 (1995): 314–35; and Stanley Feldman and John Zaller, "The Political Culture of Ambivalence: Ideological Responses to the Welfare State," *American Journal of Political Science* 36, no. 1 (1992): 68–307. For the definitive work on the role of ideology and race, see Michael C. Dawson, *Black Visions: The Roots of Contemporary African-American Political Ideologies* (Chicago: University of Chicago Press, 2001).

19. See Pamela Johnston Conover and Stanley Feldman, "The Origins of Liberal/Conservative Self-Identifications," *American Journal of Political Science* 25, no. 4 (1981): 617–45. The quote is located on 640.

20. For examples, see Rick Perlstein, *Before the Storm: Barry Goldwater and the Unmaking of the American Consensus* (New York: Hill and Wang, 2001); and J. Allen Broyles, *The John Birch Society*.

21. See, among others, Alan I. Abramowitz and Kyle Saunders, "Ideological Realignment in the U.S. Electorate," *Journal of Politics* 60, no. 3 (1998): 634–52; and their "Exploring the Bases of Partisanship in the American Electorate: Social Identity vs. Ideology," *Political Research Quarterly* 59, no. 2 (2006): 175–87; Matthew Levandusky, *The Partisan Sort: How Liberals Became Democrats and Conservatives Republicans* (Chicago: University of Chicago Press, 2009).

22. Samuel P. Huntington, *American Politics: The Promise of Disharmony* (Cambridge, MA.: Harvard University Press, 1981), 33.

23. For more, see Bernard Bailyn, *The Ideology of the American Revolution* (Cambridge, MA: Harvard University Press, 1992), 347.

24. Donald R. Kinder and Lynn M. Sanders, *Divided by Color: Racial Politics and Democratic Ideals* (Chicago: University of Chicago Press, 1996).

25. All of these numbers are consistent with roughly contemporaneous polls undertaken in which support for the Tea Party is assessed. See table A2.1 in the appendix, "Comparison of MSSRP 2011 with contemporaneous national polls by Tea Party support and selected demographics."

26. This serves as a proxy for policies like health care reform and the bank reform law, which the Tea Party rejects.

27. George E. Marcus, W. Russell Neuman, and Michael Mackuen, *Affective Intelligence and Political Judgment* (Chicago: University of Chicago Press, 2000).

28. Theodor W. Adorno, Else Frenkel-Brunswik, Daniel Levinson, and Nevitt Sanford, *The Authoritarian Personality* (New York: Harper and Row, 1950).

29. Stanley Feldman, "Enforcing Social Conformity: A Theory of Authoritarianism," *Political Psychology* 24, no. 1 (2003): 41–72.

30. Karen Stenner, *The Authoritarian Dynamic* (New York: Cambridge University Press, 2005), chapter 1. For an alternative approach, one based on social learning theory, see Bob Altemeyer, *The Authoritarian Spectre* (Cambridge, MA: Harvard University Press, 1996).

31. For comparisons between ethnocentrism and authoritarianism, see Donald R. Kinder and Cindy D. Kam, *Us Against Them: Ethnocentric Foundations of American Opinion* (Chicago: University of Chicago Press, 2009); and William A. Cunningham, John B. Nelzek, and Mahzarin R. Banaji, "Implicit and Explicit Ethnocentrism: Revisiting the Ideologies of Prejudice," *Personality and Social Psychology Bulletin* 30, no. 10 (2004): 1332–46.

32. For the emphasis on "in-group love," see Marilyn B. Brewer, "The Psychology of Prejudice: Ingroup Love, or Outgroup Hate," *Journal of Social Issues* 55, no. 3 (1999): 429–44.

33. For the "Us" versus "Them" interpretation, see Kinder and Kam, *Us Against Them*. For the conscious and unconscious dimensions of ethnocentrism, see Cunningham, Nelzek, and Banaji, "Implicit and Explicit Ethnocentrism."

34. But see Leonie Huddy and Stanley Feldman, "On Assessing the Political Effects of Racial Prejudice," *Annual Review of Political Science* 12 (2009): 423–47.

35. See Cheryl R. Kaiser, Benjamin J. Drury, Kerry E. Spalding, Sapna Cheryan, and Laurie T. O'Brien, "The Ironic Consequences of Obama's Election: Decreased Support for Social Justice," *Journal of Experimental Social Psychology* 45 (2009): 556–59.

36. Kinder and Sanders, *Divided by Color: Racial Politics and Democratic Ideals*.

37. Michael Hughes, "Symbolic Racism, Old-Fashioned Racism, and Whites' Opposition to Affirmative Action," in *Racial Attitudes in the 1990s: Continuity and Change*, ed. Steven A. Tuch and Jack K. Martin (New York: Praeger, 1997), 45–75. For a similar interpretation of symbolic racism as status defense, see also, "Whites' Opposition to Busing: Symbolic Racism or Realistic Group Conflict?," *Journal of Personality and Social Psychology* 45, no. 6 (1983): 1196–1210.

38. For more on the psychological properties of social dominance orientation, see Felicia Pratto, Jim Sidanius, Lisa M. Stallworth, and Bertram F. Malle, "Social Dominance Orientation: A Personality Variable Predicting Social and Political Attitudes," *Journal of Personality and Social Psychology* 67, no. 4 (1994): 741–63; see 741 for the quote.

39. The larger theory to which SDO belongs is social dominance theory. Social dominance theory synthesizes individual-level factors (SDO), institutional, and structural explanations to explain the persistence of inequality. For the most complete explanation of the theory, see Jim Sidanius and Felicia Pratto, *Social Dominance* (New York: Cambridge University Press, 1999). For an explanation of the evolutionary roots of social dominance theory, see Jim Sidanius, "The Psychology of Group Conflict and the Dynamics of Oppression: A Social Dominance Perspective," in *Explorations in Political Psychology*, ed. Shanto Iyengar and William J. McGuire (Durham, NC: Duke University Press, 1993), 183–224.

40. An allied model of intergroup relations, one fairly close to the social dominance model, is group position theory. Sociologist Lawrence Bobo uses it to great effect as an explanation of prejudice toward blacks and American Indians. Among other things, as Bobo argues, group position theory stresses intergroup competition and threat; social dominance theory is really more about maintaining social stability, about maintaining group dominance. We

sought to go with the social dominance model instead of group position model because we think right-wing movements are really about maintaining the prestige associated with their constituencies. We also sought to draw on a model whose reach exceeds race-based prejudice. For more on group position theory, see Lawrence D. Bobo and Mia Tuan, *Prejudice and Politics: Group Position, Public Opinion, and the Wisconsin Treaty Rights Dispute* (Cambridge, MA: Harvard University Press, 2006). For a comparison between the social dominance model and the group position model, see Lawrence D. Bobo, "Prejudice as Group Position: Microfoundations of a Sociological Approach to Racism and Race Relations," *Journal of Social Issues* 55, no. 3 (1999): 445–72.

41. Rory McVeigh, *The Rise of the Ku Klux Klan*, chapter 4.

42. These results remain valid in a multivariate setting where economic anxiety *depresses* support for the Tea Party among whites compared to non-whites in our sample. Results are available upon request.

43. Gauging perceptions of the national economic climate is another way of getting at economic anxiety. This isn't observed in our data. Therefore, we cannot completely rule out economic anxiety as a factor. Still, perceptions of the national economy and one's personal economic circumstances are related, tied together by class. We can account for both. For more, see M. Stephen Weatherford, "Economic Voting and the 'Symbolic Politics' Argument: A Reinterpretation and Synthesis," *American Political Science Review* 77, no. 1 (1983): 158–74. For an alternative in which perception of the national economic picture trumps individual economic experiences, see Donald R. Kinder and D. Roderick Kiewet, "Sociotropic Politics: The American Case," *British Journal of Political Science* 11, no. 2 (1981): 129–61. Again, however, the latter view doesn't test for the linkage of the two through class.

44. Richard J. Hofstadter, *The Paranoid Style in American Politics* and Gusfield, *Symbolic Crusade*.

45. We use what's called an ordered logistic regression model to estimate the association between support for the Tea Party and all of the other factors discussed so far.

46. Based on Skocpol and Williamson's work, we controlled for whether or not people watch Fox News, and political sophistication. While both affected support for the Tea Party, it failed to impact the substantive results.

47. Jennifer A. Whitson and Adam D. Galinsky, "Lacking Control Increases Illusory Pattern Perception," *Science* 322 (October 2008): 115–17.

48. Daniel Sullivan, Mark J. Landau, and Zachary K. Rothschild, "An Existential Function of Enemyship: Evidence that People Attribute Influence to Personal and Political Enemies to Compensate for Threats to Control," *Journal of Personality and Social Psychology* 98, no. 3 (2010): 434–49.

49. Additional analysis supports the reactionary conservative charge in that on a scale from 1 to 7 that ranges "extremely liberal" (1) to "extremely conservative" (7), two-thirds of believers consider themselves "extremely conservative." This is consistent with Rossiter's reactionary conservatives, a distinction from mainstream conservatives we made clear in chapter 1.

50. Skocpol and Williamson, *The Tea Party and the Remaking of Republican Conservatism.*

51. We also estimated the model without including Fox in the specification; the substantive results remain the same.

52. Sidanius and Pratto, *Social Dominance Theory.*

53. Gary C. Jacobsen, "The President, the Tea Party, and Voting Behavior in 2010." See also, Kevin Arceneaux and Stephen P. Nicholson, "Steeping the Tea Party" (unpublished manuscript, 2011).

54. R. Michael Alvarez and John Brehm, *Hard Choices, Easy Answers: Values, Information, and American Public Opinion* (Princeton: Princeton University Press, 2002), 15.

55. Even a casual perusal of the literature makes clear that each of the scholars responsible for introducing these concepts, or sought to adjust them in some way, first identified the sources of the concept, after which the explanatory power of each was tested.

CHAPTER THREE

1. Of course, some may argue that the connection between Obama and the Tea Party may also be about a perception that the president isn't looking out for whites, or that he favors blacks over whites. Our analysis in chapter 2 fails to include direct measures for either one. However, in both cases, the issue seems to be one of fairness. Fairness, in turn, is associated with conservatism. Our inclusion of ideology as part of the analysis should, therefore, mitigate any concern about race-based bias. For the relationship between conservatism and fairness, see John Graham, Jonathan Haidt, and Brian A. Nosek, "Liberals and Conservatives Rely on Different Sets of Moral Foundations," *Journal of Personality and Social Psychology* 96, no. 5 (2009): 1029–46.

2. For more on predispositions, see Alvarez and Brehm, *Hard Choices, Easy Answers,* chapter 2. For a pithy explanation, see also Karen Stenner, *The Authoritarian Dynamic* (New York: Cambridge University Press, 2005). For what qualifies as symbolic predispositions, see David O. Sears, "Symbolic Politics: A Socio-Psychological Theory," in *Explorations in Political Psychology,* ed. Shanto Iyengar and William J. McGuire (Durham, NC: Duke University Press, 1993), 113–49. Also, some may argue with our definition of authoritarianism as a predisposition. Feldman and Stenner argue that threat must be

present. However, our impression is more in line with Hetherington's in that authoritarianism is always present, not contingent upon perceived threat. For more on these differences, see Stanley Feldman and Karen Stenner, "Perceived Threat and Authoritarianism," *Political Psychology* 18, no. 4 (1997): 741–70; see also Stenner, *The Authoritarian Dynamic*. For the alternative, see Marc J. Hetherington and Jonathan D. Weiler, *Authoritarianism and Polarization in America* (New York: Cambridge University Press, 2009).

3. For Ron Paul's resistance, see Shane D'Aprile, "Ron Paul Slams Patriot Act; Backers Drown Out Jeers at Conference," The Hill, http://thehill.com /blogs/ballot-box/gop-primaries/143605-ron-paul-slams-patriot-act-backers -drown-out-jeers-at-cpac; on Rand's resistance, see David Weigel, "Rand Paul's Noble Defeat on the Patriot Act," http://www.slate.com/blogs/weigel /2011/05/26/rand_paul_s_noble_defeat_on_the_patriot_act.html.

4. On the normative importance of civil liberties, see Herbert McClosky and Aida Brill, *Dimensions of Tolerance* (New York: Russell Sage Foundation, 1983).

5. For an excellent example of this concept applied across time and space, see J.G.A. Pocock, *The Machiavellian Moment: Florentine Political Thought and the Atlantic Republican Tradition*, rev. ed. (Princeton: Princeton University Press, 2003).

6. Under normal circumstances in which the people aren't forced to choose between civil liberties and security, support for free speech is much higher, around 70 percent. See Christopher S. Parker, "Symbolic versus Blind Patriotism: Distinction without Difference?" *Political Research Quarterly* 63, no. 1 (2010): 97–114.

7. Darren W. Davis, *Negative Liberty: Public Opinion and the Terrorist Attacks on America* (New York: Russell Sage Foundation, 2007).

8. For the classical work on freedom as the absence of constraints, see Isaiah Berlin, "Two Concepts of Liberty," in *Four Essays on Liberty* (Oxford, UK: Oxford University Press, 1969), 118–72; for a more recent treatment, see Eric Nelson, "Liberty: One or Two Concepts," *Political Theory* 33, no. 1 (2005): 58–78.

9. Bernard Bailyn, *The Ideological Origins of the American Revolution* (Cambridge, MA: Harvard University Press, 1992); and Pocock, *The Machiavellian Moment*.

10. Milton Rokeach, *The Nature of Human Values* (New York: Free Press, 1973).

11. For an exceptional review of the values literature from the perspective of political science, see Stanley Feldman, "Values, Ideology, and the Structure of Political Attitudes," in the *Oxford Handbook of Political Psychology*, ed.

David O. Sears, Leonie Huddy, and Robert Jervis (New York: Oxford University Press, 2003), 477–510.

12. The ten value types are self-direction, stimulation, hedonism, achievement, power, security, conformity, tradition, benevolence, and universalism. See Shalom H. Schwartz, "Universals in the Content and Structure of Values: Theoretical Advances and Empirical Tests in 20 Countries," in *Advances in Experimental Social Psychology*, ed. Mark P. Zanna (New York: Academic Press, 1992), 1–66. The quotes are on 5.

13. See Herbert McClosky and John Zaller, *The American Ethos: Public Attitudes toward Capitalism and Democracy* (Cambridge, MA: Harvard University Press, 1984), chapter 2.

14. Ibid., chapters 2–4.

15. See among others, Seymour Martin Lipset, *The First New Nation: The United States in Historical and Comparative Perspective* (New York: W. W. Norton, 1979); see also, Rokeach, *The Nature of Human Values*, and McClosky and Zaller, *The American Ethos*.

16. McClosky and Zaller, *The American Ethos*, 264.

17. Ibid., 15.

18. Some argue that value conflict isn't as commonplace as many believe. In fact, William Jacoby argues that value conflict is largely confined to the unsophisticated. See William G. Jacoby, "Value Choices and American Public Opinion," *American Journal of Political Science* 50, no. 3 (2006): 706–23.

19. For the pioneering work on making a choice among conflicting values, see Philp E. Tetlock, "A Value Pluralism Model of Ideological Reasoning," *Journal of Personality and Social Psychology* 50, no. 4 (1986): 819–27; for an updated version, see Philip E. Tetlock, "Coping with Trade-Offs: Psychological Constraints and Political Implications," in *Elements of Reason: Cognition, Choice, and the Bounds of Rationality*, ed. Arthur Lupia, Samuel L. Popkin, and Matthew D. McCubbins (New York: Cambridge University Press, 2000), 239–63.

20. Davis, *Negative Liberty*.

21. See Akhil Reed Amar, *The Bill of Rights: Creation and Reconstruction* (New Haven: Yale University Press, 2000); Bernard Bailyn, "Postscript," in *The Ideological Origins of the American Revolution* (Cambridge, MA: Harvard University Press, 1992); and Gordon S. Wood, *The Creation of the American Republic, 1776–1787* (Chapel Hill: University of North Carolina Press, 1969).

22. On the overlap between civil liberties and the broader study of political tolerance, see Herbert McClosky and Aida Brill, *Dimensions of Tolerance:*

What Americans Believe about Civil Liberties (New York: Russell Sage Foundation, 1983); and John L. Sullivan, James Pierson, and George E. Marcus, *Political Tolerance and American Democracy* (Chicago: University of Chicago Press, 1982). For the Stouffer quote, see Samuel A. Stouffer, *Communism, Conformity, and Civil Liberties* (New York: John Wiley and Sons, 1966).

23. For Gibson's work on the Nazis in Skokie, see James L. Gibson and Richard D. Bingham, *Civil Liberties and Nazis: The Skokie Free-Speech Controversy* (New York: Praeger, 1985); for his work on the Klan, see James L. Gibson, "Homosexuals and the Ku Klux Klan: A Contextual Analysis of Political Tolerance," *Western Political Quarterly* 40, no. 3 (1987): 427–48.

24. On the point that liberals are more staunch defenders of civil liberties than conservatives, see the exhaustive work on the subject of civil liberties conducted by McClosky and Brill, *Dimensions of Tolerance*, chapter 7.

25. For the classic study on values in general, see Milton Rokeach, *The Nature of Human Values*; for more recent work, see Schwartz, "Universals in the Content and Structure of Values."

26. For an excellent comparative study of value conflict, see Paul M. Sniderman, Joseph F. Fletcher, Peter H. Russell, and Philip E. Tetlock, *The Clash of Rights: Liberty, Equality, and Legitimacy in Pluralist Democracy* (New Haven: Yale University Press, 1996).

27. Michael C. Dawson, *Not in Our Lifetimes: The Future of Black Politics* (Chicago: University of Chicago Press, 2011); see also, Michael Tesler and David O. Sears, *Obama's Race: The 2008 Election and the Dream of a Post-Racial America* (Chicago: University of Chicago Press, 2010).

28. Katherine Y. Barnes, "Assessing the Counterfactual: The Efficacy of Drug Interdiction Absent Racial Profiling," *Duke Law Journal* 54, no. 5 (2005): 1090–1141.

29. On perceived black criminality in colonial America, see Richard Middleton, *Colonial America: A History, 1565–1776* (New York: Wiley-Blackwell, 2002).

30. Barnes, "Assessing the Counterfactuals."

31. On the (un)constitutionality of racial profiling, see Samuel R. Gross, "Racial Profiling under Attack," *Columbia Law Review* 102, no. 5 (2002): 1413–38. On the empirical "effectiveness" of racial profiling, see Barnes, "Assessing the Counterfactual." On the social costs of racial profiling, see R. Richard Banks, "Beyond Profiling: Race, Policing, and the Drug War," *Stanford Law Review* 56, no. 3 (2002): 571–603; and Bernard E. Harcourt, "Rethinking Racial Profiling: A Critique of the Economics, Civil Liberties, and Constitutional Literature, and Criminal Profiling More Generally," *University of Chicago Law Review* 71, no. 4 (2004): 1275–1381.

32. When the question was framed as one that "require[ed] Arabs, including those who are U.S. citizens, to undergo special, more intensive security checks before boarding airplanes," 58 percent of Americans signaled their support. See Gallup, "Attack on America: A Review of Public Opinion," *Gallup Poll*, September 14–15, 2001. When the question was framed more generally, omitting references to "Arabs," far fewer sanctioned racial profiling: 18 percent. See Davis, *Negative Liberty*, chapter 3.

33. See Section 2(B) of Arizona's Senate Bill 1070; for the Georgia statue, see Section 5 of House Bill 87. Alabama: HB56 (Beason-Hammon Taxpayer and Citizen Protection Act) and HB658 signed into law on May 18, 2012. Rewrite of Alabama Immigration Law House Bill 56. Signed by Governor Bentley; South Carolina: Passed into law (South Carolina Illegal Immigration and Reform *Act*), January 1, 2012, S.B. 20 and Act No. 69; Utah: HB497 (Utah Immigration Accountability and Enforcement Act), federal judge puts a hold on ruling till decision is made on SB 1070; Georgia: Governor Nathan Deal signed (Illegal Immigration Reform and Enforcement Act), Bill HB 87 into law in May, takes effect July 1; Indiana: SB 590 signed into law May 10, 2011 by Mitch Daniels.

34. Stephanie Condon, "Sarah Palin Launches Site Targeting Democrats Who Backed 'Obamacare,'" CBSNews.com, http://www.cbsnews.com/8301 -503544_162-20017459-503544.html; Andrew Malcolm, "Now, It's Sarah Palin's Turn to Target Democrats," *Los Angeles Times* online, http://latimesblogs .latimes.com/washington/2010/03/sarah-palin-searchlight-hit-list.html.

35. Keith Olbermann, "Olbermann: Violence and Threats Have No Place in Politics," NBCNews.com, http://msnbc.msn.com/id/40981503.

36. For these interpretations of the amendments, see McClosky and Brill, *Dimensions of Tolerance*, chapter 4.

37. Davis, *Negative Liberty*, chapter 3.

38. For all comparisons, see Davis, *Negative Liberty*, chapter 3.

39. For general treatments of the Far Right and their suspicion of others, see David H. Bennett, *The Party of Fear: The American Far Right from Nativism to the Militia Movement* (New York: Vintage Books, 1995); Chip Berlet and Matthew N. Lyons, *Right-Wing Populism in America: Too Close for Comfort* (New York: Guilford Press, 2000); and Lipset and Raab, *The Politics of Unreason*.

40. For more, see Jacob Weisberg, "The Tea Party and the Tuscon Tragedy," Slate, http://www.slate.com/id/2280711/; see also Evan McMorris-Santoro and Jillian Rayfield, "Tucson Tea Party Leader: We Won't Change Our Rhetoric after Giffords Shooting," http://tpmdc.talkingpointsmemo. com/2011/01/tucson-tea-party-leader-we-wont-change-our-rhetoric-after -gifford-shooting.php; and Sandhya Somashekhar, "Gabrielle Giffords Shooting in Tuscon: Did It Stem from State of Political Discourse?" *Washington Post*

online, http://www.washingtonpost.com/wp-dyn/content/article/2011/01/08/AR2011010803652.html.

41. See McClosky and Brill, *Dimensions of Tolerance*; and Parker, "Symbolic versus Blind Patriotism."

42. For the relationship between ideology and civil liberties, see McClosky and Brill, *Dimensions of Tolerance*. For more on the connection between partisanship and ideology, see Carol Sharp and Milton Lodge, "Partisan and Ideological Belief Systems," *Political Behavior* 7, no. 2 (1995): 147–66. For the effect of partisanship and ideology on civil liberties, see Davis, *Negative Liberty*, chapter 4.

43. McClosky and Brill, *Dimensions of Tolerance*, chapter 6.

44. These results refer to our Washington Poll (2011). Results available upon request.

45. If we move beyond concepts of theoretical import, we discover—among the sociodemographic we've included—interesting results. African Americans are 7 percent less likely than all other racial groups to support free speech. Likewise, gender also affects the public's support for free speech. In this case men are 9 percent more likely than women to support civil liberties over a perception of security.

46. Since racial profiling invokes race, we added racial resentment to the model in a separate specification. It was significant, but it didn't affect the substantive impact of support for the Tea Party on racial profiling.

47. In a separate analysis, we discovered that the relationship between Tea Party support and indefinite detainment is affected by gender. In other words, the relationship we observed in our preliminary analysis is really a matter of whether or not one is a male or female.

48. Among sociodemographic factors, only gender promotes resistance to detainment, in which men are 6 percent less likely than women to support indefinite detention.

49. Santa Ana, *Brown Tide Rising*.

50. For perhaps the most well-known expression of this point of view, see Samuel P. Huntington, *Who Are We? The Challenges to American National Identity* (New York: Simon & Schuster, 2004). Moreover, it doesn't matter whether or not we're discussing Latino legal or illegal immigrants. Americans, mainly whites, are firmly against Latinos coming to America. See Efrén O. Pérez, "Explicit Evidence on the Import of Implicit Attitudes: The IAT and Immigration Policy Judgments," *Political Behavior* 32, no. 4 (2010): 517–45.

51. Tetlock, "Coping with Trade-Offs," 250.

52. Schwartz, "Universals in the Content and Structure of Values," 9.

53. In a separate analysis, we added the limited government scale to the model. It was significant and depressed support for free speech, but it failed to affect the substantive relationship between Tea Party support and free speech. We didn't include it in the model we reported in the text because limited government and ideological self-placement are theoretically and empirically similar r = .55. That is, if one considers oneself a conservative, they're also likely to prefer small government.

54. In separate analysis, we controlled for preference for limited government. But this failed to have any substantive impact on the results. Results available upon request.

55. See T. W. Adorno, E. Frenkel-Brunswik, D. J. Levinson, and R. N. Sanford, *The Authoritarian Personality* (New York: Harper, 1950).

56. For the comments on the meaning of patriotism, see Maurizio Viroli, *Republicanism* (New York: Hill and Wang, 2002) and *For Love of Country: An Essay on Patriotism and Nationalism* (New York: Oxford University Press, 1995).

57. For a recent articulation of the connection between civic activism, sacrifice, and freedom, see R. Claire Snyder, *Citizen-Soldiers and Manly Warriors: Military Service and Gender in the Civic Republican Tradition* (Lanham, MD: Rowman and Littlefield, 1999).

58. Morris Janowitz, *The Reconstruction of Patriotism: Education for Civic Consciousness* (Chicago: University of Chicago Press, 1983).

59. We realize that some scholars have no use whatsoever for patriotism. See, among others, George Kateb, *Patriotism and Other Mistakes* (New Haven: Yale University Press, 2006); and Martha C. Nussbaum, "Patriotism and Cosmopolitanism," in *For Love of Country?*, ed. Martha C. Nussbaum (Boston: Beacon Press, 2002), 3–20.

60. Christopher S. Parker, *Fighting for Democracy: Black Veterans and the Struggle against White Supremacy in the Postwar South* (Princeton: Princeton University Press, 2009).

61. Jennifer E. Brooks, "Winning the Peace: Georgia Veterans and the Struggle to Define the Political Legacy of World War II," *Journal of Southern History* 66, no. 3 (2000): 563–604. The quote can be found on 572.

62. Dietz, "Patriotism: A Brief History of the Term." See also Merle Curti, *The Roots of American Loyalty* (New York: Atheneum, 1968); Viroli, *Republicanism* and *For Love of Country*.

63. Ervin Staub, "Blind versus Constructive Patriotism: Moving from Embeddedness in the Group to Critical Loyalty and Action," in *Patriotism*, ed. Daniel Bar-Tal and Ervin Staub (Chicago: Nelson-Hall, 1997), 213–28.

64. Robert T. Schatz, Ervin Staub, and Howard Lavine, "On the Varieties

of National Attachment: Blind versus Constructive Patriotism," *Political Psychology* 20, no. 1 (1999): 151–74.

65. McClosky and Brill, *Dimensions of Tolerance*; Leonie Huddy and Nadia Khatib, "American Patriotism, National Identity, and Political Involvement," *American Journal of Political Science* 51, no. 1 (2007): 63–77.

66. Huddy and Khatib, "American Patriotism, National Identity, and Political Involvement"; Schatz, Staub, and Lavine, "On the Varieties of National Attachment."

67. Huddy and Khatib, "American Patriotism, National Identity, and Political Involvement."

68. As long as those in need are perceived as authentic, prototypical Americans (white, Christian, native-born) simply in need of a helping hand, those who feel a strong attachment to American ideals support government help for those who are in need. Theiss-Morse, *Who Counts as an American?*

69. Schildkraut, *Americanism in the Twenty-First Century.*

70. Adorno et al., *The Authoritarian Personality.*

71. For interracial examples of the principle/policy gap, see Howard Schuman, Charlotte Steeh, and Lawrence D. Bobo, *Racial Attitudes in America: Trends and Interpretations* (Cambridge, MA: Harvard University Press, 1985). For intraracial differences around integration, see Parker, *Fighting for Democracy.*

72. Adorno et al., *The Authoritarian Personality*, 107.

73. For the effect of ideology on varieties of American patriotism, see Huddy and Khatib, "American Patriotism, National Identity, and Political Involvement."

74. Among the controls for which we needed to account, education increases by 8 percent and political sophistication by 9 percent regarding the likelihood that people see patriotism more as a duty to criticize the country when necessary than to blindly accept it at face value (over those who are less well educated or politically sophisticated).

75. In a separate specification, we also controlled for preference for limited government. While it's an important predictor, it failed to affect our substantive results.

76. Among the controls, income and political sophistication also contributed to an explanation of patriotism framed in this way. As Americans become increasingly better off financially, it increases the probability that they'll put themselves before country by 7 percent over people who are less well off. In contrast, political sophisticates are 13 percent more likely than people who are less sophisticated to put country first.

77. If we throw in the effects associated with controls such as age and race, we discover that as Americans age, the likelihood decreases by 15 percent that they'll embrace the idea that the country needs to push harder to realize the goal of equality for all. Race is also important in that African Americans are 18 percent more likely than other racial groups to believe that patriotism includes stopping at nothing to ensure equality.

78. Critics might say—quite reasonably—that individualism, another important American value, is also a competing explanation, one that we must also consider. In a separate analysis we did just that, and included individualism. It didn't matter: Tea Party sentiment remained an important factor.

79. Walter F. Berns, *Making Patriots* (Chicago: University of Chicago Press, 2002).

80. Robert T. Schatz and Ervin Staub, "Manifestations of Blind and Constructive Patriotism: Personality Correlates and Individual-Group Relations," *Patriotism: In the Lives of Individuals and Nations*, ed. Daniel Bar-Tal and Ervin Staub (Chicago: Nelson-Hall, 1997), 229–45.

CHAPTER FOUR

1. See, among many others, Perlstein, *Before the Storm*.

2. William B. Hixon Jr., *Search for the American Right Wing: An Analysis of the Social Science Record, 1955–1987* (Princeton: Princeton University Press, 1992), part 4.

3. Conover and Gray, *Feminism and the New Right*.

4. Burghart and Zeskind, "Tea Party Nationalism."

5. "Census Data Reveals Dramatic Population Increase among Minority Groups," *PBS Newshour Extra* online, April 1, 2001, retrieved April 1, 2011, available at http://www.pbs.org/newshour/extra/features/us/jan-june11/census_04-01.html.

6. "Census Shows America's Diversity," Census 2010 News, March 24, 2011, http://2010.census.gov/news/releases/operations/cb11-cn125.html.

7. Gary J. Gates, "How Many People Are Lesbian, Gay, Bisexual, and Transgender?" *The Williams Institute*, April 2011.

8. "Lawsuit Alleges Texas Congressional Redistricting Plan Discriminates against Latinos, African Americans," *Chron Blog, Houston Chronicle* online, July 16, 2011, available at http://blog.chron.com/txpotomac/2011/07/lawsuit-alleges-texas-congressional-redistricting-plan-discriminates-against-latinos-african-americans/.

9. Joe Garofoli, "Redistricting Worries California Black Leaders," *San Francisco Chronicle* online, July 25, 2011, available at http://www.sfgate.com/cgi -bin/article.cgi?f=/c/a/2011/07/24/MN531KDMII.DTL.

10. Marisa Lagos, "Legislature More Supportive of Gay Rights Bill," *San Francisco Chronicle* online, September 2, 2011, http://articles.sfgate.com /2011-09-03/bay-area/30108819_1_gay-rights-equality-california-lgbt; and Ed O'Keefe, "Activists Offer Guidance on Celebrating End of 'Don't Ask, Don't Tell,' " *Washington Post* online, September 12, 2011, http://www.washingtonpost .com/local/dc-politics/activists-offer-guidance-on-celebrating-end-of-dont -ask-dont-tell/2011/09/12/gIQAX0aJOK_story.html.

11. "About Tea Party Patriots," http://www.teapartypatriots.org/about.

12. See, among others, Smith, *The Right Talk*; Rossiter, *Conservatism in America*.

13. This argument derives from an earlier article in *Political Power and Social Theory*; see Matt A. Barreto, Betsy L. Cooper, Benjamin Gonzales, Christopher S. Parker, and Christopher Towler, "The Tea Party in the Age of Obama: Mainstream Conservatism or Out-group Anxiety?" *Political Power and Social Theory* 22 (2011): 105–36.

14. Skocpol and Williamson, *The Tea Party and the Remaking of Republican Conservatism*.

15. Mayhill Fowler, "Obama: No Surprise that Hard-Pressed Pennsylvanians Turn Bitter," *Huffington Post* online, April 11, 2008, retrieved from http://www.huffingtonpost.com/mayhill-fowler/obama-no surprise-that-ha_b _96188.html.

16. Roland Martin, "Commentary: Deans' 50-state Strategy is a Plus for Obama," CNN Politics, October 28, 2008, retrieved from http://articles.cnn .com/2008-10-28/politics/martin.election_1_50-state-strategy-howard-dean -democratic-party?_s=PM:POLITICS.

17. Thomas Frank, *What's the Matter with Kansas? How Conservatives Won the Heart of America* (New York: Metropolitan Books, 2004); Joe Bageant, *Deer Hunting with Jesus: Dispatches from America's Class War* (New York: Three Rivers Press, 2007).

18. Please refer to "Content Analysis and Interviews" under the chapter 1 results in the appendix for details on the sampling frame for the content analysis.

19. Peggy S. Judd, "Campaigning is Fun! Almost as Fun as a Great TEA Party!" ArizonaTeaParty.com, June 27, 2010, http://arizonateaparty.ning.com /profiles/blogs/campaigning-is-fun-almost-as.

20. Arizona Tea Party, "Ted Nugent: The Declaration of Defiance," Arizona TeaParty.com, June 24, 2010, http://arizonateaparty.ning.com/profiles/blogs /ted-nugent-the-declaration-of.

21. Amanda Herrera, "Illegal Aliens are Bankrupting America," Arizona TeaParty.com, May 25, 2010, http://arizonateaparty.ning.com/profiles/blogs /illegal-aliens-are-bankrupting.

22. Robin VanDerWege, "My Version of the State of the Union," Arizona TeaParty.com, June 27, 2010, http://arizonateaparty.ning.com/profiles/blogs /my-version-of-the-state-of-the.

23. Ibid.

24. "Gay Marriage: Remaining Intellectually Honest Amidst Collective Support," *Tea Party Tribune* online, July 8, 2011, http://www.teapartytribune .com/2011/07/08/ny-gay-marriage/.

25. Brian Tashman, "Tea Party Nation: Gay Rights Will Doom America," June 24, 2011, http://www.rightwingwatch.org/content/tea-party-nation -gay-rights-will-doom-america.

26. Juan Williams, "Tea Party Anger Reflects Mainstream Concerns," *Wall Street Journal* online, April 2, 2010, http://online.wsj.com/article/SB20001424 05270230425270457515594205483252.html.

27. Ibid.

28. Cathy Young, "Tea Partiers Racist? Not So Fast," Real Clear Politics, http://www.realclearpolitics.com/articles/2010/04/25/tea_partiers_racist_not _so_fast_105309.html.

29. Lee Fang, "Billionaire Koch Brothers Fulfill Father's Campaign to Segregate Public Schools," AlterNet, January 12, 2011, http://www.alternet.org /newsandviews/article/435264/billionaire_koch_brothers_fulfill_father%27s _campaign_to_segregate_public_schools,_end_successful_integration _program_in_nc/.

30. Epstein and Foster, *The Radical Right.*

31. Jane Mayer, "Covert Operations: The Billionaire Brothers Who Are Waging a War Against Obama," *New Yorker* online, August 30, 2010, http://www .newyorker.com/reporting/2010/08/30/100830fa_fact_mayer?printable=true.

32. "Mapping the 2010 U.S. Census," *New York Times* online, http://projects .nytimes.com/census/2010/map.

33. Sabrina Tavernise, "New Numbers, and Geography, for Gay Couples," *New York Times* online, August 25, 2011, http://www.nytimes.com/2011/08 /25/us/25census.html?_r=1&pagewanted=all.

34. As we have already noted in chapter 3, much of SB 1070 has failed to go into effect. In a July 2010 opinion, District Court judge Susan Bolton granted injunctive relief at the request of the Department of Justice.

35. On June 25, 2012, the Supreme Court ruled that Sections 3, 5(C), and 6 are preempted by federal law.

36. Sharron Angle TV AD: "Best Friends" video, YouTube, http://www.youtube.com/watch?v=tb-zZM9-vB0&feature=channel.

37. Ibid.

38. J. D. Hayworth, *Whatever It Takes: Illegal Immigration, Border Security, and the War on Terror* (Washington, DC: Regnery Press, 2005), 30.

39. Paul Harris, "JD Hayworth's Republican Challenge to John McCain Grows as Anti-immigrant Anger Spills onto Arizona's Streets," *Guardian* online, http://www.guardian.co.uk/world/2010/jul/25/jd-hayworth-arizona-immigration-anger.

40. Devin Burghart and Leonard Zeskind, "Beyond Fair: The Decline of the Established Anti-Immigrant Organizations and the Rise of Tea Party Nativism," IREHR, 2012.

41. "Tea Party Seeks to Spotlight the "Horrors" of Illegal Immigration," FoxNews.com, http://www.foxnews.com/politics/2010/08/03/tea-party-seeks-stories-horrors-illegal-immigration/.

42. Americans for Legal Immigration, http://www.alipac.us/content.php.

43. John Tomasic, "Tea Party Groups Rallying in Support of Arizona Immigration Law," *Colorado Independent* online, May 6, 2010, http://coloradoindependent.com/52903/tea-party-groups-rallying-in-support-of-arizona-immigration-law.

44. See, among others, Ted Brader, Nicholas A. Valentino, and Elizabeth Suhay, "What Triggers Public Opposition to Immigration? Anxiety, Group Cues, and Immigration Threat," *American Journal of Political Science* 52, no. 4 (2008): 959–78; and Pérez, "Explicit Evidence on the Import of Implicit Attitudes: The IAT and Immigration Policy Judgments."

45. Jeffrey M. Jones, "Slim Majority of Americans Would Vote for DREAM Act Law," Gallup Politics, http://www.gallup.com/poll/145136/Slim-Majority-Americans-Vote-DREAM-Act-Law.aspx.

46. "House Republicans Introduce Bill to Repeal Birthright Citizenship Amendment," FoxNews.com, http://www.foxnews.com/politics/2011/01/06/house-republicans-introduce-repeal-birthright-citizenship-amendment/.

47. John Hill, "Airborne 'Anchor Baby' Attempt Shows Folly of U.S. 'Birthright Citizenship,'" *Party Tribune* online, http://www.teapartytribune .com/2011/09/22/airborne-%E2%80%98anchor-baby%E2%80%99 -attempt-shows-folly-of-u-s-%E2%80%98birthright-citizenship%E2%80%99/.

48. Mark Dennis, "Defending the Tea Party, Op-Ed," *Houston Chronicle* online, October 2, 2011, http://www.chron.com/opinion/letters/article /Defending-the-tea-party-2197411.php; *Conservative Sifu Blog*, "The Tea Party and Sexual Freedom," August 6, 2010, http://conservativesifu.blogspot .com/2010/08/tea-party-and-sexual-freedom.html.

49. "Sharron Angle: No on Abortion, Same-Sex Adoption," *CBS News* online, http://www.cbsnews.com/stories/2010/08/05/politics/main6748062.shtml.

50. "Sharron Angle: Make Gay Adoption Illegal, Allow Clergy to Endorse Candidates from Pulpit," *Huffington Post* online, http://www.huffingtonpost .com/2010/08/05/sharron-angle-make-gay-ad_n_672549.html.

51. Michelle Goldberg, "My Ex-gay Life with the Tea Party Queen," *U.S. News* online, http://www.thedailybeast.com/blogs-and-stories/2010-09-16 /christine-odonnells-gay-former-aide-speaks-out/.

52. S. G. Massey, "Polymorphous Prejudice: Liberating the Measurement of Heterosexuals' Attitudes toward Lesbians and Gay Men," *Journal of Homosexuality* 56 (2009): 147–72.

53. "Don't Ask, Don't Tell, Don't Pursue," commonly referred to as "Don't Ask, Don't Tell," was a policy put in place December 21, 1993, by President Clinton that prohibited discrimination of homosexuals in the military by not allowing servicemen and women to be asked about their sexual orientation nor to openly discuss their sexual preferences. For more information, refer to David F. Burrelli, "Don't Ask, Don't Tell": The Law and Military Policy on Same-Sex Behavior," Congressional Research Service, October 14, 2010, available at http://www.fas.org/sgp/crs/misc/R40782.pdf.

54. K. B. Dugan, *The Struggle over Gay, Lesbian, and Bisexual Rights: Facing Off in Cincinnati* (New York: Routledge, 2005).

55. See Earl Black and Merle Black, *Politics and Society in the South* (Cambridge, MA: Harvard University Press, 1987).

56. The Gallup Poll, December 9, 2010; and the *Washington Post*/ABC Poll, December 9–12, 2012.

57. We considered the possibility of endogeneity, and ran a Hausman test on the models. There's nothing to report.

58. The models for attitudes toward immigrants (presented in table A4.1 in the appendix) included the following covariates: age, education, income, gender, race, partisanship, ideology, economic anxiety, authoritarianism, ethnocentrism, social dominance, racial resentment, and Tea Party support.

59. The full models for attitudes toward sexual minorities (presented in table A4.2 in the appendix) included the following covariates: age, education, income, gender, race, partisanship, ideology, authoritarianism, ethnocentrism, social dominance, born-again Christian, moral traditionalism, and Tea Party support.

CHAPTER FIVE

1. Liz Robbins, "Tax Day Is Met with Tea Parties," *New York Times* online, April 15, 2009, http://www.nytimes.com/2009/04/16/us/politics/16taxday .html; these were preceded by smaller "Porkulus" protests that expressed dissatisfaction with the stimulus package.

2. Kenneth Vogel, "'Money Bomb': Ron Paul Raises $6 Million in 24-Hour Period," *USA Today* online, December 17, 2007, http://www.usatoday.com /news/politics/election2008/2007-12-17-ronpaul-fundraising_N.htm.

3. Devin Burghart and Leonard Zeskind, *Special Report to the NAACP on the Tea Party Movement: Tea Party Nation*, IREHR, August 24, 2010, http:// justanothercoverup.com/wp-content/uploads/2010/11/TeaPartyNationalism .pdf.

4. "Libertarian Party of Illinois: We Gave Rick Santelli the Idea for the Tax Day Tea Parties," Independent Political Report, http://www.independent politicalreport.com/2009/04/libertarian-party-of-illinois-we-gave-rick-santelli -the-idea-for-the-tax-day-tea-parties/).

5. "Libertarians Cordially Invite You to a Tea Party," Libertarian Party, April 8, 2009, http://www.lp.org/news/press-releases/libertarians-cordially -invite-you-to-a-tea-party.

6. Burghart and Zeskind, "Tea Party Nationalism."

7. Robbins, "Tax Day Is Met with Tea Parties."

8. President Obama: Job Ratings, PollingReport.com, http://www.polling report.com/obama_job.htm and President Obama: Favorability, PollingReport .com, http://www.pollingreport.com/obama_fav.htm.

9. Robbins, "Tax Day Is Met with Tea Parties."

10. Sam Stein, "Tea Party Protests: 'Ni**er,' 'Fa**ot' Shouted at Members of Congress," *Huffington Post* online, http://www.huffingtonpost.com/2010 /03/20/tea-party-protests-nier-f_n_507116.html.

11. Leonard Zeskind, "Tea Party Protest the NAACP in Los Angeles— Little Talk about Fiscal Issues," IREHR, July 25, 2011.

12. Peter Wehner, "The GOP and the Birther Trap," *Wall Street Journal* online, http://online.wsj.com/article/SB1000142405274870355130457626607 73968228358.html.

13. Jerome Corsi, *Where's the Birth Certificate? The Case that Barack Obama Is Not Eligible to Be President* (New York: WND Books, 2011).

14. "Reward for Obama's Birth Certificate ($25 million reward)," Audacity of Hypocrisy, http://www.audacityofhypocrisy.com/2009/04/26/reward-for-obamas-birth-certificate-25-million-dollars-reward/.

15. Ben Armbruster, "Tancredo's Conspiracy Theory: Obama Hides Birth Certificate to Stir Up the Right and Make Us Look Crazy," Think Progress, http://thinkprogress.org/politics/2010/04/28/94156/tancredo-obama-birther/.

16. Jeff Lichter, "Arizona Tea Party Groups Overwhelmingly Pass Motion for Rep. Franks to Open Congressional Investigation into Obama's Eligibility," Williams Tea Party, http://williamsteaparty.com/2011/07/27/arizona-tea-party-groups-overwhelmingly-pass-motion-rep-franks-open-congressional-investigation-obamas-eligibility/.

17. George C. Edwards III, *Presidential Approval* (Baltimore: Johns Hopkins University Press, 1991).

18. Michael B. MacKuen, Robert S. Erikson, and James A. Stimson, "Peasants or Bankers? The American Electorate and the U.S. Economy," *American Political Science Review* 86 (September 1992): 597–611.

19. Harold Clarke and Marianne Stewart, "Prospections, Retrospections, and Rationality: The 'Bankers' Model of Presidential Approval Reconsidered," *American Journal of Political Science* 38 (1994): 1104–23.

20. George C. Edwards III, William Mitchell, and Reed Welch, "Explaining Presidential Approval: The Significance of Issue Salience," *American Journal of Political Science* 39 (February 1995): 108–34.

21. For example, see papers presented at the 2011 American Political Science Association Annual Conference: Arthur Lupia, "A Theory of Prejudice and Why It Persists (or to Whom is Obama Still Black?)"; Michael Dawson and Julie Merseth, "Racial Pessimism in the Early Obama Era: An Analysis of Individual-Level Change and Racial Group Differences"; Candis Watts Smith, "'I'm not Racist. I Voted for Obama'": Youth White Racial Attitudes in a Time of Prominent Black Politicians"; Alan Abramowitz, "Bitter Tea: Partisanship, Ideology, and Racial Resentment in the Tea Party Movement"; Joseph Lowndes, "Racial Libertarians: The Antistatist Politics of the Tea Party Movement."

22. We freely admit that we cannot account for another important ingredient for presidential approval: retrospective economic voting in which citizens use past economic performance of the American economy as a basis for political judgment. Still, perceptions of the national economy and one's personal economic circumstances are related, tied together by class. We can account for both. For more, see M. Stephen Weatherford, "Economic Voting and the 'Sym-

bolic Politics' Argument: A Reinterpretation and Synthesis," *American Political Science Review* 77, no. 1 (1983): 158–74. For an alternative in which perception of the national economic picture trumps individual economic experiences, see Donald R. Kinder and D. Roderick Kiewet, "Sociotropic Politics: The American Case," *British Journal of Political Science* 11, no. 2 (1981): 129–61.

23. Juan Williams, "Tea Party Anger Reflects Mainstream Concerns," *Wall Street Journal* online, April 2, 2010.

24. Young, "Tea Partiers Racist? Not So Fast."

25. Brian Newman, "The Polls: Presidential Traits and Job Approval," *Public Opinion Quarterly* 34, no. 2 (2004): 437–48; Jeffrey E. Cohen, "Change and Stability in Public Assessments of Personal Traits, Bill Clinton, 1993–99," *Presidential Studies Quarterly* 31, no. 31 (2001): 733–41.

26. Donald Kinder, "Presidential Character Revisited," in *Political Cognition*, ed. Richard Lau and David Sears (Hillsdale, NJ: Lawrence Erlbaum Associates, 1986), 235.

27. James David Barber, *The Presidential Character: Predicting Performance in the White House* (Englewood Cliffs, NJ: Prentice Hall, 1972).

28. Faiz Shakir, "Eric Cantor Tries to Distance Himself from Rush: 'I Don't Think Anyone Wants Anything to Fail,'" Think Progress, March 1, 2009, http://thinkprogress.org/politics/2009/03/01/36489/cantor-v-limbaugh/.

29. Mark Levin, "Santorum at CPAC: 'Absolutely We Hope that' Obama Fails, 'I Believe His Policies Will Fail,'" Think Progress, February 28, 2009, http://thinkprogress.org/politics/2009/02/28/36479/santorum-cpac-obama/; and Ryan Powers, "Pence: 'You Bet' We Want Obama's Policies to Fail," Think Progress, March 3, 2009, http://thinkprogress.org/politics/2009/03/03/36544/pence-hopes-failure/.

30. Results available upon request.

31. Donald Trump repeatedly went on national TV and said he doesn't believe the president has a valid birth certificate. Likewise, Tea Party author Jerome Corsi dedicated two years of work in writing an entire book titled *Where's the Birth Certificate?*, which acknowledges the president's claims that he was born in Hawaii, but offers an opposing theory that disagrees with the evidence.

32. As a precaution, we ran a Hausman test for endogeneity. The results suggested that endogeneity is not a problem.

33. Skocpol and Williamson, *The Tea Party and the Remaking of Republican Conservatism.*

34. Kathleen Hall Jamieson and John N. Capella, *Echo Chamber: Rush Limbaugh and the Conservative Media Establishment* (New York: Oxford University Press, 2008).

35. Results available upon request.

36. The alpha for this index = 0.87.

37. For ease of explanation, standardized beta coefficients are used so that variances can be compared across variables that are measured using different units of measurement. However, unstandardized coefficients are reported in the full regression results in table A5.1 in the appendix.

38. One objection to these findings is that people don't know what it means to be a self-identified conservative (or liberal). This, however, isn't true. As it turns out, people do know what it means. See Pamela Johnston Conover and Stanley Feldman, "The Origins and Meaning of Liberal/Conservative Self-Identifications," *American Journal of Political Science* 25, no. 4 (1981): 617–45.

CHAPTER SIX

1. We borrow from Cathy Cohen's work for our reference to marginalized groups. See her *The Boundaries of Blackness: Aids and the Breakdown of Black Politics* (Chicago: University of Chicago Press, 1999).

2. For another example, see Kenneth Andrews, *Freedom Is a Constant Struggle: The Mississippi Civil Rights Movement and Its Legacy* (Chicago: University of Chicago Press, 2004).

3. Frank Baumgartner and Bryan Jones, *Agenda and Instability in American Politics* (Chicago: University of Chicago Press, 1993); Frank Baumgartner and Christine Mahoney, "Social Movements, the Rise of New Issues, and the Public Agenda," in *Routing the Opposition,* ed. David Meyer, Valerie Jenness, and Helen Ingram (Minneapolis: University of Minnesota Press, 2002).

4. Jim Acosta, "Tea Party Fuels Republican Edge in Enthusiasm," CNN online, October 10, 2010, http://politicalticker.blogs.cnn.com/2010/10/11 /tea-party-fuels-republican-edge-in-enthusiasm/.

5. "Republicans Win House Majority, Make Senate Gains in Wave Election," FoxNews.com, November 2, 2010, http://www.foxnews.com/politics /2010/11/02/poll-closing-key-east-coast-races-balance-power-line/.

6. For a list of the House Tea Party caucus, and how they voted, see Tea Party Voters, http://bachmann.house.gov/News/DocumentSingle.aspx?DocumentID =226594; Final Vote Results for Roll Call 379, http://clerk.house.gov /evs/2011/roll379.xml; and Final Vote Results for Roll Call 638, http://clerk .house.gov/evs/2010/roll638.xml.

7. Skocpol and Williamson, *The Tea Party and the Remaking of Republican Conservatism,* chapter 2.

8. Timothy P. Carney, "Election 2010: A Correction, Not a Revolution," *Washington Examiner* online, October 31, 2010, http://www.therightreasons .net/index.php?/topic/26502-election-2010-a-correction-not-a-revolution/.

9. Dave Cook, "With Democrats Lacking Enthusiasm, Will Tea Party Help or Hurt?" *Christian Science Monitor* online, April 15, 2010, http://www .csmonitor.com/USA/Politics/monitor_breakfast/2010/0415/With-Democrats -lacking-enthusiasm-will-Tea-Party-help-or-hurt.

10. Doug McAdam, John McCarthy, and Mayer Zald, *Comparative Perspectives on Social Movements* (Cambridge: Cambridge University Press, 1996).

11. As an example, see Kenneth T. Andrews, *Freedom Is a Constant Struggle: The Mississippi Civil Rights Movement and Its Legacy* (Chicago: University of Chicago Press, 2004).

12. Jack Citrin, "Political Alienation as a Social Indicator: Attitudes and Action," *Social Indicators* 4 (1977): 381–419. Edward McDill and Jeanne Clare Ridley, "Status, Anomia, Political Alienation, and Political Participation," *American Journal of Sociology* 68 (1962): 205–13.

13. David Riesman, *The Lonely Crowd* (New Haven: Yale University Press, 1950); Morris Rosenberg, "Some Determinants of Political Apathy," *Public Opinion Quarterly* 18 (Winter 1954): 349–66.

14. Jack Citrin, Herbert McClosky, J. Merrill Shanks, and Paul M. Sniderman, "Personal and Political Sources of Political Alienation," *British Journal of Political Science* 5 (1975): 1–31.

15. Fredric Templeton, "Alienation and Political Participation: Some Research Findings," *Public Opinion Quarterly* 30, no. 2 (1966): 249–61.

16. Steven J. Rosenstone and John Mark Hansen, *Mobilization, Participation, and Democracy in America* (New York: Macmillan, 1993), chapter 2.

17. Joris Lammers, Adam D. Galinsky, Ernestine H. Gordijn, and Sabine Otten, "Illegitimacy Moderates the Effects of Power on Approach," *Psychological Science* 19, no. 6 (2008): 558–64.

18. Citrin, "Political Alienation as a Social Indicator: Attitudes and Action."

19. Rory McVeigh, *The Rise of the Ku Klux Klan.*

20. For the influence of the John Birch Society, see among others, Lisa McGirr, *Suburban Warriors: The Origins of the New American Right* (Princeton: Princeton University Press, 2001); and Rick Perlstein, *Before the Storm.*

21. Campbell, Converse, Miller, and Stokes, *The American Voter*; Lewis-Beck, Jacoby, Norpoth, and Weisberg, *The American Voter Revisited.*

22. Matt Barreto, Loren Collingwood, Ben Gonzalez, and Christopher Parker, "Tea Party Politics in a Blue State: Dino Rossi and the 2010 Washington Senate Election," in *Stuck in the Middle to Lose: Tea Party Effects on 2010 U.S. Senate Elections*, ed. William Miller and Jeremy Walling (Lanham, MD: Rowman & Littlefield, 2011).

23. For more on political engagement and the importance of political interest, see Sidney Verba, Kay L. Schlozman, and Henry E. Brady, *Voice and Equality: Civic Volunteerism in American Politics* (Cambridge, MA: Harvard University Press, 1995).

24. Ibid.

25. Ibid.

26. Stephanie Condon, "Tea Party: 4 in 10 are Dems, Independents, Survey Says," http://www.cbsnews.com/8301-503544_162-20001743-503544.html.

27. Verba, Schlozman, and Brady, *Voice and Equality*, 1995.

28. Steven J. Rosenstone and Raymond E. Wolfinger, *Who Votes?* (New Haven: Yale University Press, 1980); Sidney Verba and Norman H. Nie, *Participation in America: Political Democracy and Social Equality* (Chicago: University of Chicago Press, 1972).

29. Other factors, such as age, education, and income, are all related to a propensity to vote. As would be expected, explanations that bear directly on politics also help explain voting. Indeed, partisanship, concerns over the economy, and ideology are all important predictors of voting in 2010 (please see table A6.1 in the appendix).

30. Richard S. Lazarus, *Emotion and Adaptation* (New York: Oxford University Press, 1991), 218.

31. Henri Tajfel, *Social Identity and Intergroup Relations* (New York: Cambridge University Press, 1982).

32. Marcus, Neuman, and Mackuen, *Affective Intelligence and Political Judgment*.

33. Lazarus, *Emotion and Adaptation*, chapter 6.

34. For our references to emotions and their behavioral consequences, see Catherine A. Cottrell and Steven L. Neuberg, "Differential Emotional Reactions to Different Groups: A Sociofunctional Threat-Based Approach to Prejudice," *Journal of Personality and Social Psychology* 88, no. 5 (2005): 770–89; Jennifer S. Lerner and Dacher Keltner, "Fear, Anger, and Risk," *Journal of Personality and Social Psychology* 81, no. 1 (2001): 146–59; Diane M. Mackie, Thierry Devos, and Eliot R. Smith, "Intergroup Emotions: Explaining Offensive Action Tendencies in an Intergroup Context," *Journal of Personality and Social Psychology* 79, no. 4 (2000): 602–16; and Larissa Z. Tiedens, "The Effect of Anger on the Hostile Inferences of Aggressive and Nonaggressive

People: Specific Emotions, Cognitive Processing, and Chronic Accessibility," *Motivation and Emotion* 25, no. 3 (2001): 233–51.

35. Wilcox, *God's Warriors*.

CONCLUSION

1. Richard Hofstadter, *The Paranoid Style in American Politics*, 45.

2. We have mentioned Skocpol and Williamson's work several times. Lepore's work is also important, as is Foley's book. There are others who, like us, take a more empirical approach but lack the ability to account for all of the competing explanations that we do. For more, see Lepore, *The Whites of Their Eyes*; Price Foley, *The Tea Party*; and Skocpol and Williamson, *The Tea Party and the Remaking of Republican Conservatism*. For the more empirical approaches, see Kevin Arceneaux and Stephen P. Nicholson, "Reading Tea Party Leaves: Who Supports the Tea Party Movement, What Do They Want, and Why?" (unpublished manuscript, 2011); see also, Jacobsen, "The President, the Tea Party, and Voting Behavior in 2010." Finally, see Maxwell, "Tea Party Distinguished by Racial Views and Fear of the Future."

3. Geoffrey Kabaservice, *Rule and Ruin: The Downfall of Moderation and the Destruction of the Republican Party; From Eisenhower to the Tea Party* (New York: Oxford University Press, 2012). As a matter of fact, one might even call moderate conservatives *principled conservatives*, insofar as they're more about limiting the influence of government in American life, law and order, fiscal responsibility, and liberty. In other words, intolerance has little to do with the policy preferences associated with conservatism. Instead, their preferences are driven by adherence to conservative principles. Reactionary conservatives' preferences, on the other hand, are driven by what they believe are threats to their social prestige. For more on principled conservatism, see Paul M. Sniderman and Thomas Piazza, *The Scar of Race* (Cambridge, MA: Harvard University Press, 1993).

4. We make no value judgments about conservatism, but the literature on the subject is voluminous. Having said that, if we take conservatives at their word, and it's really about small government, social conservatism, and national defense, for more recent work consistent with "mainstream" conservatism, see Matthew Lassiter, *The Silent Majority: Suburban Politics in the Sunbelt South* (Princeton: Princeton University Press, 2006); McGirr, *Suburban Warriors*; and Joseph Crespino, *In Search of Another Country: Mississippi and the Conservative Counterrevolution* (Princeton: Princeton University Press, 2007). For recent work that questions the sincerity of conservatives, that modern, mainstream conservatism is hopelessly bound up with racism, see, among others, Kevin Kruse, *White Flight: Atlanta and the Making of Modern Conservatism* (Princeton: Princeton University Press, 2005); and Joseph Lowndes, *From the New Deal to the New Right: Race and the Southern Origins of Modern Conservatism* (New Haven: Yale University Press, 2008).

5. Perlstein, *Before the Storm*.

6. Hofstadter, *The Paranoid Style in American Politics*, 3.

7. See, among others, John D. Skrentny, *The Minority Rights Revolution* (Cambridge, MA: Harvard University Press, 2004).

8. Lipset and Raab, *The Politics of Unreason*, 6.

9. Please see table A2.1 in the appendix, "Comparison of MSSRP 2011 with contemporaneous national polls by Tea Party support and selected demographics" for the relevant surveys.

10. There are too many examples to cite, so we'll only reference those closest to our work. For authoritarianism, see Karen Stenner, *The Authoritarian Dynamic* (New York: Cambridge University Press, 2005); for ethnocentrism, see Kinder and Kam, *Us Against Them*; for social dominance orientation, see Sidanius and Pratto, *Social Dominance Theory*.

11. James M. Jasper, *The Art of Moral Protest: Culture, Biography, and Creativity in Social Movements* (Chicago: University of Chicago Press, 1997).

12. Available at Political Correction, http://politicalcorrection.org/blog /201105130001.

13. See Chris Edwards, "George W. Bush: Biggest Spender since LBJ," available at http://www.cato-at-liberty.org/george-w-bush-biggest-spender-since -lbj/; see also, Veronique de Rugy, "Spending under President George W. Bush," Working Paper No. 09-04, Mercatus Center, George Mason University, March 2009.

14. Please see table A2.1 in the appendix, "Comparison of MSSRP 2011 with contemporaneous national polls by Tea Party support and selected demographics."

15. For a catalog of both, see Hixon, *Search for the American Right Wing*.

16. Broyles, *The John Birch Society*, chapter 1; see also, Alan Crawford, *Thunder on the Right: The New Right and the Politics of Resentment* (New York: Pantheon Books, 1980), chapter 3.

17. See Peter Viereck, "The Philosophical 'New' Conservatism," in *The Radical Right*, ed. Daniel Bell, 185–207.

18. For more on the clash between the JBS and the *National Review*, see Perlstein, *Before the Storm*.

19. Paul Burstein, *Discrimination, Jobs, and Politics* (Chicago: University of Chicago Press, 1985).

20. See Jon Agnone, "Amplifying Public Opinion: The Policy Impact of the U.S. Environmental Movement," *Social Forces* 85, no. 4 (2007): 1593–1620; Burstein, *Discrimination, Jobs, and Politics*; and Doug McAdam and

Yang Su, "The War at Home: Antiwar Protests and Congressional Voting, 1965 to 1973," *American Sociological Review* 67 (2002): 696–721. For the effect of movement, public opinion, and the congressional agenda, see Frank R. Baumgartner and Bryan D. Jones, *Agendas and Instability in American Politics* (Chicago: University of Chicago Press, 1993). For the importance of issue salience and how it's related to public opinion and representation, see Stuart N. Soroka and Christopher Wlezien, *Degrees of Democracy: Politics, Public Opinion, and Policy* (New York: Cambridge University Press, 2010).

21. For more on polarization, see, among others, Alan I. Abramowitz, *The Disappearing Center: Engaged Citizens, Polarization, and American Democracy* (New Haven: Yale University Press, 2010); Morris P. Fiorina, *Disconnect: The Breakdown of Representation in American Politics* (Norman: University of Oklahoma Press, 2009); Matthew Levendusky, *The Partisan Sort: How Liberals Became Democrats and Conservatives Became Republicans* (Chicago: University of Chicago Press, 2009); and Nolan McCarty, Keith T. Poole, and Howard Rosenthal, *Polarized America: The Dance of Ideology and Unequal Riches* (Cambridge, MA: MIT Press, 2006).

22. Terri L. Givens, *Voting Radical Right in Western Europe* (New York: Cambridge University Press, 2005).

23. For the latest on this approach, see Pippa Norris, *Radical Right: Voters and Parties in the Electoral Market* (New York: Cambridge University Press, 2005).

24. For an exemplar of this type of work, see Bert Klandermans and Nonna Mayer's edited volume, *Extreme Right Activists in Europe: Through the Magnifying Glass* (London: Routledge, 2006).

25. "Are Tea Partiers Right to Distrust Mitt Romney?" *American Prospect*, http://prospect.org/article/are-tea-partiers-right-distrust-mitt-romney.

26. "Mitt Romney Better Move to Right, Says Emboldened Tea Party," ABC News, August 1, 2012, http://abcnews.go.com/Politics/OTUS/mitt-romney-move-emboldened-tea-party/story?id=16906367#.UBqCJ2FR3T4.

27. "Tea Party Claims 'Seat at the Table' with Romney's Paul Ryan Pick for VP," *Christian Science Monitor*, August 11, 2012, http://www.csmonitor.com/USA/Elections/President/2012/0811/Tea-party-claims-seat-at-the-table-with-Romney-s-Paul-Ryan-pick-for-VP.

28. Available at FoxNews.com, http://www.foxnews.com/politics/elections/2012-exit-poll.

29. Entering 2012, the Tea Party caucus had 59 members in the House of Representatives. Before the November election, two members retired, two lost in primaries, Todd Akin and Denny Rehberg left the House to run for Senate (and both lost), and Mike Pence left to become governor of Indiana. Of the 52 remaining Tea Party caucus members in the general election, 48 won reelection

with one more heading for a runoff election. Notable losses include Allen West of Florida, Joe Walsh of Illinois, and Roscoe Bartlett of Maryland. Many races, including that of Tea Party caucus chair Michele Bachmann were much closer than in 2010. http://www.irehr.org/issue-areas/tea-party-nationalism /tea-party-news-and-analysis/item/439-tea-party-caucus-and-election-2012.

30. "House GOP Freshmen Present New Challenges for Boehner," *Washington Post* online, January 14, 2013, http://www.washingtonpost.com/politics /house-gop-freshmen-present-new-challenges-to-boehner/2013/01/14 /2557a3e4-5c1a-11e2-9fa9-5fbdc9530eb9_story.html?tid=wp_ipad; http://www .washingtonpost.com/opinions/the-worst-year-in-washington-the-tea-party /2012/12/28/f41da4d0-4f8b-11e2-950a-7863a013264b_story_1.html.

31. "Election Leaves Republicans at Loss for Answers," CNN Politics, November 9, 2012, http://www.cnn.com/2012/11/09/politics/gop-disarray /index.html. "Post Obama Win, Tea Party Not Backing Down," Townhall.com, November 7, 2012, http://townhall.com/tipsheet/katiepavlich/2012/11/07 /post_obama_win_tea_party_not_backing_down.

32. "Texas GOP Official Pushes Secession, Calls Obama Voters 'Maggots,' " The Grio, November 9, 2012, http://thegrio.com/2012/11/09/texas-gop -official-pushes-secession-call-obama-voters-maggots/.

33. "Triumph of the Tea Party Mindset," Salon.com, December 27, 2012, http://www.salon.com/2012/12/27/triumph_of_the_tea_party_mindset/.

APPENDIX

1. C. A. Cameron, J. B. Gelbach, and D. L. Miller, "Robust Inference with Multi-way Clustering," National Bureau of Economic Research, NBER Working Paper No. 327, September 2006, http://www.nber.org/papers/t0327; Mahmood Arai, "Cluster-Robust Standard Errors using R," Stockholm University Department of Economics and SULCIS, January 31, 2011, http://people .su.se/~ma/clustering.pdf.

2. Tom Snijders and Roel Boske, *Multilevel Analysis: An Introduction to Basic and Advanced Multilevel Modeling* (Thousand Oaks, CA: Sage, 1999); Marc Aerts, Helena Geys, Geert Molenberghs, Louise Ryan, *Topics in Modelling of Clustered Data* (New York: Chapman and Hall/CRC, 2002); J. M. Wooldridge, "Cluster-Sample Methods in Applied Econometrics," *American Economic Review* 93, no. 2 (2003): 133–38.

3. Unless otherwise reported, all coefficients are unstandardized.

INDEX

activism, Tea Party, 229–31; barriers to, 17, 77; citizen activists, 44, 48; commitment to, 74–75; discourse employed by activists, 2, 8, 12, 22, 48, 63–64, 160, 276–77; membership and, 16–17, 74; motives for (*see* motives for Tea Party support); negative perceptions of, 70–71, 76; political participation and, 219, 224–25, 229, 231; as reactionary, 50, 66; and "real" American identity, 37; sympathy and support as more widespread than, 16–18, 44, 52, 74–77, 241–43

Adorno, Theodor, 22, 87, 139

Affordable Care Act, xiii, 38, 73, 194, 197, 222, 255

alienation, political, 222–23

Americans for Legal Immigration PAC (ALIPAC), 167

anger, as response to social change: identity threats and intergroup anger, 238; immigration and, 186–87; Obama as target of, 191, 221; and political participation, 222–26, 240; survey to assess, 53; and Tea Party support, 48–49, 60–61, 159, 186–87, 191, 221, 238–39

Angle, Sharron, 115–16, 166, 173, 187

anti-Semitism, 21, 25–26, 30–31, 87, 252, 270

anxiety: and decline in social prestige, 86, 184; economic, 86, 90–94; election of Obama and, 10, 22, 35, 45; "illegal" immigration as source of, 56; and "loss of America," 184, 240; Obama as

source of (*see* Obamaphobia); "out-group" hostility and, 94–97, 122, 190, 192; and political engagement, 238; and reactionary conservatism in Tea Party, 48–49; right-wing movements and, 3, 23–24, 32; sexual minorities as source of, 58; and subversion, 150; survey to assess, 53, 272

approval ratings, for Obama, 59–61, 196, 201–2; among Tea Party sympathizers, 202–12; difference between Tea Party and non-Tea Party conservatives, 210–11; economic factors and, 201–2, 342n22; political predispositions and, 192–93; Tea Party influence on, 202–3

approval ratings, for Tea Party, 69–72, 73, 75

Armey, Dick, 3, 44, 196

Ashcroft, John, 114

authoritarianism (social conformity): defined and described, 87–88; minority rights and, 180–86; patriotism and, 145–50; as predisposition, 103, 126; and right-wing movements, 66, 77; Social Dominance Orientation and, 125–26; survey index questions, 271; Tea Party support and, 91–92, 100, 103, 124–29, 131–34, 145–50, 183–86, 290, 292–99

Bachmann, Michele, 8, 44

Bailyn, Bernard, 82–83

believers, Tea Party: authoritarianism and, 91–93, 92,